P9-EBY-201

CiTY·SMaRT™
GUIDEBOOK

Chicago

Adam Langer

John Muir Publications
Santa Fe, New Mexico

John Muir Publications, P.O. Box 613, Santa Fe, New Mexico 87504

Copyright © 1999 by John Muir Publications
Cover and maps copyright © 1999 by John Muir Publications
All rights reserved.

Printed in the United States of America.
First edition. First printing February 1999.

ISBN: 1-56261-450-9
ISSN: 1521-2386

Editors: Dianna Delling, Chris Hayhurst
Graphics Editor: Heather Pool
Production: Janine Lehmann
Design: Janine Lehmann
Cover Design: Suzanne Rush
Map Illustration: Laura Perfetti
Printer: Publishers Press
Front cover: © T. J. Florian/Photo Network — The El in Chicago's Loop
Back cover: © Leo de Wys, Inc./Steve Vidler — Chicago's skyline from Lincoln Park

Distributed to the book trade by
Publishers Group West
Berkeley, California

While every effort has been made to provide accurate, up-to-date information, the author and publisher accept no responsibility for loss, injury, or inconvenience sustained by any person using this book.

CONTENTS

MAP CONTENTS

See Chicago the CiTY·SMaRT™ Way

The Guide for Chicago Natives, New Residents, and Visitors

In *City•Smart Guidebook Chicago*, local author Adam Langer tells it
like it is. Residents will learn things they never knew about their city,
new residents will get an insider's view of their new hometown, and
visitors will be guided to the very best Chicago has to offer—whether
they're on a weekend getaway or staying a week or more.

Opinionated Recommendations Save You Time and Money

From shopping to nightlife to museums, the author is opinionated about
what he likes and dislikes. You'll learn the great and the not-so-great
things about Chicago's sights, restaurants, and accommodations. So
you can decide what's worth your time and what's not; which hotel is
worth the splurge and which is the best choice for budget travelers.

Easy-to-Use Format Makes Planning Your Trip a Cinch

City•Smart Guidebook Chicago is user-friendly—you'll quickly find
exactly what you're looking for. Chapters are organized by travelers'
interests or needs, from Where to Stay and Where to Eat, to Sights
and Attractions, Kids' Stuff, Sports and Recreation, and even Day Trips
from Chicago.

Includes Maps and Quick Location-Finding Features

Every listing in this book is accompanied by a geographic zone desig-
nation (see pages vi–vii for zone details) that helps you immediately
find each location. Staying on North Michigan Avenue and wondering
about nearby sights and restaurants? Look for the "Near North" label
in the listings and you'll know that statue or café is not far away. Or
maybe you're looking for the Museum of Science and Industry. Along
with its address, you'll see a "South Side" label, so you'll know just
where to find it.

All That and Fun to Read, Too!

Every City•Smart chapter includes fun-to-read (and fun-to-use) tips
to help you get more out of Chicago, city trivia (did you know the first
all-star baseball game was held at Comiskey Park in 1933?), and illumi-
nating sidebars (for the lowdown on Chicago gangster Al Capone, for
example, see page 53). And well-known local residents provide their
personal "Top Ten" lists, guiding readers to the city's best theaters,
bars, smells, and more.

Chicago Zones

Downtown
The area bordered by Lake Michigan to the east, Halsted Street to the west, Randolph Street to the north, and Roosevelt Road to the south. Includes the Loop and Printer's Row, as well as Little Italy and Greektown.

Near North
The area bordered by Lake Michigan to the east, Halsted Street to the west, North Avenue to the north, and Randolph Street to the south. Includes the Magnificent Mile, Navy Pier, and the Oak Street Shopping district.

North Side
The area bordered by Lake Michigan to the east, Kedzie Avenue to the west, Irving Park Road to the north, and North Avenue to the south. Includes the Lincoln Park, Lakeview, and Wrigleyville neighborhoods.

Far North
The area bordered by Lake Michigan to the east, Kedzie Avenue to the west, Howard Street to the north, and Irving Park Road to the south. Includes Andersonville, Rogers Park, and Edgewater.

West Side
The area bordered by Halsted Street to the east, Kedzie Avenue to the west, North Avenue to the north, and Roosevelt Road to the south. Includes Greektown, Little Italy, and Wicker Park.

Near South
The area bordered by Lake Michigan to the east, Kedzie Avenue to the west, Roosevelt Road to the north, and 35th Street to the south. Includes Pilsen, Chinatown, and Bridgeport.

South Side
The area bordered by Lake Michigan to the east, Kedzie Avenue to the west, 35th Street to the north, and 71st Street to the south. Includes Hyde Park, the South Shore, and Black Metropolis.

O'Hare
The Rosemont, Illinois, area immediately surrounding O'Hare International Airport. This zone appears in Chapter 3, Where to Stay, only.

Greater Chicago
The City of Chicago proper that is west of Kedzie Avenue, plus other nearby suburbs, including Oak Park and Evanston.

CHICAGO ZONES

© Robb Helfrick

1

WELCOME TO CHICAGO

The wind whistles as gray-blue Lake Michigan waves crash against the jagged rocks beyond the harbors. Steel and glass office buildings don't scrape the sky, they knife through it, slicing through clouds and hulking over the city like omnipotent giants peering down their dark beanstalk bodies at the hustle and bustle on the streets below.

It may no longer be the "hog butcher of the world" or "stacker of wheat" that Chicago poet Carl Sandburg once described. Neither the rat-a-tat of tommy guns nor the sloshing of bathhouse gin are heard anymore on this city's streets. The fires that blazed through Chicago in 1871 and again during the sixties riots have long since been quenched. But it's still a tough town, one that owes its reputation not to Sinclair Lewis' *Main Street* but to Upton Sinclair's *The Jungle*—a brawny, strutting, honest, no-frills kind of place.

Nobody here knows what Frank Sinatra meant when he called this town "toddling." That shattering, crackling, popping sound isn't gunfire; it's the crash of cymbals in Chicago Symphony Orchestra's percussion section. It's the yelp of the blues harmonica in 43rd Street's Checkerboard Lounge. It's the sound of thousands of footsteps descending on Milwaukee Avenue to push their way into crowded, sweaty clubs where Smashing Pumpkins defined the Chicago rock 'n' roll sound. It's the sound of hands clapping in Wrigley Field bleachers as the Cubs battle an 89-year curse. It's the sound of bodies hurtling across the stage at Steppenwolf Theater, where John Malkovich and Gary Sinise transformed the brawny school of Chicago theater. It's the beat of poetry at the Green Mill Tavern, the crunch of deep-dish pizza at Gino's, the growl of lions in Brookfield Zoo. That sea of people rushing down Madison

Chicago: City of Nicknames

Chicago has been called many things. Some of them are even printable. "Queen and Guttersnipe of the Cities," according to film director George Stevens; "City of Boundless Prairies," according to writer George Putnam Upton; "City Without Cobwebs," said writer Robert Shackleton; and "San-Fran-York," according to late lamented newspaper columnist Mike Royko. Some of the city's other nicknames:

The Windy City. *When Chicago hosted the World's Colombian Exposition in 1893, those weary of Chicago's air of self-congratulation for pulling off the successful world's fair dubbed it "The Windy City."*

City of Broad Shoulders. *From the famous Carl Sandburg poem "Chicago." Sandburg also used the phrases "hog butcher for the world," "tool maker," "stacker of wheat," "player with railroads," and "the nation's freight handler."*

The Second City. *Coined by New Yorker A. J. Liebling, in a 1952 essay in the* New Yorker.

Literary Capital of America. *According to H. L. Mencken in a 1920 issue of* The Nation.

City on the Make. *The title of a 1951 book by legendary Chicago author Nelson Algren.*

Place of Wild Onions. *The translation of the Indian word* Checagou.

The Jazz Baby. *Coined by one of Chicago's native sons: screenwriter, author, newspaperman, and playwright Ben Hecht.*

Urbs In Horto ("City in a Garden"). *The city's official motto.*

That Toddlin' Town. *The phrase comes from the 1922 song "Chicago" penned by Fred Fisher.*

City of I Will. *A tribute to the city's can-do spirit, coined in 1891 as a city slogan.*

The Petrillo Music Shell during the Grant Park Music Festival

Chicago Park District

Street hasn't come to fight the National Guard; they're jostling for a glimpse of the Chicago Bulls.

This isn't 1929 Chicago with its mobsters and bathhouse gin. This isn't the Windy City of 1968 with its protests and pellet-gun fire. Chicago has grown up to emerge as one of the country's most vibrant and livable cultural capitals. From the Drake Hotel's swanky ballrooms to Cabaret Metro's underground dance hall, from Marshall Field's glittering shop windows to Lake Michigan's sizzling beaches, from the Sears Tower's sun-drenched observation deck to the subway's comforting chill, this is Chicago at the end of the 20th century. It's not the "Second City" anymore.

Getting to Know Chicago

Though it still ranks second in size behind New York City and in population has slipped to third place, Chicago is nevertheless the quintessential American city. Neither an overstuffed island of high-rises and taxicabs nor a sprawl of faceless suburbs, Chicago provides the perfect urban experience: a shimmering lakefront, a jam-packed Downtown, flavorful ethnic neighborhoods, high-class shopping districts, breathtaking architecture, towering skyscrapers, majestic boulevards, acres of splendid parks, and a warm and friendly population. Once called "the most livable city in America," Chicago is a triumph of civic planning, truly living up to one of its many mottoes: "The City That Works."

To know the city, you must first acquaint yourself with four things: Lake Michigan, the Sears Tower, the El, and Michael Jordan. Knowing about each of these, you will understand how the city feels, how it works, how it plays, and how it sees itself.

Viewed from a distance, Lake Michigan appears a gleaming blue canvas on which the city has been painted. Marking Chicago's easternmost point and racing more than 20 miles from the city's northernmost point to its southern border, the lakefront is a free recreational paradise of bike trails, beaches, baseball and soccer fields, and parks, not to mention vista for some of Chicago's toniest homes. This is the placid city, the stretch of land that invites year-round play.

Rising 110 stories above Downtown, the Sears Tower pays homage to Chicago's reputation as the architectural capital of the United States. Challenged for the title of world's tallest building by Malaysia's Petronas Towers, the Sears Tower is an apt symbol for a city that boasts three of the ten tallest buildings in the world and is home to the masterpieces of such architectural greats as Mies van der Rohe, Louis Sullivan, Frank Lloyd Wright, and Helmut Jahn. This is the businessman's Chicago, site of some of the world's largest corporations and the Chicago Board of Trade.

The elevated train system, looping around Downtown and snaking through the city's cornucopia of ethnic neighborhoods, is the essence of Chicago. Strong, functional, and gleaming with superb craftsmanship, the El (as it's known) offers one of the best ways to see the city, from its Loop office buildings to the charming houses and apartment buildings of Uptown to the friendly confines of Wrigley Field in Lakeview to the groovy nightclubs and restaurants on the North Side. This is the tough Chicago, the city that gave birth to Nelson Algren, Studs Terkel, and Ernest Hemingway.

And then there's Michael Jordan: not just an athlete but a symbol of a city in transition. For years Chicago suffered from a strange sort of inferiority complex. Blessed with perhaps the most beautiful city skyline in the country, remarkable architecture, and a stunningly diverse population, Chicago nevertheless eyed New York and Los Angeles with competitive jealousy. This attitude was reflected in its sports teams, the woeful Chicago Cubs and Chicago White Sox, whose combined futility stretches back nearly fifty years. Even when Chicago sports teams did attain success, it always seemed to be a one-year fluke: the 1960 Chicago Black Hawks, the 1985 Chicago Bears and their lauded Shufflin' Crew. But the arrival of Michael Jordan and the Bulls' subsequent five championships have given Chicago a new winning attitude and a new sense of pride. This is the Chicago of the sports lover. No longer a weak sister or pale imitation of other, larger cities, Chicago has at last attained, in the view of many, first place, and not just in basketball but in culture, environment, and livability as well.

Chicago History

Chicago's history has been marked by an almost continuous process of self-reinvention. But perhaps that's only natural for a city that, while well on its way to international prominence as a trade and cultural center, almost entirely burned to the ground more than 125 years ago.

Chicago-ese

A number of words and phrases used commonly by Chicagoans may seem strange to folks from elsewhere. Here, a Chicago lexicon.

Back-of-the-yards: *A less-than-desirable neighborhood.*

Bleacher bums: *Those who spend their summer days in the bleachers of Wrigley Field instead of searching for gainful employment.*

Broasted: *A method of preparing chicken by broiling and roasting.*

Da coach: *The title still held by former Chicago Bears skipper, Mike Ditka.*

Deep-dish: *A thick-crusted pizza with a heavy layer of cheese and assorted toppings. Invented by Ike Sewell of Pizzeria Uno and Due.*

El: *An abbreviation for the city's elevated train system.*

Frango: *A delicious, minty, chocolate confection. Invented and produced by Marshall Field and Company.*

Heavy ticket: *One who votes more than once in a city election.*

Holy cow!: *An expression of elation. Popularized by late Chicago White Sox and Chicago Cubs announcer Harry Caray.*

Insinuendo: *A combination of "insinuation" and "innuendo." Coined by the king of the malapropism, former Mayor Richard J. Daley, who once stated, "I resemble that insinuendo!"*

Joliet Josie: *A woman below the age of consent, referencing the Joliet Correctional Center.*

Mickey Finn: *A knockout drink served by an unscrupulous bartender. Named after an infamous Chicago barkeep.*

Neighborhood shirt: *A flannel shirt, one to be worn around the neighborhood.*

Pop: *As in soda pop. "Soda" here means an ice cream soda.*

Slats Grobnik: *A street-smart, plain-speaking man-of-the-streets. A character created by columnist Mike Royko.*

Submarine: *A long sandwich on a roll. Called a "hoagie" in other parts of the country.*

Walking around money: *Spare change or bills.*

For centuries the Potawatomis and other area tribes made their home in *Checagou*, the "city of wild onions," so named for the onions that grew along the banks of the Chicago River. The first European visitors to Chicago were fur traders and missionaries such as Father Jacques Marquette and Louis Jolliet, who came in the 17th century from France. The year 1779 brought the first non–native American settler, Jean Baptiste Pointe du Sable, a black man who established a trading post on the north bank of the Chicago River. Fourteen years later, in 1793, United States and Indian tribal leaders signed the Treaty of Greenville, which gave the United States control of the region in the Old Northwest that included Chicago. Skirmishes continued between the Indians and the new settlers; the Indians killed 50 Americans at Fort Dearborn during the War of 1812. By 1833, in accordance with a provision of the Treaty of Greenville, the United States had taken ownership of all Indian land in northern Illinois and southern Wisconsin.

Chicago's history as an industrial center began as early as 1829, when Archibald Clybourne established the city's first meat-packing plant. From then on, Chicago continued to solidify its hard-nosed reputation. In the early to mid-19th century, Chicago was a sprawling city of railways and factories, of grain and wheat. The Board of Trade is graced by a statue of Ceres, the goddess of grain, a tribute to a city where, in 1870, more than 60 million bushels of grain changed hands. At about the same time, familiar names like Libby, Armour, and Swift had taken hold of the packing industry, and the Union Stockyards on the South Side housed more than 100,000 sheep, cattle, and hogs.

But Chicago was not just a rough-and-tumble meat packer's paradise. Its emergence as an industrial epicenter gave birth to high society elegance. Cotton speculator Potter Palmer purchased three-quarters of State Street, beginning the transformation that would earn it the nickname "That Great Street" and make it a hub for transportation and commerce, best exemplified by the 225-room Palmer House hotel and the Field, Leiter and Company Store.

The Water Tower

Chicago Architecture Foundation

Dreams of a swank "Paris of the Midwest" literally burned to cinders on October 8, 1871, in the infamous Great Chicago Fire. Legend has it that, at a few minutes past 9 p.m., a certain bovine creature on the O'Leary farm gave a firm hoof to a lantern, sparking a blaze that raged for three days and leveled nearly all

CHICAGO TIMELINE

1673	French missionaries and fur traders visit the area.
1779	Jean Baptiste Pointe du Sable arrives in Chicago.
1796	First Chicago birth is recorded: Eulalia Pointe du Sable, daughter of Jean Baptiste Pointe du Sable.
1803–12	The first Fort Dearborn is established.
1818	Illinois becomes the 21st state admitted to the Union.
1833	Chicago is incorporated as a town with a population of 350.
1837	Chicago is incorporated as a city. William B. Ogden is elected mayor.
1847	The first issue of the *Chicago Tribune* is published.
1848	City Hall opens on State Street; the Chicago Board of Trade is established.
1855	The Chicago Police Department is founded.
1860	The first national political convention is held in the "Wigwam," and Abraham Lincoln nominated for president.
1861–65	The Civil War rages.
1863	Mercy Hospital, Chicago's first hospital, is established.
1868	Ulysses S. Grant receives the Republican presidential nomination at Crosby's Opera House.
1869	The Chicago Water Tower is built.
1871	The Great Chicago Fire levels nearly one-third of the city.
1872	The Chicago Public Library is founded. Montgomery Ward is established.
1879	The Chicago Art Institute is founded.
1880	James A. Garfield receives the Republican presidential nomination at Exposition Hall.
1884	Grover Cleveland receives the Democratic presidential nomination at Exposition Hall.
1886	The Haymarket Riot breaks out.
1888	Benjamin Harrison receives the Republican nomination for presidency at the national convention in Civic Auditorium.
1889	Jane Addams establishes Hull House. Chicago Auditorium opens.
1891	The city's elevated railway (the El) is established.

1893	World's Colombian Exposition draws 27 million visitors. First Ferris wheel is created here.
1896	William Jennings Bryan makes famous "cross of gold" speech at the Democratic National Convention at the Coliseum.
1900	The Chicago River's flow is reversed to reduce epidemics caused by poor drainage system. The notorious Everleigh sisters, Minna and Ada, open a high-class bordello in the First Ward.
1901	Walt Disney is born in Chicago.
1903	Iroquois Theater fire kills more than 600.
1904	Theodore Roosevelt receives the Republican nomination for president at the national convention at the Coliseum.
1907	Albert A. Michelson, of the University of Chicago, becomes the first American to win the Nobel Prize in Physics.
1908	William Howard Taft wins the Republican presidential nomination at the Coliseum.
1909	Daniel H. Burnham unveils the Plan for Chicago.
1915	The Eastland Disaster claims 844 lives.
1916	Theodore Roosevelt receives the presidential nomination of the Progressive Party at Auditorium Theatre.
1919	Chicago Black Sox scandal occurs. The first Fannie May candy store opens.
1920	Warren G. Harding receives the Republican presidential nomination at the Coliseum.
1924	Nathan Leopold and Richard Loeb kill cousin Bobby Franks in notorious "thrill killing."
1925	Tribune Tower is completed.
1929	Seven members of Bugs Moran's gang are killed in a Clark Street garage in the infamous St. Valentine's Day Massacre.
1930	The Merchandise Mart is opened.
1931	Al Capone is found guilty of income tax evasion.
1932	Herbert Hoover receives the Republican presidential nomination at Chicago Stadium. Franklin Delano Roosevelt receives the Democratic nomination, also at the Stadium.
1933–34	The Century of Progress World's Fair takes place.
1933	Mayor Anton Cermak is assassinated in an attempt on FDR's life.
1934	John Dillinger is shot in the alley beside Biograph Theater.

The first controlled atomic reaction is conducted by Dr. Enrico Fermi and team.	**1942**
The Chicago subway opens.	**1943**
Thomas Dewey receives the Republican presidential nomination at Chicago Stadium. FDR wins the Democratic presidential nomination, also at the Stadium.	**1944**
The Chicago Cubs earn their last trip to the World Series.	**1945**
The Chicago Transit Authority is founded.	**1947**
Dwight Eisenhower receives the Republican presidential nomination at Chicago Amphitheater.	**1952**
Hugh Hefner founds *Playboy*.	**1953**
Mayor Richard J. Daley is elected to his first term.	**1955**
Adlai Stevenson receives the Democratic presidential nomination at Chicago Amphitheater.	**1956**
The Chicago White Sox win the pennant. Second City opens.	**1959**
Richard Nixon receives the Republican presidential nomination at Chicago Amphitheater.	**1960**
Chicago Black Hawks win the Stanley Cup.	**1961**
Picasso statue is unveiled at Civic Center (now Daley Center) Plaza.	**1967**
Hubert Humphrey wins the Democratic presidential nomination at Chicago Amphitheater while more than 5,000 anti-war demonstrators converge on Democratic headquarters at the Conrad Hilton Hotel (now Chicago Hilton and Towers).	**1968**
John Hancock building opens.	**1969**
Sears Tower is completed.	**1973**
Mayor Richard J. Daley dies at age 74. Jane Byrne is elected mayor.	**1976**
State Street Mall opens.	**1979**
Harold Washington is elected mayor.	**1983**
State of Illinois Center opens.	**1985**
The Chicago Theater reopens; Chicago Bears win Super Bowl.	**1986**
Mayor Harold Washington dies.	**1987**
Richard M. Daley is elected mayor.	
	1989
President Bill Clinton receives the Democratic presidential nomination at United Center.	**1996**

of Downtown Chicago. Burning at a rate of 65 acres per hour, the fire reduced the chamber of commerce, department stores, gas works, mills, houses, and mercantile buildings to rubble. When the smoke finally cleared, more than $200 million in property had been destroyed and 100,000 Chicagoans were homeless.

Even more remarkable than the fire itself was how quickly Chicago rebounded. Just a few years after the blaze, Chicago had almost entirely rebuilt itself. In many ways, the great conflagration ultimately proved to be a boon, as it gave city planners the opportunity to rethink the metropolis's design, setting it on course to become the cultural and architectural marvel that it is today.

Twenty years later, the destruction wrought by the Chicago Fire was no longer even slightly discernible. In 1893, Chicago hosted the World's Colombian Exposition, the most spectacular of all world's fairs, visited by more than 27 million people over a six-month period. In the early part of the 20th century, Chicago saw the formation of its world-renowned art institute, public library, opera, and symphony orchestra, garnering its long-standing reputation as a cultural capital. Daniel Burnham's Plan for Chicago, an urban blueprint for the city's future organization, was published in 1909, and much of it is still functional today. Among Burnham's contributions were calls for an unobstructed lakefront, an elaborate forest preserve and park system (from which the city derives one of its mottoes: *Urbs In Horto*, "City in a Garden"), a system of superhighways, and an intricate network of tunnels and multi-leveled streets to keep deliveries from interfering with everyday city life. Not surprisingly, Burnham's motto was

The Ferris Wheel at the 1893 World's Colombian Exhibition

Special Collections and Preservation Division/Chicago Public Library

"Make No Little Plans," still a point of civic pride.

With Burnham's plan in place, Chicago was well on its way to becoming an international capital. In 1927, the Chicago Municipal Airport (now Midway) opened, remaining for many years the world's busiest airport until that title passed to O'Hare International Airport. The year 1933 kicked off the two-year-long Century of Progress World's Fair, the legacy of which is still visible in the John G. Shedd Aquarium and Field Museum of Natural History. And although the era of Prohibition and Al Capone initiated a history of lawlessness within the city (a history Hollywood still exploits to some extent), even the gangsters and their molls and crooked First Ward aldermen could not put a damper on Chicago's remarkable growth.

TRIVIA

Chicago's ethnic composition:

African American: 39%
Caucasian: 38%
Hispanic: 19%
Asian: 4%

Based on most recent census data.

Chicago's post-war years belonged largely to Richard J. Daley. Elected mayor in 1955, the man dubbed "Boss" by legendary *Chicago Tribune* columnist Mike Royko would hold the post until he died in 1976. Daley's reign was notorious for its corruption and political machinations—he is largely credited with tipping the 1960 presidential election toward John F. Kennedy by supplying the requisite number of votes so JFK could take Illinois. The Boss will perhaps be best remembered for his lowlights, among them the 1968 Democratic National Convention, where a television camera caught him yelling an anti-Semitic slur at Abe Ribicoff for questioning his handling of anti-war protesters, and the controversial slaying of Black Panther leaders Fred Hampton and Mark Clark, which happened under Daley's watch. On the plus side, his administration oversaw the erection of some of the world's tallest buildings, including the Sears Tower, the Standard Oil Building (now the Amoco Building), and the John Hancock Center.

Political turmoil followed Daley's death in 1976. Bilandic succeeded Daley, but his re-election was dealt a significant blow when his administration could not clean up the city after a freak blizzard. He lost to Jane Byrne, Chicago's first female mayor, who presided over a racially divided city where tensions became seriously acrimonious. Harold Washington was elected the city's first black mayor in 1983. A noted reformer, Washington's first administration was stymied by white politicians who, for a time, successfully divided the city. Washington was on his way to becoming a significant healing force in the city when he died of a heart attack in 1987, sending the city once again into political upheaval.

Today, Chicago is presided over by Richard M. ("Mayor For Life") Daley, the son of Richard J. Daley. Under Daley's administration, Chicago has become a much more peaceful place. Tourism is at an all-time high.

The People of Chicago

Chicago has a reputation as one of the country's most segregated cities. There is a certain amount of truth to this, although the city seems a veritable model of integration when compared with Boston and other cities. Since peacemaker Harold Washington was elected mayor in 1983, many of the Chicago's racial divides have been bridged. The multiplicity of ethnic neighborhoods, while arguably a remnant of segregation, at the same time allows the city to showcase its remarkable diversity.

Irish Americans still maintain a stronghold in working-class Bridgeport, on the Near South Side, where both legendary mayor Richard J. Daley ("The police aren't here to create disorder; they're here to preserve disorder") and his son, current mayor Richard M. Daley, were born. People of eastern European descent can still be found on the city's Southwest Side, and Italian Americans predominate in Chicago's famed Little Italy on Taylor Street. The Jewish community resides in the city's northernmost neighborhood beside Russian and Indian immigrants in Rogers Park. Shopkeepers in the Lincoln Square neighborhood are frequently bilingual, conducting trade in both English and German. Just south of the Loop lies the tightly knit Chinatown community, while newer Asian immigrants have congregated into the largely Korean Albany Park neighborhood and the Vietnamese enclave in Uptown. African Americans, who came to Chicago in great numbers in the early 20th century, make up more than a third of the city's population and live predominantly in often-neglected South and West Side neighborhoods. The ever-growing Latino community thrives in the West Side Pilsen community. The West Side also boasts the largest urban Polish population outside of Warsaw.

When to Visit Chicago

Chicago is a city of extremes. During winter the Lake Michigan winds cut through the highest quality Gore-Tex coats like Ginsu knives through sheets of paper. Summer withers under a ferocious sun that beats down through the wet, sponge-like atmosphere, and the only respite seems to be the still knee-knockingly chilly waters of the lake. Chicago is not a city for people who like their beer lukewarm or their salsa mild. When to visit may simply be a question of which delightful extreme you prefer.

During the sizzling summers the city pulsates with excitement. Grant Park, the world's largest free outdoor auditorium/carnival, explodes with outdoor classical music concerts and the best in blues, jazz, rock 'n' roll, gospel, Latin music, and cuisine during Chicago's Blues Fest, Jazz Fest, and the two-week gastronomic delight known as "The Taste of Chicago." In the summer the pristine beaches shimmer beside the crystalline lakefront, and the beer at the baseball stadiums is refreshingly ice-cold. The streets are alive with art fairs and book sales and neighborhood celebrations. The whir of bicycle wheels speeds along lakefront trails. The parks host soccer matches and baseball games. With its vibrancy and electricity, one almost could mistake Chicago for Nice or some other Mediterranean jewel.

If anything, the legendary Chicago winters, which frequently make national news with their wind-whipping blizzards and lip-freezing sub-zero temperatures, are even more spectacular than the summers. The cold, icy city lights up like a Christmas tree. There is no better way to see a football game than bundled up in dozens of layers at Soldier Field, gazing out at a frozen Lake Michigan. With its lovely Christmas shop windows and the State Street ice skating rink, the Loop is a bustling fireplace of holiday cheer. Winter enjoys all the joys of summer but moves them indoors to the music clubs, dancehalls, fine dining establishments, and enclosed stadiums.

The Chicago Board of Trade

Chicago Architecture Foundation

Perhaps the best time to visit Chicago is neither winter nor summer, but just before summer begins and just after it ends. In late May the beaches are open but they're not overrun by sun worshippers; baseball is played at Comiskey Park and Wrigley Field but school is still in session. In September there's a cool breeze in the air, but the nights are still long and the leaves on the trees at Morton Arboretum have just begun to turn color. In May and September you can walk by the lake forever without either freezing or breaking a sweat. These are Chicago's best months.

Calendar of Events

Chicago is a city of festivals, celebrations, and cultural events showcasing some of the best sports teams, theater companies, musicians, and artists in the country. Following are some events to look for during the month you'll be visiting Chicago.

JANUARY
Chicago Boat, Sports & RV Show, 312/946-6262

FEBRUARY
Chinatown New Year's Parade, 312/744-3315
Chicago Auto Show, 630/954-0600

MARCH
St. Patrick's Day Parade, 312/744-3370

APRIL
Baseball Opening Day:
    Chicago Cubs, 773/404-CUBS
    Chicago White Sox, 773/831-CUBS
Art Chicago exhibition, 312/587-3300
Chicago Latino Film Festival, 312/431-1330

MAY
Printer's Row Book Fair, 312/987-9896

JUNE
Grant Park Blues Festival, 312/744-4763
Chicago Country Music Festival, 312/744-4763
Gospel Fest, 312/744-4763
Heart of Italy Street Fest, 312/744-3370
Celebrate on State Street arts and crafts festival, 312/744-3370
Andersonville Midsommarfest, 773/728-2995
Old Town Art Fair, 312/951-6106
Japanese Cultural Arts Festival, 312/744-3315

JULY
Taste of Chicago Food and Music Festival, 312/744-4763
Third of July Fireworks Celebration in Grant Park, 312/744-4763
Chicago Historical Society Fourth of July Celebration, 312/642-4600
Old St. Patrick's World's Largest Block Party, 312/744-3370
Sheffield Garden Walk, 312/744-3315
Chinatown Summer Fair, 312/744-3315
Fiesta Del Sol in Pilsen, 312/744-3315
Taste of Lincoln Avenue, 312/744-3315
Gay Pride Parade, 773/384-8243

AUGUST
Chicago Underground Film Festival, 773/866-8660
Venetian Night Boat Parade and Fireworks Celebration, 312/744-3370
Chicago Air and Water Show 312/744-3315
Bud Billiken Parade and Picnic, 312/744-3370
Wicker Park Greening Festival, 312/744-3315
Korean Street Festival in Albany Park, 312/744-3315
Taste of Polonia, 312/744-3315
Grant Park Jazz Festival, 312/744-4763

SEPTEMBER
Viva Chicago Latin Music Festival, 312/744-3315

Celtic Fest Chicago, 312/744-3315
Berghoff Oktoberfest, 312/427-3170
Feast of San Gennaro in Little Italy, 312/744-3315
Mexican Independence Day Parade, 312/744-3315
Chinatown Moon Festival, 312/744-3315
German-American Fest, 312/744-3315

OCTOBER
Chinese Independence Day Parade, 312/744-3315
Chicago International Film Festival, 312/425-9400
Chicago International Children's Film Festival, 773/281-9075
Columbus Day Parade, 312/744-3370
Chicago Marathon, 312/243-0003

NOVEMBER
State Street Christmas Tree Lighting Festival, 312/744-3315
Zoo Lights Festival at Lincoln Park Zoo, 312/742-2000
Veterans' Day Parade, 312/744-3370

DECEMBER
New Year's Eve Fireworks Celebration at Navy Pier, 312/595-5100
Do-It-Yourself Handel's Messiah at Orchestra Hall, 312/435-8122
Christkindlmarket at Daley Center Plaza, 312/744-3315

Chicago Weather

	Ave. High Temps degrees Fahrenheit	Ave. Low Temps degrees Fahrenheit	Ave. Monthly Precipitation in inches
January	32	18	2
February	34	20	2
March	43	29	2.6
April	55	40	2.8
May	65	50	3.4
June	75	60	3.5
July	81	66	3.3
August	74	65	3.2
September	75	58	3.1
October	61	47	2.6
November	47	34	2.4
December	36	23	2.0

Source: U.S. Department of Commerce,
National Oceanic and Atmospheric Administration.

Chicago Weather

There are few major cities with climates more volatile than Chicago's. Come here in the dog days of summer and you'll think the foreboding news about global warming is not only absolutely true but happening most quickly in Chicago. Heat waves breaking the 100-degree mark have become relatively common in July and August and, to paraphrase what all the old elevator operators used to say here, if you think the heat's bad, just wait 'til you feel the humidity. But if you're dreading the August heat, you'll be aching for it in the teeth-chattering month of January, when temperatures are known to dip well below zero and the cold winds blowing off Lake Michigan can make venturing out without layers of sweaters and socks a truly chilling experience. For the most part, though, despite the occasional heat waves, winter blizzards, and deep-freezes, Chicago enjoys a relatively temperate climate where different seasons change the face of the city at different times of the year. And, after all, the climate changes make life even more exciting and unpredictable here in Chicago. How many cities do you know that can turn from St. Tropez to Anchorage, Alaska, in just a few short months?

Dressing in Chicago

Unless you're going to one of the swanky-swankier-swankiest dining spots in town, chaperoning a nephew's high school prom, stepping out at a slick jazz club, or hobnobbing at a Downtown convention, there's one sure-fire way to get spotted as a tourist in this city: wear a suit and tie or an evening gown for a night on the town. Chicagoans pride themselves on their lack of pretension, and that charmingly straightforward steak-and-potatoes attitude carries over into the dress code (or lack of one). In 98 percent of the city about 98 percent of the time, blue jeans or well-pressed Gap slacks are just fine. Chicagoans aren't big into showy jewelry, oversized purses, high-heeled shoes, or even hats (unless of the baseball variety). In the bone-numbing winters and the hot barbecue summers, comfort always takes precedence over fashion. When dressing up to go out, keep in mind this general rule: if it's neither comfortable nor functional, few Chicagoans would consider wearing it.

Cost of Living

Unlike many other major cities, Chicago offers a variety of price ranges. No matter how much money you have, you can find a way either to spend it or save it here. Search for the most elegant, upscale establishments in Chicago and you'll come away thinking this is one of the most expensive cities in the world. But with a careful eye to bargains, you'll realize it is also one of the most affordable. Dinners for two for $100 are by no means un-

TOP TEN

Ten Great Things That Started in Chicago

1. The Hostess Twinkie (invented in 1930 in suburban Schiller Park)

2. Spray paint (devised by Edward Seymour of Sycamore)

3. Roller skates (invented by Levant Richardson of Chicago)

4. The McDonald's hamburger (devised by Ray Kroc, who opened the first McDonald's ever in Des Plaines, Illinois, in 1955)

5. The zipper (invented by Whitcomb Judson in 1896 in Chicago)

6. Cracker Jacks (invented by F. W. Rueckheim in Chicago in 1893)

7. The detective agency (founded by Allen Pinkerton in the 19th century)

8. The Weber grill (invented by George Stephens of Palatine in 1951)

9. Wrigley's Spearmint Gum (devised by Chicago's William Wrigley Jr. Company)

10. Lava Lamps (devised in Chicago in 1965)

Source: Metro Chicago Almanac

common, but at the same time, a trip to Pilsen can get you a fabulous Mexican dinner for two for about ten bucks. True, the toniest cinemas near the Magnificent Mile will run you $8.25 per seat. But take a ride off the beaten path into some of the more affordable neighborhoods and you can see a flick for two bucks.

Five-mile taxi ride:	$4.80
Average dinner for two:	$30
Daily newspaper:	50 cents
Movie admission:	$8
Gallon of gas:	$1.35
Hot dog with fries:	$2

The Local Economy

Nowhere is Chicago's remarkable resilience more evident than in its economy. While many cities have seen their luck fall with the departure of manufacturing jobs, Chicago has merely retooled and realigned itself with businesses more relevant to the 21st century. Though Chicago's days as a meat-packing giant are long gone and big steel no longer plays a significant role in the city's economy, Chicago has recently seen an explo-

Chicago's Top Ten Private Companies

Montgomery Ward & Company

Marmon Group, Inc.

Alliant Foodservice, Inc.

Kemper National Insurance

Topco Associates.

Hyatt Hotels Corp.

Ace Hardware Corp.

Cotter & Co.

Budget Rent-A-Car Corp.

OLS Industries

Source: *Crain's Chicago Business*, April 14, 1997

Chicago's Top Ten Public Companies

Sears, Roebuck & Company

Amoco Corp.

Motorola, Inc.

Allstate Corp.

Sara Lee Corp.

CNA Financial Corp.

Caterpillar, Inc.

UAL Corp.

Ameritech Corp.

Archer Daniels Midland Co.

Source: Standard and Poor's Compustat Services, Inc., from *Crain's Chicago Business*, May 12, 1997

sion in the fields of insurance, real estate, health care, and business services, as well as in the transportation and telecommunications industries. In terms of sheer numbers, Chicago's largest industries are now in the business services and health care fields. Additionally, there are more than 25 Fortune 500 businesses headquartered in and around the Chicago area. These include Abbott Laboratories, Ace Hardware, Allstate, Ameritech, Amoco, Aon Baxter International, Brunswick, Dean Foods, First Chicago NBD Corp., FMC, General Instrument, WW Grainger, Illinois Tool Works, IMC Global, McDonald's, Morton International, Motorola, Navistar International, Quaker Oats, R.R. Donnelley & Sons, Sara Lee, Sears Roebuck, Servicemaster, Stone Container, United Airlines, Unicom, USG, Walgreens, Whitman, and WMX Technologies. On a slightly less serious note, Chicago is also a major manufacturing center for cookies and candy, boasting the presence of both the Tootsie Roll Company and the Nabisco Corporation, home of Chicago's perhaps greatest invention: the Oreo.

Taxes

Like the citizens of virtually every other American city, Chicagoans like to bellyache and moan about exorbitant city taxes. Yet when compared with other cities, Chicago comes in just about average. An average family of four in 1995 paid approximately $4,017 in income tax, just slightly below the national average of $4,304 and considerably less than that paid by their counterparts in New York City, Boston, and Philadelphia. Sales tax in Chicago is 8.75 percent, property taxes approximately 9.5 percent. Illinois residents pay a 3 percent income tax.

Housing

Once priding itself on being one of the more open and accessible cities in the country, Chicago has in the past decade become more and more crowded. Many of the most popular neighborhoods, particularly North and Near North Side ones like Lincoln Park and Old Town, are running at 99 percent capacity. As prices in the suburbs have risen, many new families have chosen to remain in Chicago, pushing housing costs up in many once highly affordable neighborhoods. Still, on the outskirts of town and outside the very desirable neighborhoods near Lake Michigan, it is possible to find affordable homes and apartments, and despite the glut of potential renters and buyers, the housing situation is not yet dire, just somewhat difficult.

Average prices for homes vary widely depending on neighborhood. The median value of a house in Chicago is approximately $78,000. In working-class Bridgeport, one-time home to many a member of the Daley family, the price for an average home is slightly under $96,000. In the coveted Lincoln Park neighborhood, the average is more than $615,000. Reflecting the volatility of the city's housing market, housing prices have more than doubled in the past ten years in hot neighborhoods such as Wicker Park (a gentrifying arts community) and Wrigleyville (home to the Chicago Cubs). The same may be said of the rental situation, where the median monthly rent is still a highly affordable $377, but in Lincoln Park it's hard to find a one-bedroom apartment for under $900.

Education

Chicago public schools (the third-largest public school system in the country) have long ranked lower in quality than the national average. Notoriously underfunded, despite a $3 billion budget, and plagued by strikes, gang conflict, and poverty (83 percent of public school students come from low-income families), the public schools are long overdue for an overhaul. Many city politicians send their own kids to private and parochial schools. But things may be looking up. Most recent statistics cite a 62 percent high school graduation rate, the highest in a decade, and school attendance in the 1990s has been on the upswing as well. And the city has a nationally lauded program of magnet schools for its finest students. As for higher education, Chicago is home to a number of well-respected institutions, including the University of Chicago, Northwestern University, DePaul University, the University of Illinois at Chicago, Loyola University, Roosevelt University, and Columbia College.

Chicago Transit Authority

2

GETTING AROUND CHICAGO

A population of nearly 3 million in the city of Chicago, and more than 6 million in the Chicago metropolitan area. More than 3 million drivers in the county. Two-hundred-twenty-eight square miles of surface area in the city. More than 3,500 miles of streets. It sounds like a nightmare, but the truth of the matter is, finding your way around Chicago is a lot easier than you might think.

It helps that the city is flat. And it also helps that in 1871, there was a huge fire. That way, the city's leaders were able to map out a plan of attack to keep the city flowing freely once it had been rebuilt from the ground up. True, this is still a massive city and those not used to the spectacle of millions of automobiles heading home during a three-hour rush hour might find Chicago overwhelming.

But blessed with a very easy-to-comprehend city layout and an effective public transportation system, with a little bit of patience Chicago is simple and even fun to navigate.

City Layout

For the geographically challenged, Chicago is a dream come true. There is no city that is simpler to navigate. Not New York City, not Washington, D.C., not Los Angeles. Not even Pawtucket, Rhode Island, or Poughkeepsie, New York. It wouldn't even be outlandish to say that getting around Chicago is easier than any of its neighboring suburbs.

The only prerequisite for getting around Chicago is a fourth-grader's knowledge of math. The city is laid out like a grid. The corner of State Street and Madison Street in the Loop represents ground zero. Each block from this point represents 100. One block west of State and Madison is 100 West. Two blocks north is 200 North. Three blocks south is 300 South. And six blocks east is somewhere below the surface of Lake Michigan. The further south you go, the simpler things get. Once you get to 1200 South, all the east-west streets are numbered. Each block roughly corresponds to more than $1/2$ of a mile, so the distance from 12th Street south to 28th Street is about two miles. It doesn't get much simpler than that, although the city has developed a troubling penchant for vanity addresses (One Magnificent Mile, Three Illinois Center) and the Chicago City Council has become a little too enamored of late with renaming streets in honor of celebrities (Irv Kupcinet Bridge, Siskel and Ebert Way, Gandhi Street), which makes life slightly more complicated—though not complicated enough to confuse the fourth-grade math whiz in all of us.

Some Major Streets

North Avenue (1800 North)
Fullerton Avenue (2400 North)
Belmont Avenue (3200 North)
Irving Park (4000 North)
Montrose Avenue (4400 North)
Wilson Avenue (4600 North)
Lawrence Avenue (4800 North)
Foster Avenue (5200 North)
Devon Avenue (6400 North)
Howard Street (7600 North—northern border between
    Chicago and Evanston)
Halsted Street (800 West)
Ashland Avenue (1600 West)
Damen Avenue (2000 West)
Western Avenue (2400 West)
California Avenue (2800 West)
Kedzie Avenue (3200 West)
Cicero Avenue (4800 West)
Harlem Avenue (7600 West)

Another hint for navigating Chicago: The lake is always east. (Of course, for those of us who like to spend as much of the summer as possible on the spectacular lakefront, the truth is that the city is always west.)

TRIVIA

Western Avenue (2400 West) is the longest street in Chicago and the only one that goes from the north edge of the city to the south edge of the city and beyond. Stretching the nearly 25-mile length of Chicago, Western also crosses over the northern border into Evanston (where it changes its name and becomes Asbury Street) and goes through Blue Island, Illinois, to the south before it becomes Dixie Highway. Unfortunately, lined from north to south with car dealerships, it is also one of the least scenic streets.

Public Transportation

It's hard to criticize the Chicago Transit Authority (CTA), the city's public transportation system. Though notoriously under-funded and forever contemplating closures of its stations, any public transportation system that can manage to service approximately 425 million passengers every year without suffering some sort of meltdown has to be doing something right.

If you're not traveling to some obscure area of the city, the CTA is pretty much the way to go. The trains are reliable and fast. The buses are less so. But if you allow enough time, you should have no trouble getting where you want to go between around 7 in the morning and 9 at night. Past dark, though, and when the streets begin clearing out, the public transportation system runs its buses and trains less frequently and safety becomes more of a serious question.

Prices on board the CTA are reasonable. One train or bus ride costs $1.50. If you want a transfer (a pass that allows you to transfer to two more buses or trains within two hours), it'll cost you an extra 30 cents. But make sure up front that you tell your bus driver or the person at the sales window at the train station that you want a transfer when you pay your fare. Recently, the CTA has introduced transit card vending machines at its stations, on which you can charge up to $100 worth of travel. CTA cards and passes are also available at currency exchanges and Dominick's or Jewel food stores.

Subway (The El)

Chicago's "El" (short for elevated train) has been a key thread in the city's fabric for more than one hundred years. Beginning in 1892, El trains carried passengers to the 1893 World's Columbian Exposition for a nickel a throw. Over the course of the next century, new train lines were added steadily. The CTA was founded in 1947, leading up to the present train transportation system. There are five major train lines now and they are identified by color:

The **Red Line**, which is, incidentally, one of the cheapest and best ways to get a feel for the city, begins on the Far North Side at the Chicago–Evanston border and goes all the way south to 95th Street. One

EL/SUBWAY STOPS

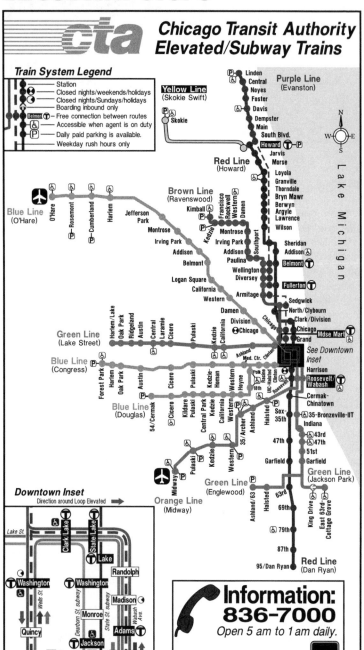

Chicago Transit Authority
Elevated/Subway Trains

Train System Legend
- Station
- Closed nights/weekends/holidays
- Closed nights/Sundays/holidays
- Boarding inbound only
- Free connection between routes
- Accessible when agent is on duty
- Daily paid parking is available.
- Weekday rush hours only

Yellow Line (Skokie Swift)
Skokie

Purple Line (Evanston)
Linden
Central
Noyes
Foster
Davis
Dempster
Main
South Blvd.
Howard

Red Line (Howard)
Jarvis
Morse
Loyola
Granville
Thorndale
Bryn Mawr
Berwyn
Argyle
Lawrence
Wilson
Sheridan
Addison
Belmont
Fullerton
Sedgwick
North/Clybourn
Clark/Division
Chicago
Grand

Brown Line (Ravenswood)
Kimball
Francisco
Rockwell
Western
Damen
Montrose
Irving Park
Addison
Paulina
Southport
Wellington
Diversey
Armitage

Blue Line (O'Hare)
O'Hare
Rosemont
Cumberland
Harlem
Jefferson Park
Montrose
Irving Park
Addison
Belmont
Logan Square
California
Western
Damen
Division
Chicago

Kedzie

Green Line (Lake Street)
Harlem/Lake
Oak Park
Ridgeland
Austin
Central
Laramie
Cicero
Pulaski
Kedzie
California

Blue Line (Congress)
Forest Park
Harlem
Oak Park
Austin
Cicero
Pulaski
Kedzie-Homan
Western
Hoyne

Blue Line (Douglas)
54/Cermak
Cicero
Kildare
Pulaski
Kedzie
Central Park
California
Western
Ashland
Polk
Racine
UIC-Halsted
Clinton
18th
Roosevelt
Ashland
Med. Ctr.
Sox-35th
35/Archer
Halsted

See Downtown Inset
Mdse Mart
Harrison
Roosevelt/Wabash
Cermak-Chinatown
35-Bronzeville-IIT
Indiana
43rd
47th
51st
Garfield

Orange Line (Midway)
Midway
Pulaski
Kedzie
Western
35/Archer
Ashland

Green Line (Englewood)
Ashland/63
Halsted
63rd
69th
79th
87th
95/Dan Ryan

Green Line (Jackson Park)
Garfield
King Drive
63rd
East 63rd-Cottage Grove

Red Line (Dan Ryan)

Downtown Inset
Direction around Loop Elevated ➡
Lake St.
Clark/Lake
State/Lake
Lake
Randolph
Wells St.
Washington
Washington
Madison
Dearborn St. subway
State St. subway
Wabash Ave.
Monroe
Quincy
Adams
Jackson
LaSalle
Library
Van Buren St.
LaSalle
Congress St.

📞 **Information:
836-7000**
Open 5 am to 1 am daily.

http://www.transitchicago.com

8/98

Chicago Transit Authority

of the most popular lines, the Red Line travels through the Far North Side Rogers Park and Edgewater neighborhoods before entering Lakeview and Wrigleyville (The Addison stop is just a block from the Chicago Cubs' Wrigley Field, which makes the Red Line particularly crowded during summer days.) From here, the Red Line continues south, making its way through Lincoln Park before going underground into the subway, where it makes a number of stops on the near North Side and in the Loop (the Chicago Avenue stop grants easy access to the Magnificent Mile and the Washington Street stop will drop you off practically in the basement of Marshall Field and Company's department store). Emerging from the tunnel, the Red Line continues down the South Side with a convenient stop at Cermak Road for Chinatown. The stop at 35th Street will drop you just a few blocks away from Comiskey Park, home of the Chicago White Sox, before heading deeper south and coming to an end at 95th. Though quite near the Robert Taylor Homes housing project, the Comiskey Park stop at 35th is well-policed and generally safe during daytime but is not recommended after dark, particularly to people unfamiliar with the area.

The **Brown Line** (also known as the **Ravenswood**) is a shorter line which provides more convenient service to certain Downtown and North Side spots and services some parts of the Far North Side of Chicago. Making a stop at the Merchandise Mart, the Brown Line travels through the Loop before snaking northwest through Lincoln Park and Lakeview and heading west through the Lincoln Square German-American neighborhood and the Korean enclave in Albany Park on Kimball Avenue, where it comes to an end. For much of the ride, this line gives an excellent street-level view of some of Chicago's ethnic neighborhoods.

The **Blue Line**, which makes stops in the Loop in the Dearborn Subway, is the best choice for traveling to O'Hare Airport, the groovy Wicker Park neighborhood, and the University of Illinois at Chicago campus on the city's West Side. A very quick and convenient line, the trains here travel efficiently to the western regions of the city, providing easy transportation to sometimes-difficult-to-get-to neighborhoods like the Latino community in Logan Square and the small Italian community in the Northwest Side's Jefferson Park.

The **Green Line** services the South and West Sides, providing much-needed but sometimes dicey transportation through some marginal areas. Traveling from Harlem and Lake to the west (convenient to suburban Oak Park and the homes of Frank Lloyd Wright), this line goes through the Loop and continues through the South Side, passing by the campus of the Illinois Institute of Technology and through the once-thriving Black Metropolis community that is now marked by poverty and public housing facilities, before ending up at 63rd and Cottage Grove. Though some people will tell you that this train line is very convenient to the University of Chicago and the sights of Hyde Park, one has to travel a few blocks through some pretty rough areas from this line to get there. If possible, other forms of transportation to the U of C and environs would be advisable.

The **Orange Line** is a relatively short line that allows quick, convenient

TRIVIA

Though Chicago basically looks like a huge tic-tac-toe board with an infinite number of squares, there are a certain number of angled streets, which provide significant short-cuts for crossing the city. In Chicago public grade schools, they used to teach that all the angled streets in the city were paved over Indian trails. There is little evidence to support this claim, but still if you want to cut some time off your trips across the city, keep an eye out for the following streets: Clybourn Avenue, Elston Avenue, Lincoln Avenue, and Milwaukee Avenue.

transportation from the Loop and through part of the South Side to Midway Airport. The CTA also has three lines that service the suburbs. The **Purple Line** (which you can catch at Howard Street) makes eight stops in suburban Evanston, providing convenient service to the city's Downtown and Northwestern University, as well as its beaches. The **Yellow Line** (which you can also catch at Howard Street) is known as the **Skokie Swift** and makes one stop in Skokie. The **Blue Line** services Oak Park, Forest Park, Rosemont, and Cicero.

The entire El and subway system is quite easy to learn. All stations and trains have maps to help you along. And, if you're stuck for travel information, give a call to the CTA at 836-7000 (no area code—the number works from whatever area code you happen to be in). Keep in mind, though, that after dark, the city's trains are less safe than its buses. If you're traveling in a group of three or more, you'll be okay in most of the well-traveled neighborhoods. But the further away you are from Downtown, Lincoln Park, or the Magnificent Mile and the fewer people you have traveling with you, the smarter you'll be if you catch a cab or take a car.

Metra Trains

A slightly more upscale option for commuter travel in the city are the double-decker Metra commuter train lines, which are quicker, cooler, roomier, and more reliable than their CTA counterparts. On the other hand, they are more expensive (the prices begin at $1.75 and go up depending on where you want to make your stop, though no ride is more than $6.60). They are also less frequent and they don't make as many stops. Offering convenient service to the Loop and the McCormick Place Convention Center, Metra makes just a few stops in Chicago, including Rogers Park and Ravenswood, before zooming into Evanston and the north suburbs. Metra does, however, have 12 different lines and some go all the way into Wisconsin and Indiana. Metra's longest route goes from Downtown Chicago to Harvard, Illinois. To get a full list of Metra's stops and schedules either stop by Union Station or call 312/322-6777 for more information.

Buses

The CTA bus system is both incredibly complicated and incredibly simple. On the one hand, there are dozens upon dozens of bus lines (about 130 in total), each signified by its own number. There are few lifelong Chicago residents who could tell you the number or the routes of more than a handful of them. On the other hand, if you just have a general direction you want to go instead of an exact destination, Chicago's bus system makes for a leisurely and effective, if somewhat imperfect science. Chances are if you get on a bus on Clark Street going south, it'll keep going south for quite some time. Keep in mind, though, that since they make very frequent stops, the buses are markedly slower than any of the train lines in the city. If you don't like this imprecise sort of approach or you're in a time crunch, there are a few excellent bus lines that are worth remembering:

The No. 136 Express begins way north in Rogers Park and continues south to Downtown, winding up at Wacker Drive and Adams Street. This is a great rush hour choice for getting Downtown quickly. The No. 147 Outer Drive Express provides relatively quick transportation between the Howard Street El (at the northern border between Chicago and Evanston) and the No. 29 State. To get back and forth between the Loop and the Magnificent Mile, get on the No. 151 Sheridan. To get from the Loop to Navy Pier, look for the downtown No. 56 Milwaukee. The No. 56 also is a good way to get back and forth between the Wicker Park arts community and Michigan Avenue downtown. The No. 8 Halsted goes all the way from Wrigleyville on the North Side to the South Side of Chicago via Halsted Street. The No. 22 Clark bus is a good, scenic way to get from the Loop to Rogers Park on the Far North Side of the city. And, to get from the North Side Lakeview and Lincoln Park neighborhoods to the Magnificent Mile and the Loop, get on either of these two very reliable lines: the No. 156 LaSalle or the No. 151 Sheridan.

CTA buses run every 5 to 15 minutes during morning and evening rush hours and every 8 to 20 minutes during the rest of the day. Some bus lines run 24 hours and at night those generally run every half hour.

The buses in the suburbs are run by the Pace Suburban Bus Service. Information about their routes and bus schedules may be obtained by calling 836-7000 from any Chicago area code.

TIP

If you're computer savvy and don't feel like finding a bus or a train schedule, most of the bus and train services in the city and suburbs have World Wide Web addresses with maps of their transportation lines.

- Chicago Transportation Authority: http://www.transitchicago.com
- Metra: http://www.metrarail.com
- Pace Suburban Bus Service: http://www.pacebus.com

TIP

In some cities, some daring souls step onto the train tracks to see when the next train is coming. In Chicago it's not a good idea. It's not even advised to lean. That third rail you see is electrified, and one step onto it is most likely fatal.

Taxis

If you're traveling anywhere in the Near North or Downtown areas of Chicago, taxis are no problem unless the city's in the throes of a blinding rainstorm or blizzard. On Michigan Avenue, taxis are pretty readily available at all hours of the day or night. And further north, Clark Street, Sheridan Road, and Halsted Streets are very reliable places to catch cabs. But if you want to be assured of your taxi's arrival, it's always a good idea to call ahead. The major taxi companies in Chicago are American United Cab Co. (773/248-7600), Checker Taxi (312/243-2537), Flash Cab (773/561-1444), and Yellow Cab Co. (312/829-4222).

Commuter Boats

Though Chicago hasn't quite turned into Venice, a fun and convenient form of transportation for Loop businessfolk and travelers has sprouted up in the form of boats. During the warmer months ferries operated by the Wendella Sightseeing Boats go back and forth along the Chicago River between between the Wrigley Building (on the northwest corner of the Michigan Avenue bridge) to Union Station every 10 minutes. The ride lasts about 10 minutes and costs $1.25.

Wendella Sightseeing Boats

Wendella Sightseeing Boats

Driving in Chicago

Though there are a number of expressways in the city which have a notorious reputation as some of the country's most dangerous (notably I-94, The Dan Ryan Expressway which zooms terrifyingly from Downtown Chicago south to Indiana and the Chicago Skyway, a jaw-droppingly worrisome acrophobic's nightmare at the southern tip of the city), Chicago is a relative breeze even for the newcomer.

Driving in the city is not a stop and go pinball game like it is on the streets of Boston or an adrenaline-infused rollercoaster ride like Manhattan. Drivers here are a relatively conscientious lot, particularly once you get outside the Loop and the Magnificent Mile areas, where most of the traffic is composed of taxi drivers and folks up from the suburbs checking out the sights and trying to get a glimpse of the Sears Tower or Dennis Rodman.

The pace is not exactly lackadaisical here, but it's not a fast-forward Indy

Ten Times and Places When You Should Leave the Car at Home:

Chicago is no stranger to traffic snarls. And of course there are a few strange souls out there who get a perverse thrill about finding them. But if you are like most people and want to avoid traffic jams at all costs, here is an introduction to some places where you'll be sure to find them.

1. *Any expressway at Rush Hour (between 7 and 9:30 a.m. and 4 and 6:30 p.m.)*
2. *Ashland Avenue also at Rush Hour (when it serves as an alternative to expressways)*
3. *North Clark Street on any weekend night (particularly when the Cubs are playing a night game)*
4. *Lake Shore Drive on Sundays when the Bears are in town or any evening when a major rock act is playing at Soldier Field*
5. *West Madison Street on evenings when the Bulls or Hawks are playing*
6. *The Dan Ryan Expressway during afternoons and evenings when the Chicago White Sox are playing*
7. *North Halsted Street on weekend nights*
8. *Division Street near Rush Street on weekend nights*
9. *I-55 (the Stevenson Expressway) during holiday seasons when Midway Airport is packed*
10. *I-90 near O'Hare Airport during the same holidays*

T. Bishop and M. Yossiffon

The El in Chicago's Loop

500 either. People generally pay attention to things like traffic lights and speed limits, especially if police cars are nearby. Chicago's famed Lake Shore Drive, the city's most scenic route which hugs the lakefront from the Far North to the South Side, in the grand scheme of things is a comparatively leisurely Sunday drive and the speed limits of 45 throughout the year and 40 throughout the winter are generally observed.

The thing to remember if you're in one of the heavily traveled tourist areas is that most every place is walkable or convenient to public transportation, and trying to navigate the traffic snarls of Michigan Avenue might not be worth the effort. But once you're past the Magnificent Mile, you can step on the gas, push the cruise control button, and head out home free to the nether regions of Chicago.

Parking Tips

Despite the fact that the city has gotten more and more congested with every passing year and certain drives take twice as long as they might have just a few years ago, street parking is not particularly difficult in 90 percent of the city if you're driving a reasonably sized car and you have a modicum of patience.

Downtown Chicago and the Near North Side is a different story. Street parking has been all but outlawed in the Loop and the few meter spaces you can find generally allow you to park for only about 15 minutes. The best bet is to find a city lot and leave your car there. Pay very close attention to which lot you choose, however, because certain garages could wind up costing 20 bucks or more if you stay for the whole day. The most affordable of these Downtown choices are the very convenient, if not altogether scenic, underground Grant Park garages, with several entrances located either directly on Michigan Avenue or directly north of Grant Park. The Michigan Avenue lots also offer direct underground access via a pedway to Marshall Field's, the Chicago Cultural Center, and various other important city locations. Quite convenient during the bitter days of winter. The East Monroe Street Garage at Columbus Drive and Monroe has nearly 4,000 spaces. You can park there the whole day, visit all the Loop shops and museums, and pay only $5.50. Another good choice for parking Downtown is the Field Harbor Parking Garage (165 N. Field Blvd. and Randolph Street, 312/938-8989) where you can park the whole day for six bucks.

Biking in Chicago

To say that Chicago is not a biker's paradise would be a significant under-statement. The city does have one exquisite bike trail that snakes for more than 15 miles around the lakefront from Edgewater to the outskirts of South Shore. But since this lovely trail is one of the city's only safe places to pedal in a leisurely fashion, when the mercury climbs above 60 degrees the bike trail becomes a clogged nightmare with the frequent cry of "On Your Left!" ringing in your ear. If you choose to push your way into the mayhem, bikes are available for rental at a number of lakefront locations, most notably by Lincoln Park Zoo and Oak Street Beach.

Truth be told, things have improved for cyclists over the past decade. Mayor Richard M. Daley, a man with a somewhat green outlook has spear-headed a plan to increase the number of bike lanes in the city. Unfortu-nately, many of the city's drivers (particularly the taxi operators) have not quite gotten into the swing of things and see the bike lanes as their oppor-tunity to pass on the right.

Airports

There are several airports serving Chicago. Most likely, readers of this book will be flying in and out of O'Hare International Airport or Midway Airport.

O'Hare International Airport

Though there is still some dispute over whether this is the world's busiest airport or whether it runs a close second to the one in Dallas-Ft. Worth, it is certainly a monster—but at the same time, a surprisingly convenient and well-organized one. I had always thought O'Hare was a horrific airport until I realized that it was far superior to every airport I'd ever visited. A few hours

TRIVIA

In the late 19th century and early part of the 20th century, Chicago was a major manufacturing center for the automobile. Some of the dozens of automobiles that were made here included the Hertz (built by the founder of Hertz Auto Rental), the Sears (made by Sears, Roebuck and Co.), the Rambler (probably the most successful brand built in Chicago), the Tucker (immortalized in Francis Ford Coppola's film *Tucker*), and the Yellow Cab.

Want to know what the traffic's going to be like before you get out? All-news radio stations WMAQ (670 AM) and WBBM (780 AM) offer traffic and weather information every 10 minutes. And once you're on the expressway, automated traffic information is available on AM 530 and 1610.

in JFK, Newark, LAX, Heathrow, or Charles de Gaulle should be sufficient to make even the most cantankerous traveler sing the praises of O'Hare.

Originally named Orchard Place and opened in 1955, O'Hare was named after Edward O'Hare, a Navy pilot and Congressional Medal of Honor winner who died in the Battle of the Midway. Visited by more than 60 million travelers every year, O'Hare is a state-of-the-art facility, with a spectacular glass United Airlines terminal designed by controversial architect Helmut Jahn. Terminals are linked by a speedy and convenient trolley system. Over the past decade, O'Hare has increased its number of moving walkways to make getting around the nearly 8,000-acre facility less taxing, but most trips nevertheless involve a fair amount of walking.

Midway Airport

Chicago's oldest airport (founded in 1923), Midway is not exactly a state-of-the-the-art facility. Infused with the aroma of fast food and crowded with noisy travelers, it more closely resembles a 1962 bus terminal. But it is, in fact, closer to Downtown Chicago than is O'Hare, and getting to and from Midway is somewhat more convenient. A comparatively small 10 million passengers per year use this facility. Located on the city's Southwest Side, it is only about seven miles from the heart of the Loop. In order to get from the plane to your rental car, I would conservatively estimate that you would save 3/4 of a mile in walking distance as opposed to O'Hare.

On the downside, however, Midway is not as readily accessibly from all areas of the city via public transportation (though the orange CTA line is okay) and getting there without a car involves travel through some less-than-desirable neighborhoods. Also, some of the major carriers do not serve Midway.

Meigs Field

Certainly this is the city's most scenic airport, but it doesn't really work for most travelers unless they are traveling via their own Lear Jets, in commuter airlines, or in small planes from Springfield, Illinois. Located right on the lakefront, a short walk away from the Adler Planetarium and about a mile from the Loop, the miniature airport was founded in 1923. There have been rumblings that the airport will eventually be closed down to make room for a lakefront park, but until that happens, Meigs affords the small-plane traveler some of the most breathtaking views of the city skyline.

Airlines

American Airlines, 800/433-7300
ATA (American Trans Air), 800/225-2995
Continental Airlines, 800/525-0280
Delta Airlines, 800/221-1212
Kiwi International, 800/538-5494
Northwest Airlines, 800/225-2525
Southwest Airlines, 800/445-5660
TWA (Trans World Airlines), 800/221-2000
United Airlines, 800/722-5243
US Air, 800/428-4322

Regional Train Service

Movie buffs probably best remember Union Station from Brian dePalma's homage to Sergei Eisenstein's classic film *Potemkin* in *The Untouchables*, when a baby carriage tumbles down the steps of the train station's main staircase while Andy Garcia, two guns in hand, comes sliding into frame to save the baby and eliminate a gangster. Aside from its cinematic significance, Union Station also is the city's main rail hub.

Located just west of the Loop (210 S. Canal Street), the recently

Metra Trains, p. 26

Metra Trains

refurbished 1925 facility is serviced both by commuter trains and Amtrak (800/USA-RAIL). Leisurely, if not always convenient or timely, service is offered from here to every major U.S. capital. Some of the more popular routes include the 90-minute trip to Milwaukee and the five-hour journeys to St. Louis and Detroit. Travel to and from New York City and Los Angeles is certainly more affordable than traveling through the air. But the length of these journeys can tend to be mind-numbing.

Regional Bus Service

The less respectful of us refer to it as "Riding The Dog," that time-honored practice of seeing the country through the bumpity-bump of the Greyhound bus window. Greyhound is certainly the most affordable of travel options to and from Chicago, and since the main terminal moved from a very seedy facility in the Loop to a serviceable location about a mile west of the Loop near the University of Illinois at Chicago, one is less likely to hear the rather frightening phrase that I heard uttered at the old Greyhound terminal as a youngster ("I'm gonna pick that little guy up, turn him upside-down and take all he's got."). Still, the Greyhound station in the early morning or after dark is far from the safest place in town so keep an eye out. Greyhound's main facility is located at 630 North Harrison Street, with facilities located near O'Hare and on the South Side. Call 800/231-2222 for more information.

Jaime Ardiles-Arce for the Ritz-Carlton Chicago

3

WHERE TO STAY

When shopping for a hotel, nobody likes surprises. You want the beds to be clean, the rooms to be comfortable, maybe a view and a lobby and a nice marble bathroom with a terry-cloth robe. While in some cities (like New York) quality can vary enormously from hotel to hotel, the hotel scene in Chicago is pretty standard. Except for the top-of-the-line, two-zillion-star establishments and the fleabags (those are the hotels not mentioned in this book), differences between hotels in the same price range are subtle.

That means Chicago doesn't have the groovy, artsy hotels you'll stumble upon in San Francisco and Manhattan. And you'll be hard-pressed to find any of those quirky but lovable bed-and-breakfasts with bars of avocado soap in the bathrooms and Laura Ashley coverlets in the bedrooms. But at the same time, it means that unless you stray very far afield, you won't find a roach trap in a room once inhabited by Jim Morrison, whose graffiti still adorns the bathroom mirror. Thanks to an explosion in Chicago's lodging and tourism scene over the last 20 years, choosy travelers can find almost everything they could possibly need. Even most of the once-rundown hotels have undergone facelifts and are perfectly adequate.

Most of the major chains have at least one outpost here, and they usually offer high-tech amenities that can't be found at some of the more charming independent hotels. Knowing that you're unlikely to get any big surprises when securing your Chicago hotel room, you need only to concentrate on the subtle essentials: Would you prefer to be near the heart of the Loop and the financial centers? The shops of Michigan Avenue? Somewhere off the beaten path? Do you care about fax/modem capability? Do you need an Olympic-sized swimming pool? The selection is vast; the choice is yours.

All accommodations are wheelchair accessible unless otherwise noted.

DOWNTOWN

Lake Michigan

Adler Planetarium

Shedd Aquarium & Oceanarium

Field Museum of Natural History

To 3 ↑

41

LAKE SHORE DR

Grant Park

Buckingham Fountain

COLUMBUS DR

Grant Park

Art Institute of Chicago

CONGRESS PLAZA DR

MICHIGAN AV

E HARRISON ST

E BALBO AV

E 8TH ST

E 9TH ST

E 11TH ST

WABASH ST

STATE ST

DEARBORN ST

POLK ST

LA SALLE ST

LA SALLE ST

WELLS ST ▶

Chicago River

S WACKER DR

LAKE ST

RANDOLPH ST

WASHINGTON ST

MADISON ST

MONROE ST

ADAMS ST

JACKSON BLVD

VAN BUREN ST

CONGRESS PKWY

HARRISON ST

CANAL ST ◀

W POLK ST

TAYLOR ST

ROOSEVELT RD

CLINTON ST ▶

◀ JEFFERSON ST

DES PLAINES ST ▶

HALSTED ST

University of Illinois at Chicago

MILES

KILOMETERS

N

Where to Stay in Downtown Chicago

1 Best Western Grant Park Hotel
2 Blackstone Hotel
3 Days Inn Lake Shore Drive
4 Essex Inn
5 Hilton Chicago and Towers
6 Hotel Allegro
7 Hyatt On Printer's Row
8 The Midland Hotel
9 Palmer House Hilton
10 Ramada Congress

Price Key
$ = Less than $80
$$ = $81–$125
$$$ = $126–$175
$$$$ = $176–$225
$$$$$ = More than $225

DOWNTOWN

Hotels

BEST WESTERN GRANT PARK HOTEL
1100 S. Michigan Ave.
312/922-2900 or 800/528-1234
$$

Located in a sort of no-man's-land—not quite the Loop and not quite Chinatown, the Best Western still offers easy access to the trade shows of McCormick Place as well as to the Museum Campus that features the Field Museum of Natural History, the John G. Shedd Aquarium, and the Adler Planetarium. Although it's probably the least desirable of the Best Westerns in the city as far as actual living quarters are concerned, the location and its competitive price make it a viable option for a traveler on a budget, or one who is shut out of the other major hotels during convention time. Plus, there's a pool. (Downtown)

BLACKSTONE HOTEL
636 S. Michigan Ave.
312/427-4300 or 800/622-6330
$$$

This 305-room hotel, built in 1910 and mere steps away from Grant Park, still has a sense of Old World charm about it. Its suites, which have housed several U.S. presidents over the years, are luxurious. The conference rooms are somewhat dingier than they used to be, and the once-magnificent Blackstone Theater has been taken over by DePaul University, but some traces of the glory years remain. (Fortunately, the memory of 1968 has long since faded. That was the year that George McGovern used the Blackstone as his presidential campaign headquarters.) (Downtown)

HILTON CHICAGO AND TOWERS
720 S. Michigan Ave.
312/922-4400 or 800/445-8667
$$$$

Huge beyond huge. Big beyond big. Also known as Chicago Hilton and Towers, the Hilton, built in 1927, takes up an entire city block and each year is home to countless conventions, meetings, and high school proms. Several heads of state, including Dwight D. Eisenhower, have stayed here. Conveniently located in the South Loop near Buckingham Fountain and other popular sites, the Hilton boasts a magnificent ballroom and more than 1,500 rooms outfitted with cherry-wood furnishings and brass fixtures. The Hilton is home to a wonderful world of sprightliness and luxury as tourists, convention-goers, and football and rock 'n' roll fans heading for Soldier Field keep it buzzing well into the wee hours of the morning. Recalling the days of

TRIVIA

The Hilton Chicago and Towers (originally the Stevens Hotel) was once the largest hotel in the world. During World War II it was used by the U.S. Air Force as a technical school.

The biggest night in the history of the Hotel Allegro came in 1933, when the hotel (then called the Bismarck) brought in 20,000 kegs of beer from Germany to celebrate the end of prohibition.

old-fashioned, full-service hotels, the Hilton has a fair amount of shops, including a hair salon and a drug store; several restaurants, including Buckingham's Steak House; and a bar called Kitty O'Shea's, which features live music. The hotel also has its own health club with an indoor pool. (Downtown)

HOTEL ALLEGRO
171 W. Randolph St.
312/236-0123
$$$

The Allegro—the newest and brightest addition to the Chicago hotel scene—is the city's funky answer to New York and San Francisco's art hotels. With flashy bursts of color in its decor, CD players in every room, a thespian staff, and early-morning reveilles, the Allegro is a bold and whimsical place. Remodeled from the old Bismarck Hotel, site of many a political gathering, the Hotel Allegro offers a much-needed jolt of youthful energy to the occasionally staid atmosphere of the Loop. (Downtown)

HYATT ON PRINTER'S ROW
500 S. Dearborn St.
312/986-1234 or 800/233-1234
$$$

Located in an up-and-coming South Loop neighborhood that always threatens to be the next big thing but never quite makes it, the Hyatt is just a short distance away from a variety of excellent bookshops and the ar-

chitectural marvels of the city's Loop financial district. The hotel is adjacent to the highly reputed and upscale Printer's Row restaurant. (Downtown)

THE MIDLAND HOTEL
176 W. Adams St.
312/332-1200 or 800/621-2360
$$$–$$$$

One of the only decent small hotels in the Loop, the Midland is a quaint choice with decent rooms located on a street that seems almost deserted after sundown. A daily buffet breakfast is offered, as is a complimentary evening cocktail. (Downtown)

PALMER HOUSE HILTON
17 E. Monroe St.
312/726-7500 or 800/445-8667
$$$$

While not the ultimate jewel in the Chicago hotel crown that it once was, the legendary Palmer House remains a somewhat less opulent version of New York's famed Plaza Hotel (although it is in fact the "sister hotel" of the Waldorf-Astoria). Palmer House has a long and storied history beginning with its establishment by one of Chicago's founding fathers, Potter Palmer. The hotel, for a while the largest in the city, was burned to the ground then rebuilt in the late 19th century. Boasting more than 1,600 rooms and suites, the hotel also has a fitness center with a steam room, sauna, and indoor pool. All rooms have two phone lines, a coffeemaker, and an iron and ironing board. There are five restaurants and lounges in the hotel, including the legendary Trader Vic's, a Polynesian-style throwback to the 1950s. (Downtown)

RAMADA CONGRESS
520 S. Michigan Ave.
312/427-3800 or 800/635-1666
$$$

The price is somewhat lower here than at the nearby Chicago Hilton and Towers, but then so is the quality of the surroundings. Though it's been around in one form or another since 1893, the Congress often seems to exist as a miniature imitation of the Hilton from its lobby to its shops. Location has kept it in business (easy access to the Loop and all points north and south). People-watching is also an advantage as the Congress tends to bring in some rather oddball conventions; in recent years the hotel has played host to Beatles memorabilia shows, the Society of American Magicians, Women of Size Take Pride, and a gathering of *X-Files* fans. (Downtown)

Motels/Hostels

DAYS INN LAKE SHORE DRIVE
644 N. Lake Shore Dr.
312/943-9200 or 800/541-3223
$$$

This is one of Chicago's most recognizable hotels, if not for its excellent location, reasonable prices, and far-from-shabby rooms, then at least for the revolving restaurant that stands at its pinnacle. The rotating room is now also available for private functions. Right next to Navy Pier, the lakefront bike trail, the beach, and the bars and shops of North Pier, and just a short stroll away from Michigan Avenue, this nearly 600-room Days Inn features an outdoor pool, a fitness center, shops, and a supermarket run by Treasure Island, one of the best high-end supermarket chains in the city. Offers excellent lake views, too. (Downtown)

ESSEX INN
800 S. Michigan Ave.
312/939-2800 or 800/621-6909
$

No one will ever mistake the Essex for a luxury hotel. The address may say Michigan Avenue, and the Chicago Hilton and Towers is only a couple of blocks away, but this is far from what anyone would consider a Mag Mile establishment. Even so, the basic if somewhat run-down rooms are serviceable enough, and the location is a good one for bargain-hunting McCormick Place trade show visitors. Also nearby are the football games and rock concerts at Soldier Field, as well as the free concerts and food and music festivals of Grant Park. The 250-plus room hotel also features a heated outdoor pool, a downstairs deli, and cable TV. (Downtown)

TRIVIA

In addition to being known as a hotel to many presidents, the Congress Hotel was also a major spot for opera stars in the beginning of the 20th century. Enrico Caruso and others used the famed marble tunnel in the Congress to gain access to the Auditorium Theater. The tunnel has since been sealed off.

Hotels

AMBASSADOR WEST
1300 N. State Pkwy.
312/787-3700 or 800/300-WEST
$$$$

The Ambassador West is only a couple of blocks away from the loudest and most whiskey-sodden, too-old-to-still-be-frat-boys joints on Division Street. But what a difference a couple of blocks can make. Refined, elegant, and understated, much like the other Ambassador hotel across the street, the Ambassador West marks the perfect metamorphosis from singles bar/meat-market bacchanalia to subtlety and refinement. Built in 1924, the 200-plus-room Ambassador maintains its air of 1920s grace and luxury, and offers lovely rooms and suites with well-stocked mini-bars. A barber shop and a beauty salon are located on the premises, and Beau's Bistro, on the first floor, is a pretty safe bet for decent food in an unoppressive atmosphere. Other perks include complimentary newspapers, shoe shines, and a fitness center with Life Fitness machines. Oak Street Beach and the opulent mansions of Astor Street and Burton Place are all within a short walking distance. (Near North)

BEST WESTERN INN OF CHICAGO
162 E. Ohio St.
312/787-3100 or 800/557-BEST
$$

One of the better bargain chain hotel options in the city (the inn boasts that the Zagat Survey named it "Chicago's Best Value"), the Best Western wins points for size and location, if not always for opulence. Just off of the Magnificent Mile, very conveniently

The grand lobby at The Drake, p. 43

located for public transportation, and an easy walk to Navy Pier and the beach, the 360-room hotel offers clean, comfortable rooms in a pristine, nearly antiseptic setting. There is not a lot of atmosphere here (despite the sunken tubs offered in the suites), and those who don't like the somewhat touristy and generic feel might do best to look elsewhere. But for tour groups, bargain travelers, and those in search of the simple pleasures of well-priced, spotless rooms in a prime location, this is an excellent choice. The Newsmakers Restaurant on the ground level serves acceptable food from 6:30 a.m. to 10:30 p.m. (until midnight on weekends). For a small fee, hotel guests are granted use of the nearby Grand Ohio Athletic Club. (Near North)

BEST WESTERN RIVER NORTH HOTEL
125 W. Ohio St.
312/467-0800 or 800/557-BEST
$$–$$$

This Best Western is located right in the midst of the hottest (if perhaps

NEAR NORTH

Where to Stay on the Near North Side of Chicago

1 Ambassador West
2 Best Western Inn of Chicago
3 Best Western River North Hotel
4 Claridge Hotel
5 Courtyard by Marriott
6 Doubletree Guest Suites
7 The Drake
8 Embassy Suites
9 Executive Plaza Hotel
10 The Fairmont
11 Four Seasons
12 Holiday Inn Chicago City Centre and Sports Center
13 Holiday Inn Mart Plaza
14 Hotel Inter-Continental Chicago
15 Hyatt Regency
16 Lenox House Suites
17 The Marriott
18 Motel 6 Chicago
19 Ohio House
20 Omni Ambassador East
21 Omni Chicago Hotel
22 Raphael
23 Regal Knickerbocker Hotel
24 Renaissance Chicago Hotel
25 Residence Inn by Marriott
26 Ritz-Carlton
27 Sheraton Chicago Hotel and Towers
28 Summerfield Suites Hotel
29 Sutton Place Hotel
30 Swissotel
31 The Talbott
32 The Tremont
33 Westin Hotel
34 Westin River North Hotel
35 The Whitehall

overcrowded) tourist establishments in the city: Michael Jordan's restaurant, the Hard Rock Café, the 24-hour rock 'n' roll McDonald's, Sportmart's Wall of Fame (which features handprints in cement of famous athletes), and the still-popular but no-longer-hip Excalibur nightclub. The hotel offers free cable and parking and has a health club with indoor pool, sauna, and sundeck. (Near North)

CLARIDGE HOTEL
1244 N. Dearborn Pkwy.
312/787-4980 or 800/245-1258
$$$

A charming, elegant little hotel just a trifle too close to the Rush and Division Streets intersection, the Claridge provides a classy and pleasant Gold Coast atmosphere. The approximately 170-room hotel dates back to the 1930s and, though the surroundings are somewhat cramped, comes with an appealing Park Avenue flavor. Among the perks offered are free continental breakfast and morning newspaper, and suites with fireplaces. Hotel dining is available at the Foreign Affairs Restaurant. (Near North)

COURTYARD BY MARRIOTT
30 E. Hubbard St.
312/329-2500 or 800/321-2211
$$$

With an indoor pool, sundeck, and even Pizza Hut pizzas via room service, this Marriott hotel caters primarily to business travelers but is also well-geared to family travelers. It's located just a few steps away from the Magnificent Mile and within easy walking distance of the Chicago River, House of Blues, and Andy's Jazz Club, one of the few jazz clubs in the city that offers high-quality jazz performances during the lunch hour. Though the area to the immediate east of the hotel can seem a bit dingy, this is nevertheless a very safe and comfortable choice that wins plaudits for its large, well-appointed rooms. (Near North)

DOUBLETREE GUEST SUITES
198 E. Delaware Pl.
312/664-1100 or 800/222-TREE
$$$$

Smack-dab in the middle of Magnificent Mile Hotel Central (the Drake, the Regal Knickerbocker, the Raphael, and several other hotels are within a couple of blocks), the all-suite Doubletree is a comfortable choice in a prime location. There is little here to set the hotel apart from its more storied neighbors, but the Doubletree does feature a rooftop health club free of charge to all of its guests. The club comes complete with a sauna and a pristine, aquamarine swimming pool. The other distinguishing characteristic is the hotel's first-floor restaurant, Mrs. Park's Tavern,

---

TRIVIA

As described by Rudyard Kipling in *American Notes*, the Palmer House was host to one of the most famous banquets in history when General U.S. Grant returned from an around-the-world trip. Celebrities in attendance for the event included Mark Twain.

TRIVIA

When Queen Elizabeth and Prince Philip stayed at the Drake Hotel, hotel managers brought in sod and grass to turn a conference room into an English garden party.

which offers excellent bistro cuisine and slightly obsequious service. Other perks include 24-hour room service and freshly baked chocolate chip cookies upon arrival. (Near North)

THE DRAKE
140 E. Walton Pl.
312/787-2200 or 800/55-DRAKE
$$$$–$$$$$

The Drake, located just a few steps from Oak Street Beach on the Mag Mile, has been considered the best hotel in Chicago for more than 75 years. More like a small city than a hotel, the opulent, 500-plus-room Drake, designed by Benjamin Marshall, has its own barber shop, beauty salon, art gallery, airline reservations desk, confectionery, florist, and jewelry store. It also serves the best hotel food in the city in the classic seafood restaurant The Cape Cod Room. The Coq d'Or bar features excellent sandwiches and soups, as well as entertainment provided by a perennial Chicago favorite, pianist Buddy Charles, who's known for belting out the Broadway hits and cabaret numbers. Guests at the Drake have included Queen Elizabeth, Pope John Paul II, Herbert Hoover, Dwight Eisenhower, Winston Churchill, Eleanor Roosevelt, and Walt Disney. The red-carpeted lobby

is the city's most luxurious, and the splendidly appointed rooms come complete with to-die-for beds, two telephones, and marble bathrooms with electric scales. Room service is offered round-the-clock. The Drake also offers afternoon tea and free exercise facilities. (Near North)

EMBASSY SUITES
600 N. State St.
312/943-3800
$$$$

All the comforts of Yuppie America are located here. The slick and sleek Embassy Suites offers not only plush sleeping arrangements, coffeemakers, well-stocked bars, microwave ovens, and a decent-sized swimming pool, but just downstairs and a two-step trot away from the lobby is a Starbucks and a trendy restaurant: Papagus, a Greek restaurant-cum-tourist spot run by Chicago's Lettuce Entertain You chain. The hotel boasts more than 350 suites, each of which come with a separate living room with a pull-out sofa bed. (Near North)

EXECUTIVE PLAZA HOTEL
71 E. Wacker Dr.
312/346-7100 or 800/621-4005
$$$

Perfectly situated between the Magnificent Mile and the Loop, just across the street from the splendid tourist boats of the Chicago River, the Executive Plaza boasts that it has the largest standard guest rooms in the city. Each room has its own mini-bar, coffeemaker, hair dryer, and iron. The hotel also has its own fitness facility and business center. Many years ago, when the hotel was known as the Executive House, Chicago Cubs star Joe Pepitone lived here. (Near North)

THE FAIRMONT
200 N. Columbus Dr.
312/565-8000 or 800/527-4727
$$$$

Though well located just steps away from the Hyatt Regency, the Loop, and the Magnificent Mile, and just a few steps more from the Art Institute, there is something about the Fairmont that nevertheless seems a little out of the way. Distanced from the hustle of Michigan Avenue, the Fairmont can feel a bit lonely and out of the loop (in both senses of the word). Once inside, though, things pick up with a busy and elegant lobby and luxurious rooms and suites (there are nearly seven hundred). The Fairmont also has its own athletic facility, The Sporting Club, and four restaurants and lounges including the art deco Metropole. (Near North)

FOUR SEASONS
120 E. Delaware Pl.
312/280-8800 or 800/332-3442
$$$$$

The Four Seasons is a strong contender for the best hotel in the city; if you don't believe me, ask Woody Allen or Martina Navratilova, both of whom were recently spotted here (separately, I should hasten to add). Though it's far from the cheapest in Chicago, you truly do get what you pay for in this 343-room hotel. Located above the shops of the exquisite 900 Michigan shopping mall (featuring movie theaters, a variety of restaurants, and nearly one hundred excellent stores), the Four Seasons is deluxe in every sense of the word. Even the bar is comfortable enough to sleep in. Spacious rooms with beautiful lake and city views offer big bathrooms, terry cloth bathrobes, hair dryers, and private bars. The hotel features such amenities as complimentary shoe shines and round-the-clock room service. The impressive health club facilities include a pool (if you forget your swimsuit, Four Seasons will provide you with one), jogging track, sundeck, and exercise stations with individual TVs and headsets. Afternoon tea is offered by the fireplace in the Seasons Lounge. (Near North)

HOLIDAY INN CHICAGO CITY CENTRE AND SPORTS CENTER
300 E. Ohio St.
312/787-6100 or 800/465-4329
$$$

A 500-room establishment built with the physically fit in mind (*Fitness Magazine* called it one of the "top ten hotels for fit business travelers in America"), this well-located and reasonably priced chain hotel is connected with the McClurg Court Sports Center health club. Hotel guests receive free admission to the club. All the shops and sights of Michigan Avenue and adjoining neighborhoods are within easy walking distance, as is Navy Pier. Excel-

---

Bed-and-Breakfast Chicago, Inc.—covering neighborhoods from Hyde Park to Edgewater and all points in between, including Old Town, Lakeview, DePaul, and the so-called Gold Coast—offers a wide variety of bed-and-breakfast options at generally reasonable prices. Choices include everything from Queen Anne–style homes to high-rise apartments to two-flats. Call 312/951-0085 for details.

T I P

Though some of Chicago's top hotels might seem a little bit pricey, most all of them offer special weekend rates. Call ahead to avoid missing out on the deals.

lent views of the city and the lake are available, as are both indoor and outdoor pool facilities. The rooms may not be spectacular in and of themselves, but they are certainly cozy enough, and irons, ironing boards, hair dryers, and coffeemakers are all available free of charge. The Holiday Inn also offers numerous dining choices including the Centre Cafe, the Winners Sports Bar, and the Corner Copia bakery. (Near North)

HOLIDAY INN MART PLAZA
350 N. Orleans St.
312/836-5000 or 800/465-4329
$$$
Not your typical Holiday Inn, this hotel is housed in the Apparel Center

beside the Merchandise Mart (a building once owned by the Kennedy family and so large that it has its own zip code). The 500-plus-room hotel offers excellent views of the city and is within easy walking distance to the nearby restaurant and gallery district. Amenities include an indoor pool. Sports awards and charity banquets are often held here. (Near North)

HOTEL INTER-CONTINENTAL CHICAGO
505 N. Michigan Ave.
312/944-4100 or 800/327-0200
$$$$$
Originally functioning as a private men's club (the Medinah Athletic Club) in the late '20s and early '30s,

Hilton Chicago and Towers, p. 37

Hilton Chicago and Towers

The Ambassador East is probably most famous for its restaurant, the Pump Room, which opened in 1938. Since its opening, the most sought after table has been Booth One, which was first occupied by actress Gertrude Lawrence. Others who have sat in Booth One include Salvador Dalí, who drew on the tablecloths; Burr Tilstrom (accompanied by puppet pals Kukla and Ollie); Janet Leigh and Tony Curtis; Natalie Wood and Robert Wagner; and Humphrey Bogart and Lauren Bacall, who came here on their honeymoon.

this idiosyncratic 800-plus-room hotel still maintains an air of exclusivity. Housing perhaps the most beautiful swimming pool in Chicago (Olympic-sized with a mosaic-tile design), the Intercontinental is located right in the middle of all the Michigan Avenue action. Though the rooms are somewhat pricey there is little to quarrel with in terms of elegance; the furniture is plush, the etched-wood paneling is a nice old-fashioned touch, and the rooms offer well-stocked minibars, coffeemakers, and terry-cloth bathrobes. Use of the pool and the Intercontinental's excellent health club facilities will cost you an extra $8 per day. (Near North)

HYATT REGENCY
151 E. Wacker Dr.
312/565-1234 or 800/233-1234
$$$–$$$$

More populated than many Illinois cities, the 2,000-plus-room Hyatt is constantly abuzz with activity and bills itself as one of the largest hotel convention facilities in the country. Located on Wacker Drive right next to the Chicago River, the hotel is perfectly located—equidistant from the Magnificent Mile and the Loop—and everything from Oak Street Beach to the Art Institute of Chicago is an

easy walk away. The Hyatt is adjacent to the Illinois Athletic Club, which offers a full range of health club facilities including a rock climbing wall. (Near North)

LENOX HOUSE SUITES
616 N. Rush St.
312/337-1000 or 800/445-3669
$$$

It's taken some time, but after a number of up and down years in a variety of guises, the Lenox House seems to have settled into middle age with its appealing variety of well-furnished suites. Built in 1928 and a prominent spot for big band figures like Tommy Dorsey, Harry James, and Duke Ellington when it was The Croydon, the hotel was pretty run-down before its 1985 makeover. Though even the best suites here don't rival those at some of the better-known Mag Mile establishments, they do offer good value in terms of comfort and price. Choices range from doubles with decent sitting and work areas to the far more luxurious executive studio suites with Murphy beds that disappear to make way for a more businesslike setting. The Lenox House Suites also garners favor for its proximity to the Michigan Avenue shopping district, the Ontario Street nightlife scene, the best of

Chicago-style pizza (just a block away from legendary Pizzeria Uno and Pizzeria Due), Houston's Restaurant, and Andrews Coffee Shop, rumored to have one of the world's longest breakfast counters on its first floor. The hotel also offers a fitness center and gift shop. (Near North)

THE MARRIOTT
540 N. Michigan Ave.
312/836-0100
$$$–$$$$

One of the larger hotels in Chicago, the newly redesigned 1,100-plus-room Marriott is like a shopping mall unto itself with its broad selection of sometimes elegant, sometimes tacky stores and offices. The luxurious rooms feature coffeemakers, mini-bars, hair dryers, irons and ironing boards, and fax/modem data ports. The serviceable but not particularly spectacular dining options include Allie's American Grille and JW's Steakhouse. The reason to go here is not so much the hotel itself as it is the Magnificent Mile location: all the major shopping centers and many excellent restaurants and museums are either a quick walk or a cheap taxi ride away. The Marriott offers health club facilities with an indoor pool, weight room, and outdoor deck with basketball courts. (Near North)

OMNI AMBASSADOR EAST
1301 N. State Pkwy.
312/787-7200 or 800/843-6664
$$$–$$$$

Listed as one of the Historic Hotels of America by the National Trust for Historic Preservation, this Ambassador offers 275 rooms and suites and, like its neighbor, the Ambassador West, it provides a welcome respite from the hubbub of Rush and Division Streets, nestling comfortably into one of the priciest residential areas of the city. Complementing the hotel's elegant oasis-like Gold Coast atmosphere is the famed Pump Room restaurant, which has boasted many a celebrity sighting over the years and is one of the only restaurants in the city that still requires a jacket and tie. (Near North)

OMNI CHICAGO HOTEL
676 N. Michigan Ave.
312/944-6664 or 800/843-6664
$$$$

Just off the Magnificent Mile, the all-suite Omni offers approximately 350 rooms featuring such perks as a well-stocked bar, fax machines, irons and ironing boards, and even kimonos. Guest rooms are separated from bedrooms and parlors by French doors. The fourth-floor Cielo restaurant features splendid views of the city and a clever trompe l'oeil ceiling. The Omni

Thinking of traveling to Chicago in November? Better make your reservation early. In November, during the Radiological Society of North America's annual convention at McCormick Place, thousands of radiologists descend upon the city, making hotel and restaurant reservations a relative nightmare. Keep on top of the game by planning early and by contacting the Chicago Convention and Tourism Bureau (312/567-8500) to make sure that you're not traveling during prime convention time.

also offers its own health club facilities including step-machines, stationary bikes, Nautilus equipment, a swimming pool and Jacuzzi, and a rooftop sundeck. (Near North)

RAPHAEL
201 E. Delaware Pl.
312/943-5000 or 800/821-5343
$$$

Billing itself as "Chicago's Elegant Little Hotel," the Raphael has approximately 170 rooms and suites and is located just a few steps away from the John Hancock Center and the Magnificent Mile. Taking its cue from the grand master Raphael, the hotel offers rooms that, while not priceless works of art, at least strive to be with their lovely floral-patterned bedding arrangements, sleek wooden furniture, and antique-style fixtures. The hotel also has its own restaurant (Raphael Restaurant) done up in 19th century decor. (Near North)

REGAL KNICKERBOCKER HOTEL
163 E. Walton Pl.
312/751-8100
$$$$

A member of the Historic Hotels of America, this art deco hotel, built in 1927, is located just across from the Drake Hotel in the Magnificent Mile (conveniently located for visiting the Museum of Contemporary Art). With only about 250 rooms, the Knickerbocker has finally recaptured the glory of its early, elegant days that was abandoned during its more run-down period in the '70s and '80s. Rooms feature two-line phones, modem ports, and marble bathrooms. The hotel also features the Nix restaurant, serving American cuisine with a touch of both Southwestern and Pacific Rim cooking, as well as the clubby Martini Bar, which offers a

The Ambassador West, A Wyndham Grand Heritage Hotel

The Ambassador West, p. 40

selection of more than forty different kinds of martinis. Admission to a nearby health club is an extra $10; free jogging and bike trails are just a couple of blocks to the east. (Near North)

RENAISSANCE CHICAGO HOTEL
1 W. Wacker Dr.
312/372-7200 or 800/468-3571
$$$

An excellent choice for well-heeled business travelers, the 500-plus-room Renaissance Chicago is located within easy walking distance of the major office buildings of the Loop, and offers all the necessary accoutrements for turning one's hotel room into a private office: fax machines, modems, printers, coffeemakers, and a nearby copy shop. The Renaissance Chicago sits on the grounds of what used to be the Shangri-La Restaurant, which in the 1960s was by far the best Chinese restaurant in the city. Room service is offered round-the-clock and delivery is guaranteed within 25 minutes. There is a complimentary health club with indoor swimming pool, whirlpool, sauna, and juice; it's open from 5:30 a.m. to 10 p.m. Some travelers in the advertising business need never even set foot outside as a good deal of the suites connect directly with the Leo Burnett Building. Two decent restaurants are also located in the hotel, which offers wonderful views of the Chicago River. (Near North)

RESIDENCE INN BY MARRIOTT
201 E. Walton Pl.
312/943-3800 or 800/331-3131
$$$

This luxury chain all-suite establishment is located just a block away from Oak Street Beach. Complimentary breakfast is served daily and hors d'oeuvres are available nightly. Despite the opulence of the rooms, however, the main lobby of the hotel has a too-bright graduate school –housing feel; perhaps it's the complimentary soft drink dispensers. Perks at this Marriott include complimentary grocery shopping service, continental breakfast, and an evening social hour where guests mingle and, if they're lucky, exchange room keys. All rooms, from studios to two-bedroom suites, feature a fully equipped kitchen. A good choice for the business traveler camping out in Chicago for more than a weekend. (Near North)

RITZ-CARLTON
160 E. Pearson St.
312/266-1000 or 800/621-6906
$$$$$

Every room here at the storied Ritz comes with a view. Rooms begin on the 15th floor above the tony Water Tower Place shopping mall, and offer stunning views of Lake Michigan or the twinkling fairy lights of the Magnificent Mile and the city's luxurious

TRIVIA

In 1996 4,244,121 people attended conventions, trade shows, and corporate meetings in Chicago. Their expenditures totaled $4,731,402,921!

shopping districts. Though the price may be high, the perks are many here: marble bathrooms and terry-cloth bathrobes, complimentary shoe shines, 24-hour room service, and comfortable rooms splendidly appointed with mahogany furniture. On the premises is the Ritz-Carlton's famed dining room, a cheerless but altogether excellent restaurant (one of the city's best), and the Greenhouse atrium, where cocktails and afternoon English tea are offered. The First Couple stayed here during Hillary Clinton's 50th birthday celebration. While singles run from $355 per night, if you're feeling particularly wealthy you can get the Ritz's Presidential Suite for a cool $3,500. (Near North)

SHERATON CHICAGO HOTEL AND TOWERS
Cityfront Plaza
301 E. North Water St.
312/464-1000 or 800/325-3535
$$$$

It was good enough for the president and his entourage during the 1996 Democratic National Convention. It's easy to see why Bill Clinton, in the Democratic Party's first return to Chicago since the legendary days of 1968, made this his headquarters. Located near Michigan Avenue yet still somewhat secluded in a developing tourist and office area just east of the Mag Mile, the 1,200-plus-room Sheraton is an excellent mix of luxury and

The lobby of the Palmer House Hilton, p. 38

practicality. The hotel's immense lobby and numerous well-designed executive office spaces give it the feel of a high-end hotel and elegant business center. Rooms feature mini-bars, complimentary newspapers, and an on-site health club with sauna, sundeck, and indoor swimming pool. There are five restaurant options here including the Streeterville Grille and Bar. Less inviting is Spectators, a stuck-in-the-'80s sports bar with (nevertheless) pleasing views of the Chicago River. (Near North)

SUMMERFIELD SUITES HOTEL
166 E. Superior St.
312/787-6000 or 800/833-4353
$$$
Formerly the Barclay Chicago, the atmosphere here is less that of a luxury hotel than an expensive, if somewhat cheerless, high-dollar condo building. But at least it's not as drab as it used to be. Located just around the corner from the Magnificent Mile, within easy walking distance from Neiman Marcus, Water Tower Place, and the rest of the major shops, the Summer-

field is a comfortable, mid-priced hotel featuring such amenities in its rooms as VCRs and full kitchens with microwave ovens. There is a rooftop exercise facility and a free breakfast buffet every morning. Downstairs you'll find a 24-hour convenience store. (Near North)

SUTTON PLACE HOTEL
21 E. Bellevue Pl.
312/266-2100 or 800/810-6888
$$$$
Having changed hands a couple of times in recent years, this curious hotel strives for an understated, if somewhat pompous European luxury—even though it's just a stone's throw away from some of the most vulgar and boisterous cigar-smoking, celebrity-hopping joints of Rush and Division Streets. Famous not only for having the hotel room from which this author was once booted by the hefty, one-time Crosby, Stills, Nash, and Young vocalist David Crosby, the Sutton Place offers approximately 250 tastefully decorated and ultra-comfy rooms featuring perks like

(Caption at right of image: Palmer House Hilton)

CD players, well-stocked mini-bars, 24-hour room service, and an aerobic fitness suite. Decent haute cuisine may be had on the first floor at the Brasserie Bellevue, and better-than-decent but not-so-haute cuisine is available across the street at the Original Pancake House, a long-time Chicago favorite. (Near North)

SWISSOTEL
323 E. Wacker Dr.
312/565-0565 or 800/654-7262
$$$$
Somewhat isolated and even lonely at times, this 630-room establishment just east of the Loop in an island of well-appointed and pricey hotels has an elegance that at times can border on iciness. The hotel offers a Penthouse Health Club and Spa and is also home to the Palm Restaurant, famous for its prime rib and lobster. (Near North)

THE TALBOTT
20 E. Delaware Pl.
312/944-4970
$$$$
The proximity of the quiet and elegant Talbott to the John Hancock Center and Water Tower Place on the Magnificent Mile make it a favorite of those who crave the elegance and understatement of an small, old-style luxury hotel rather than the noise and clutter of the more ritzy and gargantuan establishments nearby. With the tone of a 1920s vintage New York–style apartment building, the Talbott (actually built in 1957) offers full kitchens in a good number of its 150-odd rooms and suites and is located across the street from both The Third Coast café—which although populated by an excess of poseurs is pleasant for outdoor dining in the summer—and

Johnny Rockets, a decent '40s-style hamburger and shake joint. The Talbott features coffee and tea by the fire during Chicago's cold autumn, winter, and early spring. Complimentary continental breakfast and seasonal beverages are offered, and a sidewalk café (prime for people-watching) is located on the first floor. (Near North)

THE TREMONT
100 E. Chestnut St.
312/751-1900 or 800/621-8133
$$$$
Long-considered one of the best and most elegant of Chicago's smaller, European-style hotels, the Tremont offers superb amenities in its luxurious and tastefully appointed rooms. Mini-bars, 24-hour room service, marble-tiled bathrooms, VCRs, CD players, and their signature terry-cloth bathrobes are all included. Posh and quiet, the approximately 130-room hotel also has the advantage of being located nearby not only the Magnificent Mile, but also the excellent research facility and exhibit space of the Newberry Library, the Rush Street bar scene, and the exclusive shops and boutiques of Oak Street. (Near North)

WESTIN HOTEL
909 N. Michigan Ave.
312/943-9347
$$$$
With slightly fewer than 800 rooms, the Westin is a favorite of business travelers and wedding parties. Though there is nothing remarkable about the hotel in terms of elegance or specialized boutiques, it is difficult to go wrong with the sleek surroundings and the charming and well-appointed rooms. The Chelsea

TRIVIA

In 1998 the state of Illinois outspent every other state in the union by $35 million with its budget for tourism.

Restaurant and Bar, located in the hotel, offers decent Continental Cuisine. The Westin also offers free health club facilities. (Near North)

WESTIN RIVER NORTH HOTEL
320 N. Dearborn St.
312/744-1900
$$$$

Formerly the Hotel Nikko, this 400-room hotel offers excellent views of the Chicago River and is located within convenient walking distance of both the Loop and the Magnificent Mile. Less than a block away from the House of Blues nightclub and Harry Caray's restaurant, this Westin nevertheless feels somewhat isolated and lonely, particularly after dark. Inside, however, with the exception of the somewhat depressing piano lounge, the hotel offers all the modern conveniences including large, marble bathrooms; bathrobes; and fax machines. (Near North)

THE WHITEHALL
105 E. Delaware Pl.
312/944-6300 or 800/948-4255
$$$$

Though Mick Jagger and his ilk may have moved onto larger and more classically elegant hotels like the Four Seasons, the Whitehall maintains its subtler form of haute-couture that keeps attracting tourists and celebrities who long for a bit of quiet amid the hubbub of Michigan Avenue. Built in 1928, the Whitehall began life as a residential apartment building. It was converted into a hotel—designed in the manner of an English country house complete with Chippendale desks, marble bathrooms, and floral-patterned bedspreads—in 1972. Less redolent of the English countryside are the VCRs and CD players located in every room. Just a block away from the Water Tower shopping mall and two blocks away from Oak Street Beach, the Whitehall offers 24-hour room service, free use of its health club, complimentary coffee and newspapers, and daily afternoon tea. The Whitehall Place bistro on the first floor serves lunch and dinner. (Near North)

Motels/Hostels

MOTEL 6 CHICAGO
162 E. Ontario St.
312/787-3580 or 800/466-8356
$

No one ever came to a Motel 6 expecting the height of Old World opulence, but considering the price and location of this particular link in the chain, bargain travelers unconcerned by amenities like Olympic-sized swimming pools, bedside mints, and well-stocked bars would be hard-pressed to do better. Located just off of Michigan Avenue and an easy walk to Navy Pier, Motel 6 Chicago offers nearly two hundred cheap, no-frills rooms and suites, as well as a bistro/café and bar. (Near North)

OHIO HOUSE
600 N. LaSalle St.
312/943-6000
$

There is a certain charm in finding

The Legendary Lexington

Chicago's most legendary hotel no longer stands. But people still pause at the corner of 22nd and Michigan, once home of the Lexington Hotel, from which Al Capone maintained his headquarters.

Capone, though known throughout the world as a Chicagoan, was actually born in Brooklyn in 1899. He didn't make it to Chicago until he was 20 years old. Rising quickly in the ranks of gangster society in this notorious Chicago neighborhood (then known as the Levee District), Capone began as a bouncer at 2222 South Wabash Avenue —the Four Deuces nightclub. He worked for Johnny Torrio, nephew of Chicago crime boss Jim Colossimo; gangster lore has it that Capone was responsible for gunning "Big Jim" down.

Capone created a South Side crime syndicate based mainly on bootlegging, although he had his hands in gambling and prostitution concerns, as well. With control of the South Side assured, Capone took up residence in the Lexington, where he had two floors to himself and his gang. At the St. Valentine's Day Massacre in 1929, Capone's men burst into a Clark Street garage and gunned down seven members of one of his last competitors.

Capone's reign as syndicate boss was short-lived. Indicted in 1931 on tax-evasion charges, he was sentenced to 11 years in Alcatraz. He was released in 1939 before finally dying from syphilis in 1947 in Miami. The Lexington survived, later changing its name to the New Michigan Hotel. It was finally demolished, but not before Geraldo Rivera appeared on live national television to show America what Capone had left hidden in his vaults in the Lexington: just about nothing.

the equivalent of an Indiana highway motel in the middle of all the action of LaSalle and Ontario Streets. This back-to-basics establishment features not only the cheap but clean accommodations you'd expect off of I-55, but also decent and ultra-cheap diner food in the Ohio House restaurant right on the premises. (Near North)

NORTH SIDE

Hotels

BELDEN-STRATFORD
2300 Lincoln Park West
773/281-2900
$$$–$$$$

Calling itself "the epitome of luxury living," the Belden Stratford is a fine hotel and the permanent residence for some of Chicago's rich and not-necessarily-famous in the heart of Lincoln Park, just across the street from the Lincoln Park Zoo and Conservatory and a short walk from the beach. Guests are greeted in a handsomely furnished lobby with a piano, a gold and alabaster chandelier, and antique books held in glass cases. The hotel's high-end rooms offer elegant perks including formal dining rooms, baths with separate showers, and whirlpools. Another advantage of the Belden Stratford is the fact that two excellent restaurants are located on the premises: the high-end French restaurant Ambria, and the mid-priced Mon Ami Gabe, one of the best examples of bistro cuisine in the city. The hotel also offers its own fitness center, rooftop sundeck, and full-service beauty salon. (North Side)

CITY SUITES HOTEL
933 W. Belmont Ave.
773/404-3400
$$

Those seeking a placid getaway from the grind of city life might shiver at the thought of spending the night at a hotel that is steps away from some of the most densely populated and funky urban nightspots in Chicago. But those uninterested in Mag Mile elegance will find a good deal of 1920s charm at this quaintly rehabbed one-time mobster hangout just steps away from the hopping gay nightclub Berlin, the Belmont El stop, and the longtime teen punk hangout Dunkin' Donuts (known to locals as Punkin' Donuts). Nothing fancy here. Just clean rooms, an exciting location, and, as in other City Suites hotels, continental breakfasts from Ann Sather's Swedish diner, which is located nearby. Not wheelchair accessible. (North Side)

PARK BROMPTON INN
528 W. Brompton
773/404-3499 or 800/727-5108
$$$

Located a couple of miles from the Magnificent Mile, the Park Brompton offers one of the best bargains in one of Chicago's most inviting and unpretentious neighborhoods, Lakeview. Just steps away from miles of park land, Lake Michigan, a bike trail, a golf course, and tennis courts, as well as the funky shops of Clark Street and Broadway, the no-frills hotel, run by City Suites, offers both the secluded atmosphere of a resort and the bustling air of big-city life. Designed in the style of an English inn—complete with tapestries and four-poster beds—the Park Brompton also offers a continental breakfast featuring food from Ann Sather's restaurant, a classic Swedish Chicago diner famed for its iced cinnamon rolls. Not wheelchair accessible. (North Side)

SURF HOTEL
555 W. Surf St.
773/528-8400 or 800/787-3108
$$

Somewhat off the beaten path but within easy walking distance of the lake, the bike trail, Diversey Harbor,

NORTH SIDE

Lake
Michigan

North Av
Beach

South
Lagoon

Lincoln
Monument

North Av

Fullerton
Beach

North
Lagoon

Lincoln
Park

Diversey
Harbor

Lincoln
Park
Zoo

Lincoln Park West

LAKE SHORE DR

LAKEVIEW AV

SHERIDAN RD

Belmont
Harbor

SEDGWICK ST

Lincoln
Park

LAKE SHORE DR

Bird
Sanctuary

STRATFORD

W SURF ST

ARLINGTON PL

Oz
Park

④ ⑦

⑤

①

②

BROMPTON

⑥

BROADWAY

HALSTED ST

CLARK ST

Lincoln
Park
Campus

Graceland
Cemetery

Wrigley
Field

③

GEORGE ST

ARMITAGE AV

IRVING PARK RD

CLIFTON AV

CLIFTON AV

RACINE ST

LINCOLN AV

W WRIGHTWOOD AV

BELDEN AV

CLIFTON AV

SOUTHPORT AV

CORTLAND ST

CLYBOURN AV

ASHLAND AV

Chicago River

ELSTON AV

HERMITAGE AV

C&NW RR

DAMEN AV

Hamlin
Park

DIVERSEY PKWY

FULLERTON PKWY

HERMITAGE ST

BELMONT AV

ADDISON ST

GRACE ST

LEAVITT ST

ARMITAGE AV

LEAVITT ST

WESTERN AV

BELDEN AV

MILWAUKEE AV

CAMPBELL AV

ROSCOE ST

CAMPBELL AV

MAPLEWOOD AV

CAMPBELL AV

California
Park

Revere
Park

GEORGE ST

CALIFORNIA AV

NORTH AV

41

90
94

64

N

0   2
KILOMETERS

0   2
MILES

the beach, the Lincoln Park Zoo, and a golf driving range, as well as the shops of Clark Street and Broadway, this City Suites Hotel has a quiet neighborhood feel to it and caters to tourists who don't want to be in the middle of all of the touristy hangouts of downtown. A relic of the 1920s, the Surf—with its basic rooms and charming lobby—is a safe, affordable choice. Room service is provided by Ann Sather's Swedish diner. Not wheelchair accessible. (North Side)

Motels/Hostels

ARLINGTON HOUSE INTERNATIONAL HOSTEL
616 W. Arlington Pl.
773/929-5380 or 800/467-8355
$

In staying here you can fool your friends and business associates by making them think you're residing in a high-dollar neighborhood while shelling out next to nothing. And that's what this hostel/home for the elderly has going for it. The surroundings are drab. An unpleasant odor suggests both kitchen cleanser and what it was used to clean up. But the rooms are basically clean. Lincoln Park and the shops of Clark Street are only a couple of blocks away. There's no curfew. Since you're only spending $18 a night, don't expect to find a chocolate mint or even a package of Chuckles on your pillow. Not wheelchair accessible. (North Side)

COMFORT INN OF LINCOLN PARK
601 W. Diversey Pkwy.
773/348-2810 or 800/221-2222
$$

Located just east of the intensely cluttered Clark and Diversey intersection, this Comfort Inn is an easy walk to the many shops, supermar-

kets, bars, bookstores, and restaurants in Lincoln Park and Lakeview. The Half Shell seafood bar and the Duke Of Perth Scottish bar are only a couple of blocks away. The inn is designed in a semi-Victorian style, but once you get beyond the bricked-in, fortress-like parking lot it turns into a very familiar, clean and basic mid-priced American hotel. There's not much of a lobby but the rooms and the location are a good bet and the continental breakfast is free. Like its neighbor to the east, The Days Inn, the Comfort Inn of Lincoln Park is a frequent choice of mid-level and second-tier rock bands playing at the Metro, the Riviera, and other venues to the north. (North Side)

DAYS INN LINCOLN PARK NORTH
646 W. Diversey Pkwy.
773/525-7010 or 800/LPN-DAYS
$$$

Ignore the unpleasant and sometimes hideous flower arrangements that greet you on the walk in. Tune out the soupy Muzak that is piped into the lobby. Once you get past them, you'll find a perfectly acceptable and affordable hotel that is frequented by many a budget-conscious business traveler as well as second-tier rock 'n' roll bands heading through town for a one-nighter. Located at the Clark and Diversey intersection and around the corner from the Century Shopping Mall, the Days Inn finds itself in a neighborhood that hardly ever seems quiet or lonely. Even at three in the morning on the weekends, revelers are heading back from the nearby bars, diners, and restaurants, or ambling purposefully in search of a char-red hot from the Wiener Circle a few blocks to the south. Recently retooled for the business set, the Days Inn offers executive rooms with coffeemakers, ironing boards, mini- fridges, and fax/modem jacks. Other perks include a more-elaborate-than-usual continental breakfast and access to a health club (it's inside the Century Mall) with an indoor jogging track and Nautilus equipment. (North Side)

FAR NORTH

Motels/Hostels

CHICAGO INTERNATIONAL HOSTEL
6318 N. Winthrop Ave.
773/262-1011
$
This ultra–low budget option is certainly not housed in the best location in the city, which probably makes its curfew a good idea. The only advantage of the area is the proximity of the Loyola El stop, which makes it relatively easy to hop on a train and leave the area. The hostel, which resembles a low-budget student dorm on the outskirts of a former Eastern Bloc town, isn't much to look at, and its hours are somewhat military in nature: in by midnight, out by 10 a.m. That said, dorm life here is clean and friendly, and offers a good way to meet foreign travelers. For those without much to spend or uninterested in the comforts of posh hotel life, the price makes it all worthwhile. Not wheelchair accessible. (Far North)

WEST SIDE

Hotels

HYATT AT UNIVERSITY VILLAGE
625 S. Ashland Ave.

312/243-7200 or 800/662-5233
$$$
Formerly owned by the Rush Presbyterian St. Luke's Medical Center and recently taken over by Hyatt, this is not the most scenic of hotels, and walking to the Loop (or anywhere else for that matter) after dark is far from an intelligent idea. Still, this is probably the only option for people interested in visiting the University of Illinois–Chicago campus or any of the many medical centers (Cook County, Rush, U of I) clustered around the area. Nearby nightlife consists primarily of Little Italy on Taylor Street (great food and, in the summer, splendid Italian ice) and the wholesale and discount shops of Maxwell Street and Roosevelt Road. A health club facility is offered for hotel guests. (West Side)

Bed and Breakfast

HOUSE OF TWO URNS
1239 N. Greenview Ave.
312/810-2466 or 800/835-9503
$$
The artsy enclave of Wicker Park with its hip shops, restaurants, and galleries has become quite gentrified in the past decade; many of the artists have been replaced by high-dollar eateries and condo dwellers. But the area has not become quite so commercial that it offers much in the way of lodging. To the rescue, the House of Two Urns, a cool, Victorian-style two-flat B&B built in a 1912 former storefront. Groovy guest rooms are designed with particular themes: the Cat Room, adorned with drawings and pictures of cats; the Alcove, filled with historical mementos and a view of Downtown Chicago; and the Pea Room, with a fairy-tale theme and a bed suggested by "The Princess and the Pea." All rooms have hair dryers

and terry-cloth robes and slippers, and have access to a fridge, coffeemaker, toaster, and microwave oven. Continental breakfast consists of freshly baked breads, homemade jam, juice, coffee, and tea. The B&B also has a rooftop view and a garden. One caveat: According to the owners, "There is no handicapped access and children are welcomed on a case-by-case basis." (West Side)

SOUTH SIDE

Motels/Hostels

INTERNATIONAL HOUSE
1414 E. 59th St.
773/753-2280
$

The cheapest way possible to enjoy dorm living at the University of Chicago without actually shelling out money for tuition, the International House is located in the heart of Hyde Park on the U of C campus. Though outside the confines of the Hyde Park area (the neighborhoods are dicey at best), this hostel-like setting provides a friendly and isolated atmosphere. Not wheelchair accessible. (South Side)

RAMADA INN LAKESHORE
4900 S. Lake Shore Dr.
312/288-5800
$$

This hotel has changed hands a number of times over the past few decades and though it isn't the pinnacle of luxury, it is about as good as it gets for those seeking reasonably priced comfort near the University of Chicago and Hyde Park. Offering two hundred rooms and suites, the hotel is just a short distance from some of the most beautiful stretches of Chicago lakeshore with excellent views of the city skyline and the nearby Museum of Science and Industry. On a clear day you can see Indiana. The hotel also offers decent meals in the first-floor restaurant, free shuttle service to McCormick Place and Downtown shopping districts, and a clean (if oddly configured) outdoor pool. Muhammad Ali was once spotted here. (South Side)

Bed-and-Breakfasts

WOODED ISLE SUITES
5750 S. Stoney Island Ave.
773/288-6305 or 800/290-6844
$$

Not technically a bed-and-breakfast in the traditional sense, Wooded Isle offers vintage two-and three-bedroom apartment suites with full kitchens in the heart of Hyde Park. Located just a couple of blocks away from the Museum of Science and Industry and 57th Street Beach, the furnished apartments include such amenities as a fully equipped kitchen with coffee and tea supplies, queen-sized Murphy beds, and, in some cases, use of the owner's bicycle. It's a good choice if you're visiting the University of Chicago. Not wheelchair accessible. (South Side)

O'HARE AREA

Hotels

COMFORT INN O'HARE
2175 E. Touhy Ave., Des Plaines 60018
847/635-1300 or 800/228-7666
$$

Geared primarily to business travelers or folks traveling to the Rosemont Horizon to see Garth Brooks,

SOUTH SIDE

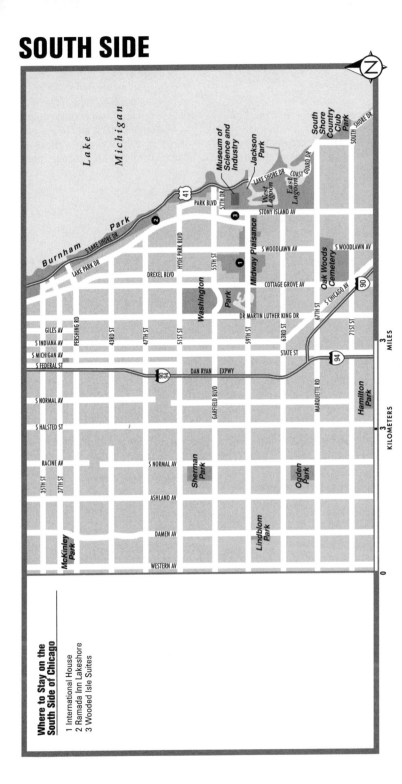

Where to Stay on the South Side of Chicago

1 International House
2 Ramada Inn Lakeshore
3 Wooded Isle Suites

O'HARE REGION

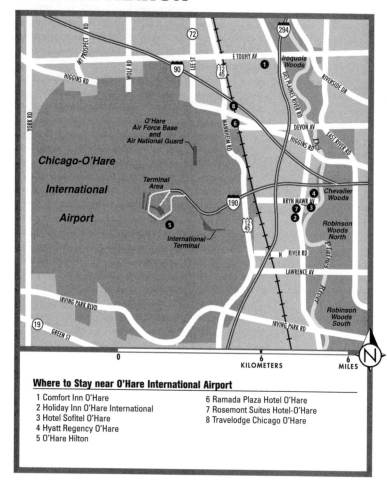

Where to Stay near O'Hare International Airport

1 Comfort Inn O'Hare
2 Holiday Inn O'Hare International
3 Hotel Sofitel O'Hare
4 Hyatt Regency O'Hare
5 O'Hare Hilton

6 Ramada Plaza Hotel O'Hare
7 Rosemont Suites Hotel-O'Hare
8 Travelodge Chicago O'Hare

the hotel offers continental break-fast, its own health club, and free 24-hour transportation to O'Hare Airport. It has about 150 standard rooms and suites. (O'Hare)

HOLIDAY INN O'HARE INTERNATIONAL
5440 N. River Rd., Rosemont 60018
847/671-6350 or 800/465-4329
$$$

Though it's far from the best home base for visiting the city, the Holiday Inn O'Hare is conveniently located near the airport, the Rosemont Convention Center, the intimate Rosemont Theatre, and the cavernous Rosemont Horizon, home to many a rock concert and college basketball game. Boasting more than five hundred rooms, the Holiday Inn has a huge ballroom, a fair number of restaurants, free shuttle service to O'Hare, and an elaborate sports complex that features a free health club, sauna, whirlpool, tanning booths, and both indoor and outdoor pools. (O'Hare)

HOTEL SOFITEL O'HARE
5550 N. River Rd., Rosemont 60018
847/678-4488 or 800/233-5959
$$$–$$$$

Though it may not offer the "Touch of France" it promises (such things are difficult in Rosemont, near the airport no matter what the literature might tell you), the 300-room Sofitel does offer a touch of comfort, class, and convenience for the business traveler. Complimentary shuttle service to and from O'Hare is offered, and only a walkway separates guests from the Rosemont/O'Hare Expo Center. Perks at the Hotel Sofitel include an indoor pool, fax/modem jacks, and truffles on the pillows. In keeping with French tradition, the hotel has in recent years held a celebration for the first shipment of Nouveau Beaujolais. (O'Hare)

HYATT REGENCY O'HARE
9300 W. Bryn Mawr Ave.,
Rosemont 60018
847/696-1234 or 800/233-1234
$$$

The first hotel in the Chicago area to feature Hyatt's signature glass elevators (my father was so excited that he bundled the family into the Thunderbird to see it when it was first built), this hotel looks like something constructed out of a child's set of Crystal Climbers building toys. With its 12-story atrium, indoor pool, health club, and four restaurants, it's a popular place for conventions. (O'Hare)

Hotel Allegro Chicago

A guest room at Hotel Allegro Chicago, p. 38

O'HARE HILTON
Box 66414
O'Hare International Airport
773/686-8000 or 800/445-8667
$$$

This is the perfect hotel if you're just passing through, if you have a particular fondness for airports, or if you're chronically late for flights. It's the only hotel located on the grounds of O'Hare Airport: Step out of baggage claim and step into the lobby. The Hilton offers round-the-clock room service and health club facilities including an indoor pool, sauna, Jacuzzi, and steam room. (O'Hare)

RAMADA PLAZA HOTEL O'HARE
6600 N. Mannheim Rd., Rosemont 60018
847/827-5131 or 800/228-2828
$$

Before stand-up comedy died a painful death in the Chicago area, this hotel would have been quite convenient to the numerous comedy venues in the vicinity. Now it provides travelers access to the Rosemont theaters and convention centers as well as the airport. Featuring more than five hundred rooms, the hotel has indoor and outdoor pools, tennis courts, and a nine-hole golf course. But golfers beware: Smack the ball too hard and you might wind up smashing into the site of a former comedy club. (O'Hare)

ROSEMONT SUITES HOTEL-O'HARE
5500 N. River Rd., Rosemont 60018
847/678-4000 or 800/333-3333
$$$
Though a little further from the airport than most other hotels in the O'Hare region, the Rosemont Suites Hotel makes up for it with its well-appointed, all-suites approach. Each suite features a separate living room and bedroom, fridge, micro-wave, two TVs, and two phones. A complimentary home-cooked breakfast is offered every morning. (O'Hare)

Motels/Hostels

TRAVELODGE CHICAGO O'HARE
3003 Mannheim Rd., Des Plaines 60018
847/296-5541 or 800/255-3050
$
The Travelodge offers no-frills lodging near O'Hare. There's nothing fancy, just cheap and safe accommodations, free coffee and newspapers, fridges, and microwaves. (O'Hare)

GREATER CHICAGO

Hotels

MARGARITA: A EUROPEAN INN
1566 Oak Ave., Evanston 60201

847/869-2273
$$
Despite it's catchy name, the Margarita's proximity to Franksville (a better than average hot dog and gyro joint) and the Tom Thumb Hobby Shop suggests suburbia more than Europe. Still, this 54-room hotel is one of the only viable options when visiting historic Evanston, a town that was incorporated before Chicago and is best known for Northwestern University and the remnants left by the powerful Women's Christian Temperance Union. Established in 1915 as a boarding house for young working women, the Margarita is now part hotel/part bed-and-breakfast, and offers both private rooms and rooms with shared bathrooms. A free continental breakfast is part of the deal. Italian dining is also available here at the highly reputed Va Pensiero restaurant. Not wheelchair accessible. (Greater Chicago)

THE OMNI ORRINGTON
1710 Orrington Ave., Evanston 60201
847/866-8700 or 800-THE-OMNI
$$$
Within easy walking distance of the campus, the downtown Evanston shopping district, and a very scenic lakefront, the Orrington boasts 280 rooms with such perks as sofa beds, irons and ironing boards, fax/modem jacks, and good-sized desks, plus a lobby that looks like it could double for a 1920s movie set. Northwestern University football fever is felt even here as the hotel restaurant has recently been renamed Gary Barnett's. (Greater Chicago)

Everest

4

WHERE TO EAT

For better or for worse, Chicago does not have a reputation for subtlety in cuisine. We're a steak-and-potatoes, deep-dish or stuffed pizza kind of town. We take burgers and frankfurters seriously and we like big portions of everything. It's hard to go a mile without finding an excellent and huge steak, a wonderfully greasy Polish sausage, a lip-smackingly scrumptious platter of barbecued ribs, or an impossibly filling deep-dish pizza bomb.

But that's not all Chicago is about. The wonderful thing about this huge melting pot of a city is that it is tough to think of any sort of cuisine that it doesn't do well. You want fine French cuisine? There are dozens of places on the Near North Side. Heaping portions of Chinese food? Chinatown's loaded. Vietnamese? Check out Argyle Street. Southern Italian? Northern Italian? Polish? Lithuanian? Everything from the simplest plate of fried chicken to the most complex bouillabaisse can be found within the city limits. Restaurant lovers who've lived here all their lives have barely scratched the surface of what Chicago has to offer. You'll find them sampling tripe in small Italian neighborhood cantinas, scarfing down chorizo in Pilsen, dashing down Milwaukee Avenue in search of the perfect pierogi. If you take them by surprise, you might find them enjoying a Chicago-style hot dog or a really juicy porterhouse steak.

This chapter begins with a list of restaurants organized by type of food. A review of these restaurants (organized by zone) follows. All restaurants are wheelchair accessible unless otherwise noted.

> **Price rating symbols:**
> $ under $10 per person
> $$$ $11 to $20
> $$$$ $21 and up

Ice Cream

Margie's Candies (NS), p. 83
Peterson's Ice Cream Parlor (GC),
    p. 97
Rainbow Cone (SS), p. 96

Indian

Moti Mahal (FN), p. 89
Klay Oven (NN), p. 73

Italian

Agostino's (GC), p. 96
Bice (NN), p. 69
Coco Pazzo (NN), p. 69
Harry Caray's (NN), p. 72
La Gondola (NS), p. 82
Italian Village (D), p. 67
Mia Francesca (NS), p. 83
New Rosebud Café (WS), p. 90
Tuscany (WS), p. 92
Vernon Tap (WS), p. 92
Vinci (NS), p. 85

Japanese

Hatsuhana (NN), p. 73
Matsuya (NS), p. 83
Sai Cafe (NS), p. 84

Korean

Gin Go Gae (FN), p. 87

Mexican/Tex-Mex

Blue Mesa (NS), p. 78
El Jardin (NS), p. 81
El Nuevo Leon (NSS), p. 93
Salpicon (NS), p. 76

Middle Eastern

Hashalom (FN), p. 87
Tel Aviv Kosher Pizza (FN), p. 89

Pizza

Bacino's (NS), p. 77
Giordano's (NN), p. 81
Gino's (NN), p. 72
Lou Malnati's (O), p. 96
Pizzeria Uno (NN), p. 75
Pizzeria Due (NN), p. 75

Seafood

The Cape Cod Room (NN), p. 69
The Half Shell (NS), p. 81
Shaw's Crab House and Blue Crab
    Lounge (NN), p. 76

Soul Food

Army and Lou's (SS), p. 95

Steaks

Eli's (NN), p. 70
Gene and Georgetti's (NN), p. 70
Gibson's Steakhouse (NN), p. 72
Myron and Phil's (GC), p. 97

Thai

Arun's (FN), p. 87

Vegetarian

Blind Faith Cafe (NS), p. 78
Heartland Cafe (FN), p. 87

DOWNTOWN

THE BERGHOFF
17 W. Adams St.
312/427-3170
$$

One of Chicago's longest-standing and most-respected dining traditions, the Berghoff has been a staple of the Chicago restaurant scene since 1898 and the atmosphere is professional and buzzing with activity. Serving a variety of expertly crafted German specialties (including a *schlachtplatte*, bratwurst, Wiener schnitzel, and sauerbraten) plus more universal fare (fish and pasta), the Berghoff has the air of an old-fashioned German dining hall, the likes of which is difficult to find even in Germany anymore. The Berghoff also serves a good deal of sides (including herring or creamed spinach) and is famous for its home-brewed beer and root beer,

DOWNTOWN

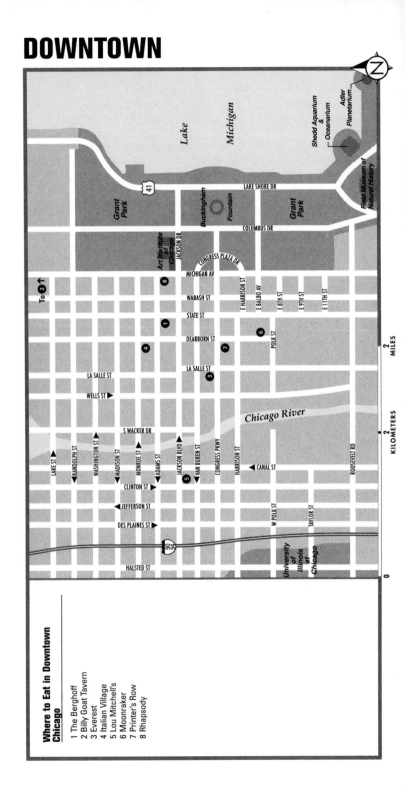

Where to Eat in Downtown Chicago

1 The Berghoff
2 Billy Goat Tavern
3 Everest
4 Italian Village
5 Lou Mitchell's
6 Moonraker
7 Printer's Row
8 Rhapsody

both of which are available in pitchers or perfectly chilled steins. Lunch, dinner daily. (Downtown)

BILLY GOAT TAVERN
430 N. Michigan Ave.
312/222-1525
$

Even before *Saturday Night Live* immortalized this bustling tavern with its famous "cheezborger, cheezborger, cheezborger" routine, it was already a Chicago favorite, especially among the staffs of the *Chicago Tribune* and the *Chicago Sun Times*, both of which have offices nearby. The burgers, paper thin and served up at a moment's notice, are not necessarily the best gourmet choices, but the loud, old-time-Chicago atmosphere is enough to keep people coming back for more. Lots of beer is available, and most of it is cheap. The Billy Goat is still a great spot for a quick bite and a brew for the after-work crowd. Lunch, dinner daily. (Downtown)

EVEREST
440 S. LaSalle St.
312/663-8920
$$$

Towering over the streets of Chicago, on the 40th floor of the One Financial Place building in the heart of the Loop, Everest (presided over by universally acclaimed chef Jean Joho) scales the heights of Chicago's culinary world as well. The accent here is on the Alsatian (a large collection of wines from the Alsace region and meals with an Alsace flavor may be found here), but a more general sense of fine European dining prevails. Foie gras and goat-cheese ravioli are highly recommended. Reservations required. Dinner only; closed Sun and Mon. (Downtown)

TRIVIA

The first Berghoff restaurant was built at the 1893 Columbian Exposition by Herman Berghoff, largely as an excuse to sell his beer.

ITALIAN VILLAGE
71 W. Monroe St.
312/332-7005
$$$

Some people may argue that the food is not quite what it was in the 1920s at this venerable Chicago institution, but the locale is so charming that it hardly matters. The second floor of this Loop building is a sparkling lover's hideaway that looks like something out of Disneyworld. The romantically inclined may dine beside the painted murals of landscapes or in the city's only secluded booths that are separated from the restaurant by means of doors. With a good selection of pastas and standard Italian fare, this is a favorite of both the theater and opera crowd, so much so that Lyric Opera conductor Bruno Bartoletti even has a veal dish named after him here. Rumor has it that Al Capone used to hang out at the spectacular bar. Lunch, dinner daily. Not wheelchair accessible. (Downtown)

LOU MITCHELL'S
565 W. Jackson Blvd.
312/939-3111
$

This is not the place to go if you were hoping for a quiet, romantic repast with a loved one. This place (a favorite of the Loop business crowd) is noisy, crowded, and a premium is not placed upon personal privacy. Diners are shoved together at a counter or

The original owner of the Billy Goat Tavern, Sam Sianis, is famous for having put a hex on the Chicago Cubs. Legend has it that an usher at the Cubs game refused to allow Sianis to take his pet goat Murphy into Wrigley Field for the 1945 World Series because of the animal's odor. After the Cubs lost the series, it is said that Sianis wrote a letter to Cubs owner P.K. Wrigley asking, "Who stinks now?"

at tiny little tables with barely any room to breathe. But nobody here seems to mind much. That's because Lou Mitchell's is a time-honored Chicago breakfast tradition and the noise and the crowds are part of the atmosphere. People come to enjoy their neighbors jostling them to pass down a jar of Lou's homemade orange marmalade served with signature Greek toast. Huge and excellent omelets are served in large metal skillets. All women customers get a free container of Milk Duds. Breakfast, lunch daily. (Downtown)

MOONRAKER
733 S. Dearborn St.
312/922-2019
$$
I can think of no better restaurant in Chicago that combines the ambiance of an old-school neighborhood bar with a fine dining establishment. The bar area is a great place for a beer and conversation with the affable barkeep about the state of Chicago's sports teams. But the dining area could pass for a pricey restaurant. Luckily, in both places, you can get great burgers and some excellent seafood specials including seafood crepes and a great Portobello mushroom sandwich. Lunch, dinner daily. (Downtown)

PRINTER'S ROW
550 S. Dearborn St.
312/461-0780
$$$
Though it boasts a good percentage of fine restaurants per capita, Printer's Row has still not quite caught on as the groovy artists' and businesspeople's South Loop mecca that it always promised to be. Nevertheless, for the past 20 years, chef Michael Foley's unique modern American kitchen creations have kept people coming back. Venison is a specialty here as are other forms of game and seafood. Though things tend to get pricey quite quickly here, the quirky middle-American flavor makes this a memorable dining experience. Lunch and dinner are served Mon–Sat. Closed Sun. (Downtown)

RHAPSODY
Symphony Center
65 E. Adams St.
312/786-9911
$$$
Located on the main floor of Symphony Center, this restaurant offers an unusual view of Wabash Avenue and, more importantly, a menu of somewhat fussy but fun American meals that change seasonally. A relatively new addition to the Chicago dining scene, Rhapsody wins raves

for its whimsical presentations, such as a Caesar salad with bibb leaf lettuce and a giant red onion ring, and shrimp in phyllo dough made to resemble shredded wheat. Lunch Mon–Sat; dinner daily. (Downtown)

NEAR NORTH

BICE RISTORANTE
158 E. Ontario St.
312/664-1474
$$$
Bice serves chic Italian cuisine in an atmosphere that recalls some of the best dining experiences in Milan. Lunch and dinner are offered in the main dining area or in the bar, where movers and shakers are seen dining alone reading the latest Martin Amis novel. The pastas and fish specialties are among the best in the city. Lunch, dinner daily. (Near North)

BISTRO 110
110 E. Pearson St.
312/266-3110
$$$
The chef here trained with Joel Robuchon, a somewhat sainted figure who has been referred to as "the chef of the century." You will not go too far wrong ordering bistro standards such as steak frites. Simple fish preparations are also quite good, though regulars recommend taking advantage of items cooked in Bistro 110's wood-burning oven and steering clear of anything complex. Ask for the signature baked garlic with your bread. Lunch, dinner daily. (Near North)

BLACKHAWK LODGE
41 E. Superior St.
312/280-4080
$$$
The last vague link Chicago has to the famous and long-lamented Loop institution The Blackhawk, this hopping Near North joint offers a wide array of regional American choices, from the not-completely-standard American (corn chowder, beef tenderloin) to the oh-so-standard American (hot apple pie, lemonade). It's one of the best restaurants in town to also offer a sizable kids' menu. Lunch, dinner daily. (Near North)

THE CAPE COD ROOM
140 E. Walton Pl.
312/787-2200
$$$
One of the oldest and most time-honored traditions of Chicago dining, neither the Cape Cod Room, located in the Drake Hotel, nor its menu have changed much since 1933. The seafood choices are uniformly good, although special points go out to Cape Cod specialties like Lobster Thermidor, Lobster Newburg, Dover Sole, and excellent clam chowder and Bookbinder red snapper soup. But what really makes the Cape Cod Room worth the extra journey (and the extra dollars) are the little touches: The delicately rendered pewter plates; the red- and white-checked tablecloths; the baskets of cheese rolls, salt sticks, and matzo; the generous and strong drinks; the regulars at the oyster bar. And, if you save room, the desserts are scrumptious, particularly the Cape Cod's famous frozen ice-cream pies. Dinner daily. (Near North)

COCO PAZZO
300 W. Hubbard St.
312/836-0900
$$$
Though the atmosphere may seem a touch corporate or touristy, the food more than makes up for it. Located

The Drake Hotel's Cape Cod Room has served many a martini to many a celebrity including Joe DiMaggio and Marilyn Monroe, who carved their initials into the bar. Incidentally, the Cape Cod Room's Table #39 was a favorite of comedian Jack Benny.

near the River North art gallery district, Coco Pazzo (the Chicago outpost of a well-respected New York restaurant) serves traditional Italian specialties with a highly professional flair. Even the rather pedestrian-sounding dishes (an appetizer of seasonal vegetables, spaghetti with garlic and oil) are uniformly excellent, and the special risottos and fish of the day are exquisitely prepared. Among the desserts, Coco Pazzo's homemade ice creams (especially banana chocolate chip and caramel) are especially noteworthy. If there is a long wait, the bar near Coco Pazzo's wood-burning stove is a good place to enjoy something from the wide selection of Italian wines. Lunch, dinner Mon–Fri; dinner only Sat and Sun. (Near North)

ED DEBEVIC'S
640 N. Wells St.
312/664-1707
$$

They say it's a restaurant, but Ed Debevic's is about as close as Chicago comes to dinner theater. This '50s-imitation diner was started by Chicago's Lettuce Entertain You corporation and has become one of the city's hottest spots for tourists and suburban girls celebrating Sweet Sixteens. Wise-cracking, in-your-face waitresses serve up burgers, chili, and chicken-fried steak with attitude, and every-so-often jump up on the counters to dance

along to '50s hit tunes. A number of Chicago's successful actors and actresses got their start here Lunch, dinner daily. No credit cards accepted. (Near North)

ELI'S
215 E. Chicago Ave.
312/642-1393
$$$

They say that Chicago politicians know a good steak. So that must be why they come here. A favorite of businesspeople and well-connected officials in Chicago city government, Eli's, founded by the late lamented Chicago restaurateur Eli Schulman, calls itself "The Place for Steak" and wins rave reviews for its special sirloin prepared with crushed peppercorns and for its generous relish trays. Eli's is also famous for having the best cheesecake in the city (the chocolate chip is a definite winner). Lunch, dinner Mon–Fri; dinner only Sat and Sun. (Near North)

GENE AND GEORGETTI'S
500 N. Franklin St.
312/527-3718
$$$

Some steak joints try to be more than steak joints, especially since meat-eating has grown less and less fashionable. But Gene and Georgetti's knows better than to keep up with trends. This is the quintessential steak house, the steak house in the tradition of those Lowenbrau com-

NEAR NORTH

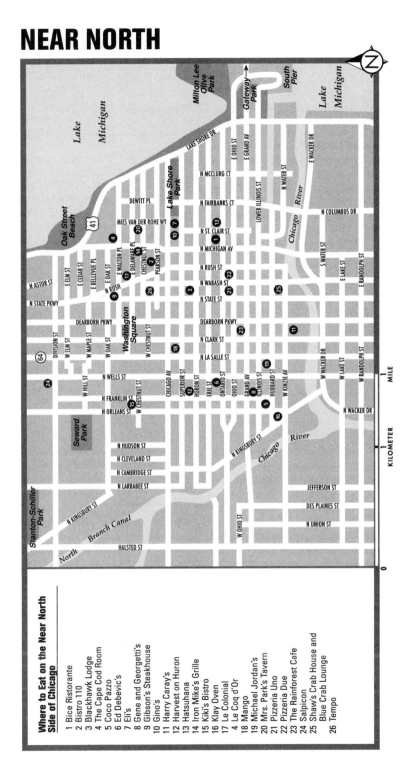

mercials where a guy named Dolan (variously referred to as a genius) orders "the biggest steak you got and a bottle of Lowenbrau." That's what you'll get here and you won't be the least bit disappointed. The "garbage" salad—a meal in itself, with greens, vegetables, salami, cheeses, and more—is also a plus. Lunch, dinner Mon–Sat. (Near North)

GIBSON'S STEAKHOUSE
1028 N. Rush St.
312/266-8999
$$$
If you're looking for where the big shots of sports dine, you'll likely find them here at Chicago's moving-and-shaking Rush Street joint where steak lovers mingle with the likes of Dennis Rodman and Charles Barkley and Chicago sportscasters. Gibson's is not cheap, but it is widely heralded as having the best steak in the city and a bustling see-and-be-seen atmosphere. Non–beef eaters with a good deal of disposable income might choose one of Gibson's absolutely huge lobster tails. Dinner daily. (Near North)

GINO'S
160 E. Superior St.
312/943-1124
$
It is sometimes possible to detect more than a few subtle differences among the great deep-dish pizza establishments of Chicago. Some people say Pizzeria Due is the best, some say it's Lou Malnati's, and some claim top honors go to this venerable spot. Like deciding whether you're a Cubs fan or a Sox fan, a lot of it depends on where you grew up and whose opinion held sway over you. Gino's is certainly as good as the rest of the deep-dish

outfits, and with the exception of the signature golden corn-meal crust, it is virtually indistinguishable. Its pizza was voted the country's best by *People* magazine and *Bon Appetit*. Lunch, dinner daily. (Near North)

HARRY CARAY'S
33 W. Kinzie Ave.
773/465-9269
$$
Chicagoans generally don't have much patience for celebrity rest-aurants, having bid not-so-fond farewells to establishments owned or endorsed by Jim McMahon, Bobby Douglass, Oprah Winfrey, and others. But because of the persistent high quality of this one, it's had staying power, even after the demise of its namesake. The accent here is on the standard Italian (the late Cubs announcer was born with the name Carabino), and the restaurant is known for its pastas, seafood, and steaks. Unlike the owners of many other celeb joints, Harry actually ate here and now you know why. Check out the Harry memorabilia while you're here so that you can reminisce about a man who was perhaps the greatest baseball announcer of all time and knew a good meal when he saw one. Lunch Mon–Sat; dinner daily. (Near North)

HARVEST ON HURON
217 W. Huron St.
Chicago
312/587-9600
$$$
One of the newest additions to the hip, groovy dining scene in Chicago, Harvest is a daring and funky eatery with one of the most original menus in town. With its brightly colored interior (eye-catching scarves function as lampshades) and its hipster

waitstaff (one member goes by the name of Cheetah), Harvest splits the difference between upscale nouvelle American cuisine restaurant and a Soho nightclub. Harvest shines particularly with its creative appetizers—chief among these, an exquisite seaweed-wrapped salmon roll speckled with fish roe and the barbecued shrimp with sugarcane. Lunch, dinner Mon–Fri, dinner only Sat, Sun. (Near North)

HATSUHANA
160 E. Ontario St.
312/280-8808
$$$
The most respectable, subdued, and expensive of Chicago's Japanese restaurants, Hatsuhana offers one of the city's widest array of sushi options and many say it's the best around. Choices aside from sushi are not particularly plentiful, though the beers here are big enough that they can constitute a meal in themselves. This is the classiest sushi bar around. Lunch, dinner Mon–Sat; closed Sun. (Near North)

IRON MIKE'S GRILLE
100 E. Chestnut St.
312/587-8989
$$$
One of the other Chicago celebrity institutions that has had staying power, Iron Mike's owes its reputation and popularity to former Chicago Bears' tight end and head coach Mike Ditka, the most popular coach in Chicago history, even now that he has moved to New Orleans. Located in the Tremont Hotel, Iron Mike's has, of course, the Ditka essentials: pork chops and pheasant sausage. While you shouldn't expect to see Da Coach here during football season, the food is strong

enough that it outweighs the downsides of unsuccessful celebrity hunting. Breakfast, lunch, dinner daily. (Near North)

KIKI'S BISTRO
900 N. Franklin St.
312/335-5454
$$$
The service here can be a little strange sometimes, but that shouldn't turn you off of the uniformly excellent bistro cuisine. Steak frites is especially well done here as are the onion soup and a variety of fish choices. Dinner Mon–Sat. Closed Sun. (Near North)

KLAY OVEN
414 N. Orleans St.
312/527-3999
$$$
Probably the classiest of Chicago's many fine Indian restaurants, this Near North location combines an elegant atmosphere with a delicious array of vegetarian and non-vegetarian choices. Chief among these are Klay Oven's tandoori specials, butter chicken curry and breads prepared in, of course, a clay oven. Lunch and dinner daily. (Near North)

LE COLONIAL
937 N. Rush St.
312/255-0088
$$$
Technically more French-Vietnamese than out-and-out French, this Rush Street favorite has fast become the choice of Chicago's glitterati and social scenesters. Vietnamese spices infuse dishes like the beef salad with lemon grass with a subtly exotic flavor. Appetizers are especially good (try the spring rolls made with shrimp). To hobnob with the rich-and-hoping-to-get-famous, check out the

bar on the second floor. Lunch, dinner daily. (Near North)

LE COQ D'OR
140 E. Walton Pl.
312/787-2200
$$

Quite possibly the classiest bar in the city, the Drake Hotel's piano lounge certainly has the best bar menu. While pianist Buddy Charles plays Broadway standards and torch songs in the evenings, Le Coq d'Or serves a full menu of dinners and snacks. The soups are always excellent, especially the Drake's signature Bookbinder red snapper. The sandwiches, too, are delicious, and the best club sandwich in the city is served here. The burgers are also quite good, seasoned and stuffed with green peppers and onions. And for that nightcap, Le Coq d'Or serves the city's largest and best martini. Lunch, dinner daily. (Near North)

MANGO
712 N. Clark St.
312/337-5440
$$$

The words "American" and "bistro" don't always go well together, but here chef Steve Chiappetti has created a restaurant that has just the right mixture of affordable food in a comfortable atmosphere with many original and inventive touches. The menu keeps changing here, but Chiappetti wins points for his preparations of lamb, pork chops, and fish, and, as an appetizer, his delectable Mediterranean fish soup. Desserts are also quite fine here, especially the banana chocolate mousse cake (when available). Lunch, dinner Mon–Fri, dinner only Sat and Sun. (Near North)

MICHAEL JORDAN'S
500 N. LaSalle St.
312/644-DUNK
$$

The fact that the food is good here comes as something of a surprise. Even if it weren't, you'd expect the huge three-dimensional Michael Jordan leaping onto LaSalle Street, the displays of memorabilia, and the constant video screenings of Jordan highlights to keep packing them in anyway. The accent here is on the southern and the rumor is that North Carolinan Jordan and his wife Juanita had a hand in crafting the menu. Catfish, crab-and-shrimp cakes, and macaroni and cheese are specialties here, as is a meal which is said to be Jordan's pre-game favorite (strip steak with garlic mashed potatoes). While you're munching down on Jordan's favorites, be sure to check out the considerable Michael arcania here, which even includes a portrait of Number 23 by Ed Paschke. Once in a while, Jordan even shows up. Lunch, dinner daily. (Near North)

MRS. PARK'S TAVERN
198 E. Delaware Pl.
312/280-8882
$$

When most other restaurants close up shop, this is where their staffs go for a late-night meal. Often populated largely by chefs, Mrs. Park's, located on the first floor of the Doubletree Guest Suites hotel, offers an excellent late-evening menu that boasts good appetizers, snacks, salads, sandwiches, and main courses. Though the service can get a trifle unctuous, the cuisine, which includes everything from a scrumptious barbecued pork chop to a splendid grilled-chicken Caesar salad, more than makes up for it. Breakfast, lunch, dinner daily. (Near North)

PIZZERIA UNO AND PIZZERIA DUE
29 E. Ohio St. and 619 N. Wabash Ave.
312/321-1000 and 312/943-2400
$ (both)

The food is the same in both of these pizzerias (located one block from each other), and it is pretty much universally agreed that both Pizzerias Uno and Due contain Chicago's, if not the world's best pizza. Here is where Ike Sewell created Chicago's legendary deep-dish pizza, the first pizza to require not only a knife and fork, but also a doggie bag. Improbably filling and ultimately satisfying, the pizza here is a Chicago culinary experience not to be missed. For meat-eaters, the Uno Special is a lip-smacking delicacy. Vegetarians, however, need not be alarmed, for pizzas are available with a variety of excellent toppings. Sometimes it takes 45 minutes for your specially made pizza to arrive, but it's worth the wait and you can bide your time taking in the atmosphere, sipping a beer, or enjoying a surprisingly excellent salad. Perhaps not a must-see, but a definite must-eat. Lunch, dinner daily. (Near North)

THE RAINFOREST CAFE
605 N. Clark St.
312/787-1501
$$

It may not be the biggest restaurant in Chicago, but the Rainforest Cafe sure has the biggest frog. There it stands, peering down goggle-eyed on Clark Street. Of the tourist establishments in this heavily populated area, this chain outlet is clearly the most fun, offering menus that will tantalize kids but should please adults as well. Pita quesadillas and

---

Ten Best Hometown Treats
by Karen Langer, director of alumni reunions, Northwestern University

1. Jay's potato chips
2. Berghoff root beer
3. Frango mints
4. Goose Island beer
5. Pizza from Pizzeria Due
6. Vienna pastrami
7. Noon Hour herring
8. Tootsie pops
9. Eli's chocolate chip cheesecake
10. Watermelon ice from Mario's Italian Lemonade

Honorable Mentions: Rainbow Cone's Palmer House ice cream, Fluky's hot dogs, Canfield's Swiss crème soda, Parky's chocolate malt, and caramel corn from Garrett Popcorn Shop.

Hot Dogs, Chicago Style

Chicagoans take their hot dogs seriously. We don't just slap mustard and sauerkraut on them and shove them at you like they do in New York. Making a Chicago hot dog is a fine art, and asking for the wrong thing can leave you the laughingstock of any true Chicagoan. The classic Chicago hot dog is served on a poppy-seed bun with mustard, pickle relish, chopped onions, slices of tomato, a wedge of dill pickle, and two hot peppers stuffed in on either end of the bun. Optional condiments include celery salt, and you are allowed to squeeze the juice from the hot pepper out on your hot dog. Sauerkraut is a possibility, though not generally recommended. If you want to be truly respected here, please don't make a fool

Portobello mushroom sandwiches are good choices and the rain forest motif should help to instill environmental consciousness in the youngsters from an early age. (Near North)

SALPICON
1252 N. Wells St.
312/988-7811
$$$
Though Mexican food in Chicago has generally come to mean cheap burritos accompanied by large vats of margaritas, this Old Town restaurant adds a touch of class to the proceedings. With its understated ambiance more reminiscent of one of Chicago's upscale French or North American *etablissements*, Salpicon offers delicious fish entrées in place of chimichangas and dumplings in place of *nachos grande*. And, of course, the guacamole is excellent. Dinner daily. (Near North)

SHAW'S CRAB HOUSE AND BLUE CRAB LOUNGE
21 E. Hubbard St.
312/527-2722
$$$
Last time I dined here, Chicago Bulls general manager Jerry Krause was seated at the next table, which gives you an idea of the dressed-for-success, high-dollar clientele that this seafood joint gets. Actually two restaurants, Shaw's offers a fine-dining, if somewhat stuffy atmosphere, while the Blue Crab Lounge next door provides the noisy and happening air of a Boston oyster bar. The best items on the menu here include the best crab cakes in the city and generous platters of oysters. A popular spot for a power lunch. Lunch, dinner daily. (Near North)

TEMPO
1 E. Chestnut St.
312/943-4373

$

From the outside this may look like any run-of-the-mill 24-hour diner. But there has to be a reason why many of Chicago's major athletes, television news personalities, and traveling rock stars still keep coming back. The reason is that it's the best 24-hour diner in town. Featuring a wide array of Greek specialties and breakfasts, Tempo is one of the city's best dining choices past midnight. Omelets are especially good here and come with Greek toast and homemade orange marmalade. Check out the collection of Polaroid photos on the wall to see which celeb you've recently crossed paths with. Breakfast, lunch, dinner daily. (Near North)

NORTH SIDE

ANN SATHER'S
929 W. Belmont
773/348-2378
$$

This North Side version of Chicago's best Swedish diner serves the same great omelets, seafood benedict, and Swedish specialties (including fruit soup and Swedish meatballs) that are found at Ann Sather's original Andersonville location (see Far North listings for more information). The famous iced cinnamon rolls are available here, too. Breakfast, lunch daily. (North Side)

BACINO'S
2204 N. Lincoln Ave.
773/472-7400
$$

Aside from having created the phenomenon of deep-dish pizza, which has resulted in the worldwide explosion of Pizzeria Uno outlets, Chicago is also home to something called stuffed pizza. Fairly self-explanatory, stuffed pizza sticks its "toppings" inside two layers of cheese rather than on top of the pizza itself. Of Chicago's many stuffed pizza joints, this Lincoln Park institution offers the best of the lot with tangy tomato sauce and flaky, almost cookie-like crusts. The spinach-stuffed pizza is a particularly strong option. Lunch, dinner daily. (North Side)

THE BAGEL
3107 N. Broadway Ave.
773/477-0330
$$

After a long stint in Chicago's most heavily Orthodox Jewish neighborhood in West Rogers Park, this classic deli moved southward to the hustle and bustle of Lakeview. The move hasn't hurt the food at all. Sandwiches of all shapes and sizes are available, but the standards are, of course, the best—the corned beef and hot pastrami on rye are definite winners. If there were a citywide contest for the best matzo ball soup, The Bagel would no doubt win outright. A great selection of ethnic desserts *(rugeleh)* and not-so-ethnic desserts (turtle cheesecake) is also available. The only downside of this rich culinary experience is the coleslaw, which, unlike everything else on the menu, is to be avoided at all costs. Breakfast, lunch, dinner daily. (North Side)

BISTROT ZINC
3443 N. Southport Ave.
773/281-3443
$$

There are very few places in Chicago which bring to mind the leisurely and luxurious atmosphere of dining at an unpretentious Parisian café or brasserie. This is about as close as you can come in this city. With the hubbub of its atmosphere and its zinc bar, this bistro does evoke the Paris of the 1930s and the cuisine certainly helps it along. Steak frites is a wise choice in the dining area and in the bustling front area; crepes and other delicacies are available at the bar. Lunch, dinner daily. (North Side)

BLIND FAITH CAFE
3300 N. Lincoln Ave.
773/871-3820
$$

In terms of high-quality vegetarian dining, this is probably the best choice in the city. With a wide variety of veggie and non-dairy options ranging from barbecued tempeh to chilaquiles with tofu, this is a vegetarian's dream. Breakfasts also come highly recommended and Blind Faith gets extra points for its cornucopia of natural sodas and homemade smoothies. Lunch and dinner are served daily. (North Side)

BLUE MESA
1729 N. Halsted St.
312/944-5990
$$

Just across the street and a block down from Chicago's esteemed Steppenwolf Theatre Company lies the best Southwestern cuisine in town. Unlike the menu at any other restaurant in the city, Blue Mesa offers a constant set of adventures for the diner from blue corn tamales to white chocolate quesadillas to more traditional offerings like fajitas, seafood enchiladas, and chiles rellenos. Even the nachos here are great. Lunch, dinner daily. (North Side)

BRETT'S
2011 W. Roscoe St.
773/248-0999

$$$

Though it is primarily known as a place for dinner, this quaint and cozy Roscoe Village establishment actually has what is arguably the best Sunday brunch in town. Here one can enjoy a perfectly prepared mimosa or a homemade smoothie with an excellent array of creative culinary options that make Brett's seem like the world's best bed-and-breakfast (without the bed). It's tough to go wrong here, though the smoked salmon is a standout and the house salad served with feta and sun-dried tomatoes approaches perfection. Best of all, though, is the complimentary bread and sweet roll basket served with homemade jam. Dinner Wed–Sun, plus brunch Sat and Sun. Closed Mon and Tue. (North Side)

CAFÉ AVANTI
3706 N. Southport Ave.
773/880-5959
$

A favorite of the pre- or post-theater or film crowd, this café is one of the friendliest in town. In the front area there is excellent people-watching out on Southport Avenue; the back is a good place for the more studious to write or read. Pastries are the usual lot, but there are intriguing coffee specialties, most notably the "Turtle," a delightful mixture of espresso and caramel flavor. Tables are also available outside in the summer. It's a perfect spot before checking out the art films at the Music Box movie theater or the entertainment at the New Mercury Theater. Open 7 a.m. to 11 p.m. daily. (North Side)

CHARLIE TROTTERS
818 W. Armitage
773/248-6228

NORTH SIDE

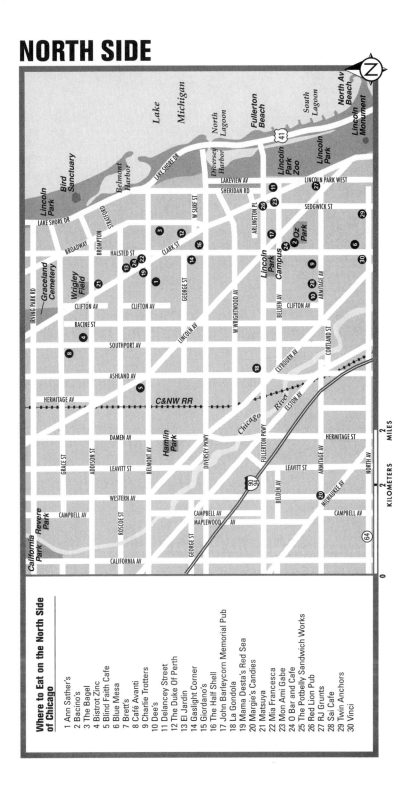

Where to Eat on the North Side of Chicago

1 Ann Sather's
2 Bacino's
3 The Bagel
4 Bistrot Zinc
5 Blind Faith Cafe
6 Blue Mesa
7 Brett's
8 Café Avanti
9 Charlie Trotters
10 Dee's
11 Delancey Street
12 The Duke Of Perth
13 El Jardin
14 Gaslight Corner
15 Giordano's
16 The Half Shell
17 John Barleycorn Memorial Pub
18 La Gondola
19 Mama Desta's Red Sea
20 Margie's Candies
21 Matsuya
22 Mia Francesca
23 Mon Ami Gabe
24 O Bar and Cafe
25 The Potbelly Sandwich Works
26 Red Lion Pub
27 RJ Grunts
28 Sai Cafe
29 Twin Anchors
30 Vinci

Superdawg, p. 97

$$$

If you've got the cash, you can get a reservation, and you've got only one meal to have in Chicago, this is the place to go. Generally thought to be the best restaurant in Chicago (it actually won honors from *Wine Spectator* readers for best chef and best restaurant in America), Charlie Trotters offers a constantly changing menu of international specialties ranging from antelope to shiitake ravioli. Make your reservations well in advance (there are only about 20 tables here) and prepare to stay a while, pay a lot, and be thankful that you did it. Reservations are required. Dinner only; closed Sun and Mon. (North Side)

DEE'S
1114 W. Armitage Ave.
773/477-1500
$$

The sad truth about most Chinese restaurants in Chicago (even some of the best ones) is that you have to forget about your health when you walk in the door and begins snarfing down

the sweet-and-sour shrimp and the egg rolls. That is happily not the case in this well-respected Lincoln Park institution, which is one of the finest upscale Chinese restaurants around. Here the vegetables are fresh and crispy, and the sauces and appetizers are thankfully devoid of grease. There is also a great selection of vegetarian choices and noodle dishes. Dinner daily. (North Side)

DELANCEY STREET
2301 N. Clark St.
773/281-9100
$$

This is the closest Chicago gets to a genuine New York deli. It's loud, hectic, and crowded, and the portions are enormous. Featuring an impossibly huge selection of sandwiches, dinners, breakfasts, and assorted Jewish specialties on its menu, It's hardly a place for the diet conscious, but it's a great place to fall off the wagon. The creatively seasoned matzo ball soup is a specialty, and it's difficult to go wrong with any of the omelets or sandwiches. The more ethnically inclined or daring might want to go for such favorites as hoppel-poppel or matzo brie. Bowls of pickles and bread accompany each meal. Breakfast, lunch, dinner served daily. (North Side)

THE DUKE OF PERTH
2913 N. Clark St.
773/477-1741
$

If you couldn't tell the Scottish motif from the huge selection of Scotch whiskeys listed on the drink menu or from the Scottish sea chanteys playing in the background, the menu should clue you in. Though most people come here for the more standard fare like the chicken sandwiches and the hamburgers (the Sean Connery Burger is a favorite), a number of Scottish touches create a delightful pub atmosphere. If you're in an adventurous mood, try the Scotch egg as an appetizer or the trifle for dessert. All meals come with a choice of French fries or pasties—a Scottish variety of mashed potatoes. A garden patio is opened in the summer months, though sometimes the wait for tables out there can be long. Lunch, dinner daily. (North Side)

EL JARDIN
3335 N. Clark St.
773/528-6775
$

Though the food here is quite delicious, most people come for the sangria and the margaritas, which are staggeringly good. Staggering is the key word here, too, for that's how most people walk out of here—stumbling blindly up Clark Street in search of Wrigley Field and the rest of the Wrigleyville nightlife scene. There isn't anything particularly unusual on the menu here—just the usual selection of cheaply priced and filling Mexican specialties. But the raucous atmosphere, the generous drinks, and the ample portions make for an affordable and memorable evening . . . if, in fact, you can remember it. Lunch, dinner daily. (North Side)

GASLIGHT CORNER
2858 N. Halsted St.
773/348-2314
$

For years, this has been one of the absolute favorite dining and drinking choices of Chicago's theater community, and not just because of the cheap beer and the pool table. Though you wouldn't know it by looking at it, the Gaslight serves surprisingly excellent burgers and quite possibly the best and most affordable bratwurst in the city. Lunch, dinner daily. No credit cards accepted. (North Side)

GIORDANO'S
1840 N. Clark St. (and numerous other locations)
312/944-6100
$$

One of the first pizzerias in Chicago to feature stuffed pizza, Giordano's has achieved meteoric success in the city and now boasts 40 locations. With 17 different stuffings to choose from, Giordano's has something to delight every palate. And, for the lighter appetite, thin-crust pizza is available here as well. Lunch, dinner daily. (North Side)

THE HALF SHELL
676 W. Diversey Pkwy.
773/549-1773
$$

This doesn't look like the place where you could get some of the best

The Cape Cod Room at The Drake, p. 69

seafood in the city, but looks are deceiving. And, though the Half Shell has the air of a dingy neighborhood bar where locals pack in to watch Monday Night Football and political debates, the menu offers a great selection of basic seafood choices. Shrimp, scallops, and king crab legs are all decently prepared here and served on paper plates with dollops of cocktail sauce and the Half Shell's own special sweet-and-sour sauce. All customers get a lollipop at the end of their meals. Lunch and dinner are served daily. (North Side)

JOHN BARLEYCORN MEMORIAL PUB
658 W. Belden Ave.
773/348-8899
$

Avoid this place like the plague on weekends, unless you feel like waiting in line with a posse of baseball hat–clad DePaul fraternity boys and dart players. Any other time, though, this is one of the most pleasant pub dining experiences in the city, particularly in summer when the spacious patio is open. Inside, as slides of famous paintings and silent movies are projected on the walls, you may choose from a slew of burger and chicken sandwich options and a more-than-adequate list of beers, then throw a few darts while you wait for your order to be filled. Lunch, dinner daily. (North Side)

LA GONDOLA
2425 N. Ashland Ave.
773/248-4433
$$$

Located in a rather unassuming neighborhood to the west of Lincoln Park, this is the sort of old-fashioned Italian dining experience the likes of which has become difficult to find. It sort of resembles a steak joint for Italian food. Salads are large and come with big dollops of creamy garlic dressing. Pastas and fish dishes are expertly prepared and served in giant portions (the seafood ravioli is an excellent special). This is the favorite choice of Chicago's bocce players whose club is just a few doors down. Dinner daily. (North Side)

MAMA DESTA'S RED SEA
3216 N. Clark St.
773/935-7561
$$

Because of the cheap prices, the unique spices, and the communal nature of the Ethiopian dining experience, Mama Desta's has long been a favorite of the Chicago theater community as well as diners of all stripes. In very intimate surroundings, diners help themselves to portions of flat, spongy, pancake-like bread with which they scoop a variety of intriguingly seasoned vegetable dishes, including green lentils, spiced chard, and mixed veggies. Chicken, beef, and fish dishes are also available in the family-style setting. Lunch, dinner daily. (North Side)

MARGIE'S CANDIES
1960 N. Western Ave.
773/384-1035
$

The oldest ice-cream parlor in the city limits, Margie's, with its pink neon sign and its antique soda fountain, is like a trip back in time to Grover's Corners of Thornton Wilder's *Our Town*. With miniature jukeboxes at each table and stuffed animals everywhere, this is a must for both ice-cream and nostalgia lovers. The usual selection of sundaes, shakes, sodas, and phosphates is available here as is what is purported to be the world's largest sundae. Back in the days of Beatlemania, the Beatles took their dates here for ice cream. Open 10–11 daily. (North Side)

MATSUYA
3469 N. Clark St.
773/248-2677
$$

Even though this restaurant is found in the heart of the ultra-mainstream Wrigleyville neighborhood, you won't hear much English spoken here. That's because Chicago's Asian community knows where to find some of the best sushi in town. Though there are other items offered on the menu, those with an aversion to sushi might best look elsewhere lest the city's widest selection of sushi and creatively designed maki rolls be wasted on them. Dinner daily. (North Side)

MIA FRANCESCA
3311 N. Clark St.
773/281-3310
$$$

Wow, this place sure is popular. If you're not fond of claustrophobic surroundings or rubbing elbows with dozens of young ad execs and other sundry yupsters, this high-traffic North Side Italian eatery might not be your bowl of clams. But as you might expect, there's a good reason for the crowds. Just try the pastas and the pizza appetizers and you'll know why. So squeeze in, try to relax, and enjoy. Dinner daily. (North Side)

MON AMI GABE
2300 N. Lincoln Park West
773/348-8886
$$

Don't let the somewhat somber surroundings of the rather staid Belden-Stratford hotel put you off. Inside, there lies a very casual and satisfying bistro dining experience. Though it is operated by the sometimes irritatingly trend-conscious Lettuce Entertain You Enterprises, their influence is not particularly visible here. What remain are superb bistro items like onion soup, steak frites, and some excellent fish preparations in a comfortable setting. Patio dining is available in the summer. Dinner daily. (North Side)

O BAR AND CAFE
3343 N. Clark St.
773/665-7300
$

The Chicago cafe scene, with its hipster poets and happening groovesters, is not generally known for its haute cuisine. But the late-night menu at this relatively new and slick North Side café is particularly good. With a multicultural crowd coming in at all hours of the evening to listen to acid jazz or Spanish guitar or to watch the plays going on in the basement, O Bar is a vibrant scene. And, as a bonus, the sandwiches (most notably Captain Ron's fish sandwich), appetizers, and side dishes are prepared quickly and professionally. O Bar also has one of the city's most creative martini menus, prepared by some of the friendliest bartenders around. Lunch, dinner daily. (North Side)

THE POTBELLY SANDWICH WORKS
2264 N. Lincoln Ave.
773/528-1405
$

Though the name of this college hangout isn't exactly appetizing, this charming hole-in-the-wall has the best submarine sandwiches in town. Located near DePaul University, students and professionals pile in here at lunch time to have one of the Potbelly's signature ham and Swiss, Italian, or vegetarian subs made in an antique oven. Excellent yogurt shakes are also available. Lunch, dinner daily. (North Side)

RED LION PUB
2446 N. Lincoln Ave.
773/348-2695
$$

This is the closest you'll come to an authentic English pub within the Chicago city limits. The Red Lion is teeming with English atmosphere—books about England in the rear bookcase, tall glasses of cider and ale, even a classic red English telephone booth. The specialties here all come from that sceptered isle as well—generous baskets filled with beer-battered fish and chips, beef stew, Welsh rarebit, scones served with whipped cream and jam. There are American items here as well (burgers and so forth), but the pride of the Union Jack is the main reason to come, as is the Red Lion's friendly black cat that keeps watch over the premises. Lunch, dinner daily. (North Side)

RJ GRUNTS
2056 N. Lincoln Park W.
773/929-5363
$$

Lettuce Entertain You is one of the most successful restaurant chains in the city, having given birth to Ed Debevic's, Papagus, and a host of other restaurants. But this was the first one, and it remains charmingly stuck in the 1970s with its health shakes, salad bar, and excellent sandwiches. Lunch, dinner daily. (North Side)

SAI CAFE
2010 N. Sheffield Ave.
773/472-8080
$$

You wouldn't necessarily expect the best sushi in town to come in a neighborhood that is known better for its population of clean-cut students who have just had one beer too many while watching the NCAA tournament on the big screen. But it does. Though it's not the cheapest sushi restaurant in Chicago, it does offer the best values with its delicious, pristine, and well-sized portions. The appetizers here, especially the *gyo-za*

Though there is no way to measure with absolute certainty, Chicago is home to both the world's largest and the world's smallest sundae. The world's largest is at Margie's Candies (1960 N. Western Ave., 773/384-1035). The world's smallest is at Ed Debevic's (640 N. Wells St., 312/664-1707).

(Japanese dumplings), are not to be missed. For those who still have not accustomed themselves to the thought of eating raw fish, Sai Cafe does very well with its tempura and teriyaki entrées. The miso soup is always served at exactly the right temperature. Dinner daily. (North Side)

TWIN ANCHORS
1655 N. Sedgwick St.
312/266-1616
$$

There's nothing quite like an authentic neighborhood bar, especially when the bar serves food as good as this one does. An Old Town local favorite for years, the regulars come in every evening to enjoy huge slabs of barbecued ribs, burgers, baskets of French-fried shrimp, and, for the more health conscious among them, surprisingly good tuna steak sandwiches. If you're looking for a place to catch the Monday Night Football game in clean, comfortable surroundings with a pitcher of beer and a cheap, good meal, this is the place to do it. Lunch, dinner daily. (North Side)

VINCI
1732 N. Halsted St.
312/266-1199
$$$

Just down the block from the Steppenwolf and the Royal George Theatre, this is a favorite of the pre- and post-theater crowd and with very good reason. Understated, elegant, and particularly stuffy, Vinci is one of the finest Italian restaurants in the city. Operated by highly respected chef Paul LoDuca, Vinci is a friendly establishment that boasts exquisite daily risottos, pizzas, and the best polenta around. Dinner daily. (North Side)

FAR NORTH

ANN SATHER'S
5207 N. Clark St.
773/271-6677
$$

If you wake up too late on the weekend, you might have to wait quite a long time for a table at Chicago's best Swedish diner located in the heart of the Swedish Andersonville North Side community. But patience has its payoffs, and here they come in the forms of delicious omelets, scrumptious eggs, seafood benedict, and great Swedish specialties like fruit soups and Swedish meatballs. Best of all are the side orders, which include the homemade applesauce, yummy rice porridge, and Ann Sather's famous iced cinnamon rolls, which are also thankfully available to go. (There's another Ann Sather's location at 929 W. Belmont on the North Side.) Breakfast, lunch daily. (Far North)

FAR NORTH

Where to Eat on the Far North Side of Chicago

1 Ann Sather's
2 Arun's
3 Fluky's
4 Gin Go Gae
5 Hashalom
6 Heartland Cafe
7 Moody's Pub
8 Moti Mahal
9 Tel Aviv Kosher Pizza
10 Tre Kronor

ARUN'S
4156 N. Kedzie Ave.
773/539-1909
$$$

Arun's, located in the burgeoning Albany Park neighborhood, has gained a reputation as one of the world's finest Thai restaurants. Though it is quite possibly the most expensive Thai place in town, there are reasons for this, including Arun's delicious *Khao kriab* (seafood filled dumplings), the yummy chicken coconut soup, and the opulent decor of the restaurant itself. Arun's also gets high marks for its pristine preparations of seafood. Arun's serves dinner Tuesday–Sunday. Closed Mon. (Far North)

FLUKY'S
6821 N. Western Ave.
773/274-3652
$

The classic Chicago hot dog experience. Bar none. If you want to know what a Chicago hot dog is all about, order a single or a double with everything, which includes mustard, onions, relish, pickle, and tomatoes. Hot chili peppers are optional, though they are highly recommended. Polish sausages are also quite good here. Fluky's is much cleaner and restaurant-like than in its old days as a hot dog stand on Maxwell Street, but the hot dog stand feel is still contained within the food itself. If for some strange reason you come to this legendary neighborhood institution not wanting a hot dog, the hamburgers are surprisingly good (served with the same toppings as a hot dog) and there is also a decent salad bar for the health-conscious. Breakfast, lunch, dinner daily. No credit cards. (Far North)

GIN GO GAE
5433 N. Lincoln Ave.
773/334-3894
$$

All of the main courses are uniformly strong and wonderfully piquant (look out for the spicy bean curd and be prepared to drink a lot of water) at what I consider to be the best Korean restaurant in the city. The appetizers are more than enough reason to come. Generously supplied in the fashion of a Korean version of a Jewish deli tray, is everything from strips of seaweed to hot pickled cabbage to pickles that come with every meal. Affordable dining in a homey, family setting. Lunch, dinner daily. (Far North)

HASHALOM
2905 W. Devon Ave.
773/465-5675
$

The Israeli rock music on the stereo sets the atmosphere. It serves as a perfect complement to the ultra-cheap and surprisingly good Moroccan and Israeli cuisine located in the midst of this multiethnic area. Populated largely by neighborhood families, Hashalom's specialties include great falafel sandwiches, *bourekas* (triangle-shaped pastries with a variety of fillings), and Israeli and Moroccan combination plates. Be sure to order the hummus and the roasted peppers as side dishes. Lunch, dinner Sun–Thurs; lunch only Fri. Closed Sat. (Far North)

HEARTLAND CAFE
7000 N. Glenwood Ave.
773/465-8005
$

Michael James—long-time revolutionary and '60s radical, one-time

Ten Best Places to Eat or Just Hang Out

by Mike North, co-host of highest-rated sports talk
show in Chicago on WSCR-AM

1. **Gibson's Steakhouse** (1028 N. Rush St., 312/266-8999)
   Best martinis in town. Great steaks and outstanding pork chops.

2. **Iron Mike's Grille** (100 E. Chestnut St., 312/587-8989)
   Great bar, salads, and pork chops, and upstairs there's a cigar bar.

3. **Basta Pasta** (6711 N. Oshkosh Ave., 773/763-0667)
   Outstanding Italian food, including chicken Parmesan and pastas.

4. **Roma's Beef** (4237 N. Cicero Ave., 773/775-2078)
   The best homemade beef in the city. They make their own
   sausage and the fries are home cut.

5. **Harry Caray's** (33 W. Kinzie Ave., 773/465-9269)
   The baby back ribs are out of this world. The bar is
   outstanding and it's just a great time.

6. **Jilly's** (1007 N. Rush St., 312/664-1001)
   Upstairs there's a beautiful bar area (with all the best beers),
   while downstairs there's a discotheque.

7. **The Wiener Circle** (2622 N. Clark St., 773/477-7444)
   It's where I like to go after one or two in the morning. I have
   two char dogs with mustard, onion, celery salt, and a tamale.

8. **Gale Street Inn** (4914 N. Milwaukee Ave., 773/725-1300)
   This newly remodeled family-run business offers delicious ribs
   that practically fall off the bone.

9. **Double Bubble Bar** (6036 N. Broadway)
   This is the best shot-and-a-beer joint in the city. They also
   serve pretty good sandwiches.

10. **Los Tacos Americanos** (Belmont and Southport)
    Come here for the city's best steak-and-cheese burritos.
    They're better than anything you could find in Mexico.

high-ranking officer of Students for a Democratic Society, and co-founder of Rising Up Angry—has turned this corner of East Rogers Park into the last bastion of Chicago hippiedom. Running a small theater, a neighborhood bar, a newspaper, and this health-food restaurant, James has maintained a foothold in both the '60s and the '90s. James is constantly updating his menu, but the cornbread and veggie burgers are long-time favorites, and it's tough to beat dining out on Heartland's spacious patio on a warm summer day. Lunch, dinner daily. (Far North)

MOODY'S PUB
5920 N. Broadway
773/275-2696
$

Many people say that the best burger in town is available here. And even if it's the second or third best, the atmosphere more than makes up for it. Located on the North Side, Moody's is a homey and cozy dark spot in the winter with its roaring fireplaces and bowls full of peanuts whose shells carpet the floor. It's even nicer in the summer when Moody's opens up its garden patio where locals linger for hours sipping on cold pitchers of beer or fruit punch and enjoying the gigantic burgers. Moody's is known especially for its blue cheeseburger. Lunch and dinner are served daily. (Far North)

MOTI MAHAL
2525 W. Devon Ave.
773/262-2080
$$

Devon Avenue is the mecca for all matters Indian, from clothing to cuisine. This pleasant little storefront is an exceptional and highly affordable choice for the area. Moti Mahal serves up delicious appetizers like vegetable *samosas* and *pakoras* (offered with a selection of sauces including a fruit chutney), as well as very cheap, family-style main courses. Vegetarians may choose from a wide range of possibilities including a terrific *sag paneer* (spinach cooked in spices with homemade cheese), and carnivores will delight in the lamb and tandoori specials. A selection of Indian breads including cheese *nan* and *poori* are highly recommended. Lunch and dinner are served daily. (Far North)

TEL AVIV KOSHER PIZZA
6349 N. California St.
773/764-3776
$

Despite what the name suggests, there's far more than just the best kosher pizza in town available here. Aside from kosher Mexican and Chinese specialties, salads, and soups, Tel Aviv also offers the best and cheapest falafel sandwich in the city. Sometimes you may have to wait a long time for a table, particularly on Saturday nights after synagogue has let out. But the atmosphere and the good cheap food makes it well worth it. Lunch, dinner Sun–Thurs; lunch only Fri. Closed Sat. (Far North)

TRE KRONOR
3258 W. Foster Ave.
773/267-9888

Homemade Danishes. Homemade cinnamon rolls. Freshly squeezed orange juice and omelets accented with havarti or danish blue cheese. For value, taste, and friendly neighborhood atmosphere, it's tough to do better than this immaculate, off-the-beaten path Scandinavian breakfast and lunch spot. Even the oatmeal is excellent. Breakfast and lunch only, closed Mon. (Far North)

WEST SIDE

GREEK ISLANDS
200 S. Halsted St.
312/782-9855
$$$

This small strip of South Halsted Street is known as Greektown. At night, dining establishments here come alive with the sounds of *bozouki* music, the roaring flames of *saganaki* bathed in ouzo, and the cry of "Opaaa!" Of all the restaurants in Greektown, this venerable institution provides the best equation of excellent Greek food plus a party atmosphere minus some of the fraternity party hijinks that mar some of the other neighborhood establishments. Best choices here include the red snapper, gyros platter, and the wonderful selection of appetizers including *tzatziki* and *taramosalata* (a bread spread made out of fish roe). Lunch, dinner daily. (West Side)

MANNY'S
1141 S. Jefferson St.
312/939-2855
$

Few places like Manny's exist anywhere in the country anymore and this is pretty much the only one left in Chicago—an old-fashioned luncheonette with cafeteria service. Owned for eons by the Raskin family, Manny's is a throwback to the good old days where short-order cooks slice the corned beef and roast beef for your sandwiches, slide freshly cut bagels onto your plastic tray, ladle sloppy portions of chicken soup into your bowl, and scoop out daily specials like chicken marsala and spaghetti and meatballs out of big metal vats. You can also select from a variety of old-fashioned desserts including Jello molds and slices of Boston cream pie. A breakfast and lunchtime favorite with the working and the business crowd, Manny's is not open for dinner. Breakfast, lunch daily. (West Side)

MARCHÉ
833 W. Randolph St.
312/226-8399
$$$

Loud, glitzy, and located in a cavernous hall in the West Randolph Street market area, Marché began as the place to go for the city's high-fashion models and photographers. And, though the initial restaurant-of-the-moment craze has died down somewhat, this is still an ultra-slick spot populated by the black-clad. What has allowed the restaurant to maintain its foothold in this trendy area is its far-above-average bistro cuisine ranging from well-prepared fish dishes to steak frites. An excellent selection of desserts is also available. Dinner daily. (West Side)

NEW ROSEBUD CAFÉ
1500 W. Taylor St.
312/942-1117
$$$

Despite the immense size of this restaurant, the wait for a table on weekends can sometimes be up to an hour. This has long been a favorite of the Taylor Street faithful. And though there are few surprises offered in and among the southern Italian specialties, there is little way to go wrong here. Especially good are the linguini with white clam sauce, served with dozens of fresh clams and homemade sausage. Portions are so huge that doggie bags are almost always necessary. Lunch, dinner Mon–Sat; closed Sun. (West Side)

SANTORINI
138 S. Halsted St.
312/829-8820
$$$

While Greek Islands takes awards for atmosphere and excitement, this other Greektown institution comes away with the prize for the best food of any in the neighborhood. Though the mood here is subdued, people aren't coming here for chef's yelling

WEST SIDE

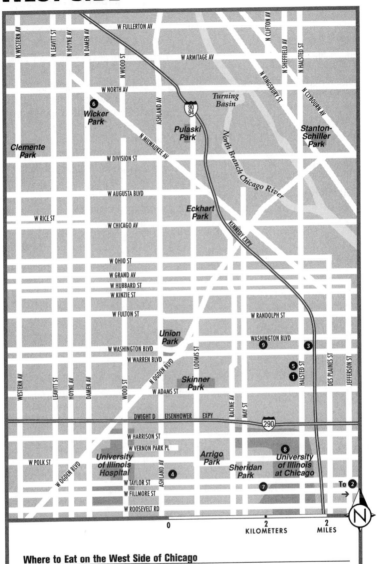

Where to Eat on the West Side of Chicago

1 Greek Islands
2 Manny's
3 Marché
4 New Rosebud Café
5 Santorini
6 Soul Kitchen
7 Tuscany
8 Vernon Tap
9 Wishbone

"Opaaa!" They come here for the seafood including red snapper, grilled octopus, and shrimp, all prepared simply but deliciously. Lunch, dinner daily. (West Side)

SOUL KITCHEN
1576 N. Milwaukee Ave.
773/342-9742
$$$
Located right smack dab in the center of Wicker Park's groove at the intersection of North Avenue, Milwaukee, and Damen, Soul Kitchen has quickly turned from a neighborhood favorite into one of the best outposts for modern American cuisine. A favorite of the Chicago Bulls and Bulls fans en route to the game, the restaurant is known for its groovy atmosphere, rock 'n' roll waitstaff, and regional American specialties including catfish with black-eyed peas and jerk chicken. Desserts are a must. Dinner daily; brunch Sun. (West Side)

TUSCANY
1014 W. Taylor St.
312/829-1990
$$$
Though Little Italy lasts for only a few blocks on Taylor Street, it is positively lined with excellent dining choices and this is one of the best. Famous for its rotisserie chicken, Tuscany also serves excellent Italian sausage as well as pastas and veal specialties. Frequently crowded, particularly before and after Chicago Bulls or Chicago Black Hawks games, the restaurant has a competent and professional Old World feel. Lunch, dinner daily. (West Side)

VERNON TAP
1073 W. Vernon Park Pl.
312/733-3393

$$
Though the food is excellent here and the portions are huge, this is not necessarily a place to go to impress a date. This is a loud joint and, in many ways, a guys' joint. This is where you hang out before you go to the Hawks game. Service here is quick and efficient, and the pastas, though there are few surprises among them, are superb. There are no menus, just a selection of items scrawled on chalkboards. But the regulars don't seem to mind. They come here all the time, as the prices are surprisingly reasonable, and they know what they like and when they want it. Lunch and dinner are served daily. (West Side)

WISHBONE
1001 W. Washington St.
312/829-3597
$$
Great Southern cooking still hasn't made much of an impact on the city, but this favorite shines out as an exception. Located near Oprah Winfrey's Harpo Studios, Wishbone is a down-home, bayou-cooking delight with its selection of Southern specialties like catfish, red beans and rice, Hoppin' Jack (like Hoppin' John but with black beans instead of black-eyed peas), crawfish cakes, and jambalaya. Most meals come with a selection of sides that can range from spinach and collard greens to ratatouille and black-eyed peas. Save room for the excellent variety of desserts. In summer, dining is available outside at Wishbone's outdoor sidewalk café. Brunch, though often quite crowded, is also highly recommended here. Lunch, dinner daily. (West Side)

EL NUEVO LEON
1515 W. 18th St.
312/421-1517
$

Located in Chicago's bustling Latino community in Pilsen, this restaurant is one of the liveliest and cheapest Mexican restaurants in the city. While Mexican pop music blasts on the jukebox, families chow down until the wee hours of dawn on quickly and expertly prepared burritos, enchiladas, and chimichangas. Complimentary nachos and salsa and a bowl of jalapeño peppers accompany each meal. The guacamole here is especially good. A delightful and authentic experience. Lunch, dinner daily. No credit cards. (Near South)

HEALTHY FOOD
3236 S. Halsted St.
312/326-2724
$

Right in the middle of Bridgeport, birthplace of both the current and former Mayor Richard Daley, lies this delightful Lithuanian diner, which serves not only healthy food, but good food as well. Although there are more than enough delicious down-home specialties to try here, the items that are especially good are the *blynai* (thin Lithuanian pancakes which come with your choice of fruit or cheese fillings) and the extra-hearty pancakes. There are also delicious health shakes available. A great spot to stop before a White Sox game at nearby Comiskey Park. Breakfast, lunch daily. No credit cards. (Near South)

HONG MIN
221 W. Cermak Rd.
312/842-5026
$$

The dim and dingy surroundings at Hong Min do not look like anything special. But this is generally thought to be the best restaurant in Chinatown and has been for some time. The usual selection of appetizers, beef, chicken, pork, and seafood dishes is available here, but the sauces and spices are surprisingly sharp and fresh. Lunch, dinner daily. (Near South)

JIM'S HOT DOG STAND
1320 S. Halsted St.
312/666-0533
$

You may not forgive yourself in the morning if you come here. But then again, if you drive by at night and you don't stop in for one of Jim's signature Maxwell Street Polish sausages, you might not forgive yourself either. Open 24 hours and a favorite of cops, college students, and late-night stragglers who live around the old Maxwell Street mar-

Pizzeria Uno, p. 75

Carolyn Crimi

NEAR SOUTH SIDE

Where to Eat on the Near South Side of Chicago

1 El Nuevo Leon
2 Healthy Food
3 Hong Min
4 Jim's Hot Dog Stand
5 Mandar-Inn
6 Moon Palace
6 Three Happiness

ket neighborhood, Jim's can be smelled from miles away—a wonderfully greasy scent of mustard and grilled onions. Though some swear by the pork chop sandwiches, the Polish sausages are what made this hot dog stand famous. Disgustingly greasy yet absolutely delicious, they are slapped into buns with grilled onions, mustard, and spicy-hot jalapeños, and come with free fries and an optional bag of salt. Open 24 hours daily. (Near South)

MANDAR-INN
2249 S. Wentworth Ave.
312/842-4014
$$

As far as the main courses go in this Chinatown mainstay, you're not liable to find many surprises. Though the name suggests exclusively Mandarin cooking, there is also a good deal of mild Cantonese and spicy Szechwan choices. What truly makes this restaurant special are the appetizers, particularly the vegetarian spring rolls and vegetarian pot stickers, which contain all the yummy wonderfulness of Chinese appetizers without the regrets the morning after. Ask for some of Mandar-Inn's famous (and just plain delicious) lemonade to accompany your meal. Lunch, dinner daily. (Near South)

MOON PALACE
216 W. Cermak Rd.
312/2255-4081
$$

If this isn't the best restaurant in Chinatown, it certainly is the friendliest one. Wisecracking waitresses serve heaping portions of traditional Chinese cuisine. The menu is huge and all the standard items are prepared respectfully and quickly. At lunch time there is often a wait due to the McCormick Place convention crowd, but it's easy to get a table for dinner. Local legend has it that one of the chefs here used to be a personal cook for Chairman Mao. Lunch, dinner daily. (Near South)

THREE HAPPINESS
209 W. Cermak Rd.
312/842-1964
and
2130 S. Wentworth Ave.
312/791-1229
$$

The two Three Happiness locations are essentially across the street from each other. The Wentworth Avenue location, with its massive dining room, is a splendid lunch choice with its great dim-sum presentations. The Cermak location is superior as a dinner option, featuring all the usual items, though sometimes the best choices are not to be found on the menu. A fellow diner once recommended that I ask for the barbecued pork *chow-teh* to me. I'm still not sure exactly what it is, but it was one of the best Chinese meals I've ever had. Lunch, dinner daily. (Near South)

SOUTH SIDE

ARMY AND LOU'S
422 E. 75th St.
773/483-3100
$$

The word around town is that Army and Lou's used to be the late mayor Harold Washington's favorite restaurant. Known especially for its fried chicken, this South Side establishment also pulls in the crowds with its catfish and its excellent selec-tion of down-home side

The Rainforest Cafe, p. 75

dishes and desserts, including collard greens and peach cobbler. Lunch and dinner are served Sun, Mon, and Wed–Sat. Closed Tues. (South Side)

RAINBOW CONE
9233 S. Western Ave.
773/238-7075
$

Snobby city dwellers might scoff at the idea of driving to the depths of the South Side for an ice-cream cone. But they aren't familiar with the pleasures of a rainbow cone, something the cognoscenti of the South Side have known ever since the early part of this century. No mere mélange of disparate flavors, the eponymous cone is a thrilling and refreshing burst of flavors featuring a tangy orange sherbet and Rainbow Cone's own mystery flavor known as Palmer House. It's definitely worth a long summer's drive. Open 1–11 daily. Not usually open in the winter but policy may change; call to check. (South Side)

GREATER CHICAGO

AGOSTINO'S
2817 N. Harlem Ave.
773/745-6464
$$$

You have to drive quite a ways from downtown to reach this Italian neighborhood on the Far West Side of the city, but the trip is well worth it for the authentic Italian fare available here. Homey, unpretentious, and unassuming, Agostino's still probably has the best Italian food in the city. Pastas and seafoods are done to perfection here and one of the nicer touches is the bowl of fruit that follows every dinner. It's a neighborhood favorite and this author's personal nomination for best restaurant in Chicago. Dinner daily. (Greater Chicago)

LOU MALNATI'S
6649 N. Lincoln Ave., Lincolnwood
847/673-0800
$

Lou Malnati's has other locations in the city that are more convenient to

Downtown, but this was the first one and it has the most homey and authentic feel to it. This is where every kid growing up on the north side of Chicago wants to have his or her birthday party and, because the deep-dish pizza is so good and cheap, parents hardly ever complain about it. For those who are peculiar enough to come here and not want some of the city's best pizza, Lou Malnati's also offers excellent salads and sandwiches. Lunch, dinner daily. (Greater Chicago)

MYRON AND PHIL'S
3900 W. Devon Ave., Lincolnwood
847/677-6663
$$$

Imagine the world's best non-kosher Bar Mitzvah and you get the basic idea of the food here at one of Chicago's top steak joints. The main courses—from juicy prime rib to huge portions of garlicky shrimp DeJonghe to the tangy barbecued ribs to the liver and onions—are outstanding, but the appetizers and relish trays are generous and delicious as well. Catering to the hearty appetites of neighborhood car dealers, card players, and sports fans, Myron and Phil's offers trays of pickled vegetables,

carrot and celery sticks, and scoops of chopped liver, and a sizable bread basket before each belt-busting meal. Said to be a favorite of Bill Clinton's and Dan Rostenkowski's. Lunch, dinner daily. (Greater Chicago)

PETERSON'S ICE CREAM PARLOR
1104 W. Chicago Ave., Oak Park
708/386-6130
$

Since the early days of Oak Park, the quaint home of a young Ernest Hemingway and Frank Lloyd Wright's architecture, this antique ice-cream parlor has been a city staple. One of the few ice-cream parlors around that still makes its own flavors, Peterson's has a wide variety of flavors. The New York Cherry and peppermint are exceedingly good, especially when topped with a silver boat of Peterson's signature hot fudge. Sandwiches and burgers are also available. Lunch, dinner daily, plus breakfast and lunch on Sat and Sun. (Greater Chicago)

SUPERDAWG
6363 N. Milwaukee Ave.
773/763-0660
$

As far as the quality of the dog it-

TRIVIA

Chicago is pretty well established as the town that invented deep-dish pizza, and we take credit for lifting the hot dog from the realm of snack food into fine culinary art. But these aren't the only contributions Chicago has made to the world of cuisine. Other food items that were born in Chicago include Cracker Jack (devised by F.W. and Louis Rueckheim in 1890) and shrimp DeJonghe (invented at DeJonghe's Restaurant). The 1893 World's Fair was also the site where many classic American products were introduced to the world, including shredded wheat and Wrigley's Juicy Fruit gum.

self, Superdawg might have to take third place to the other hot dog joints mentioned in this book. But as far as authentic retro atmosphere goes, Superdawg is unparalleled. This is the only hot dog stand left in the city with drive-in service. Pull up in the parking lot, talk into the speaker, and someone will bring your hot dog and fries directly to your car. Burgers (served on black bread) and thick shakes and malts are specialties here. Just look for the dancing hot dog on top of the restaurant for a quintessential dining experience. Lunch, dinner daily. No credit cards. (Greater Chicago)

WALKER BROTHERS PANCAKE HOUSE
153 Green Bay Rd., Wilmette
847/251-6000
$

The lines on weekend mornings sometimes go all the way outside this north suburban institution, and not just because Robert Redford used to dine here way back when he was filming *Ordinary People*. The fact is that Walker Brothers (which now has a number of locations in the northern suburbs) has great omelets and probably the best pancakes around. Walker Brothers is known especially for its incredibly sweet but still delicious apple pancakes. Its crepes are also excellent, particularly the seafood variety. Breakfast, lunch, dinner daily. (Greater Chicago)

Carolyn Crimi

5

SIGHTS AND ATTRACTIONS

For some, it's standing at the top of the John Hancock building in the observation deck, looking down at Lake Michigan and following it all the way south to Indiana as impossibly tiny automobiles curve around Lake Shore Drive. For others, it's the first swig of beer in the bleachers of Wrigley Field, looking out at an iridescent green field and a perfect diamond. It's the curve of the spectacular staircase that winds up the Rookery Building, the splendid pink neon of the sign at Phil and Son's Gas Station on North Lincoln Avenue, the laughter of ice-skaters on State Street, the view of the city from the Adler Planetarium.

Chicago is a city of a thousand perfect sights, a thousand perfect moments. One such moment can be experienced just east of the Belmont Harbor. To get there, you walk through an underpass beneath Lake Shore Drive. Sometimes, if you get there by evening, you'll hear a lone saxophonist playing Star Eyes or John Coltrane's Naima. Pass the bike path and walk along the grass until you reach the rocks. Climb over them and you'll find yourself standing in front of the deep blue lake, listening to the waves splashes below you and feeling the spray of the water on your cheeks. To the north lies the park, to the south lie the lights of the city. In front of you are lights of the boats, floating silently upon the lake. Sit down on the rocks, close your eyes, and listen to the lake.

This is but one of Chicago's special offerings. There are a thousand more sights, attractions, and little moments of perfection to guide your way.

DOWNTOWN

Sights in Downtown Chicago

1 Adler Planetarium
2 *Batcolumn* (Claes Oldenburg)
3 *The Bowman and the Spearman* (Ivan Mestrovic)
4 Buckingham Fountain
5 Chicago Board of Trade
6 Chicago Cultural Center
7 Chicago Mercantile Exchange
8 City Hall
9 Daley Center
10 Fine Arts Building
11 *Flamingo* (Alexander Calder)
12 *The Four Seasons* (Marc Chagall)
13 Lake Shore Drive
14 Marquette Building
15 *Miro's Chicago*
16 Monadnock Building
17 *The Monument with Standing Beast* (Jean Debuffet)
18 Old Fort Dearborn
19 The Rookery Building
20 Sears Tower Skydeck
21 John G. Shedd Aquarium
17 James R. Thompson Center
22 Harold Washington Library Center

DOWNTOWN

ADLER PLANETARIUM
1300 S. Lake Shore Dr.
312/922-7827
The first planetarium to open to the public in the Western Hemisphere, the Adler Planetarium is home to permanent exhibits dedicated to the history of astronomy and features artifacts gathered from human trips to outer space. Its major attractions are elaborate sky shows. Housed in its recently remodeled Sky Theatre, the frequently updated shows turn the planetarium's ceiling into an exquisite night sky. The nearby Doane Observatory, also run by the planetarium, occasionally allows visitors to gaze into the heavens, often during major astronomical events like eclipses or comet sightings. Mon–Thu 9–5, Fri 9–9, weekends 9–6. $3 adults, discounts for children and seniors. (Downtown)

BATCOLUMN
600 W. Madison St.
What, you may ask, is a 20-ton, 100-foot-tall steel baseball bat doing standing near the corner of Madison and Clinton Streets? This is the work of the witty, Swedish-born American artist Claes Oldenburg, who is noted for creating enormous sculptures of ordinary items (i.e., a clothespin or a slice of chocolate cake) outside of their usual contexts. Erected in 1977, the enormous baseball bat was chosen after Oldenburg decided against creating sculptures of a giant spoon or fireplug. (Downtown)

THE BOWMAN AND THE SPEARMAN
Michigan Ave. and Congress St.
Flanking the entrance to Grant Park, Buckingham Fountain, and the lake, these two powerful bronze statues of Indian warriors on horseback were built in 1928 by sculptor Ivan Mestrovic. Though the two seem to be in the middle of battle, neither is carrying a weapon, a symbol of Mestrovic's antiwar beliefs. *The Bowman and The Spearman* now stand almost as guardians to the city as one passes them upon entering Downtown Chicago from the Eisenhower Expressway. (Downtown)

BUCKINGHAM FOUNTAIN
Grant Park, off Lake Shore Drive
between E. Jackson Boulevard
and E. Balbo Dr.
There are few sights more attractive on a warm summer Chicago night than this 1927 fountain. Bathed in a rainbow of colors during a nightly light show, the pink marble fountain shoots out streams of water more than a hundred feet high. Designed in the style of a fountain from Versailles, Buckingham, strangely enough, is controlled by a computer in Atlanta. The fountain is operational May 1–Sept 1. Light shows nightly at 9. (Downtown)

CHICAGO BOARD OF TRADE
141 W. Jackson Blvd.
312/435-3590
With the golden statue Ceres, the solemn and graceful Roman goddess of grain, looking down on LaSalle Street from her lofty perch atop the 1930 art deco Chicago Board Of Trade, you'd almost think that the proceedings inside the building would be of a somewhat dignified nature. Alas, they are not. But if you're interested in learning more about how the world capitalist economy works, try a trip to the

Chicago Board of Trade's observation deck, where you can view the madness of gold, silver, corn, and soybean trading going on in the pits below. Tours of the Board of Trade, as well as the Chicago Mercantile Exchange and the Chicago Board Options Exchange can be arranged through Ticker Tape Tours, Ltd. (312/644-9001) Mon–Fri 8–2. Free. (Downtown)

CHICAGO CULTURAL CENTER
78 E. Washington St.
312/346-3278
An excellent facility for exhibitions, lectures, and music and dance performances, the landmark cultural center (listed in the National Register of Historic Places) is pretty much a museum on its own. Opened in 1897 as the home of the Chicago Public Library, the center is notable for its exquisite tilework and stained glass. Rooms here were modeled on the Doge's Palace in Venice, the Palazzo Vecchio in Florence, and the Acropolis. Its

stairways were immortalized in the Brian DePalma film *The Untouchables*, where they were used to represent the grandeur of an opera house. Mon–Thu 10–7, Friday 10–6, Sat 10–5, Sun 12–5. Free. (Downtown)

CHICAGO MERCANTILE EXCHANGE
30 S. Wacker Dr.
312/930-8249
Founded in 1919, the Chicago Mercantile Exchange is one of the country's greatest exchanges for futures ranging from soybeans to pork bellies. Two different visitors galleries allow the spectator to look upon the mayhem while a seemingly random and chaotic progression of hand movements help to determine the country's economic future. Daily 7:30–3:15. Free. (Downtown)

CITY HALL
121 N. LaSalle St.
312/744-4000
They say you can't fight city hall.

James R. Thompson Center, p. 109

Murphy/Jahn Inc., Architects

The Ten Best Smells in Chicago

By Terry Abrahamson, screenwriter, playwright, songwriter, and native Chicagoan. Abrahamson has written songs for Muddy Waters, Joan Jett, and George Thorogood. He gained national attention when he wrote a controversial parody advertisement about Jerry Falwell for *Hustler* magazine—the case went to the Supreme Court and was immortalized in the film *The People versus Larry Flynt.*

1. **Blommer's Chocolate Factory** The smell wafts through the air of River North and River West as the signature aroma of post-industrial Chicago.

2. **The Basement of the Museum of Science and Industry** Decades of injection-mold machine afterburn, the scent of bad cafeteria food, and South Side pomade remain virtually unchanged in spite of newly introduced McDonald's food and changing coiffure practices.

3. **Unrehabbed Chicago El Stations** Urine, rail grease, newspapers, and rodent rot harken back to the days of a grimier but gentler rapid transit.

4. **Under the Wrigley Field Bleachers** Beer, decaying wax beer cups, vapors of recycled beer, and vapors of decaying beer vendors.

5. **Unrehabbed Park District Field Houses** Like River Park, 5100 N. Francisco. Locker room meets woodshop meets gymnasium floor wax meets the ghost of the 10-cent pop machine.

6. **Lincoln Square Bowling Alley, 4874 N. Lincoln Ave.** Sweaty shoes and sweaty fingers in sweaty ball-holes combine with the scents of newsprint scoresheet pads, beer, and the signature cork bowling balls.

7. **Joe's Barbecue, 4900 W. Madison St.** If John Sebastian had been black, "Summer in the City" would have been about Joe's.

8. **Maxwell Street Depot, 31st and Canal St.** A great example of the ubiquitous Vienna hot dog stand. The smell grabs you from a block away. Take a deep breath and your cholesterol count could easily double as a Harvard-caliber SAT score.

9. **R & J Foods, 28th Pl. and Wallace** In this olfactory combination of pretzel sticks, dixie cup freezer chest, and the ghost of Vel detergent, the old IGA and Certified Grocers live on.

10. **Holden Drugs, 37th and Union** Once again, it takes a lot of inhaling, but this throwback to the pre-Rogaine pharmacy should take you back to the days when pharmacists wore Ben Casey shirts. If they only had a lunch counter!

But to know why they say it, it might be a good idea to step inside this cavernous 1911 Loop building (designed by Chicago School architects Holabird and Roche), where both the city of Chicago and the county of Cook house their offices. The building is abuzz with activity as aldermen, mayors' aides, and government officials conduct their daily affairs. To get a real feel for the way government works, check out the meetings of the Chicago City Council, where Mayor Richard M. Daley presides. Often contentious, frequently petty, and almost always entertaining, the interactions of Daley and the aldermen and alderwomen of Chicago's 50 wards make this a required tourist spot for anyone interested in the workings (or non-workings) of city government. The first Chicago City Council met more than 160 years ago in the Saloon Building and today, even in City Hall, the word "saloon" is still appropriate. City Hall is open daily from nine to five. Call ahead to see when the next meeting of the city council is being held. Free. (Downtown)

DALEY CENTER
Dearborn and Randolph Sts.
There are a great number of courts in the Daley Center building. But unless you're in town fighting a racketeering charge, that's probably not a feature that will draw you there. The real reason to visit the Daley Center is the building's outdoor plaza. Lorded over by Pablo Picasso's famed 160-ton, 1967 sculpture that is part woman, part butterfly, and part beast, the plaza is a perfect spot to cool your heels while watching the passing Loop scene or to enjoy a free summer concert. (Downtown)

FINE ARTS BUILDING
410 S. Michigan Ave.
Aside from housing the Fine Arts movie theaters, an excellent used bookshop, and a café, this 1892 structure is also an architectural marvel in its own right. Formerly a showroom for Studebaker automobiles, the Fine Arts Building now houses music classrooms, a music shop, and picturesque recital rooms. It also features one of the city's only remaining manually operated elevators. (Downtown)

FLAMINGO
219 S. Dearborn St. between Jackson Blvd. and Adams St.
Outside the Federal Center and plaza designed by Ludwig Mies van der Rohe, this reddish-orange steel sculpture stands proudly, looking almost as if it were folded out of origami paper. In truth, this is the 1974 work of noted whimsical artist, mobile maker, and circus enthusiast Alexander Calder and is one of the city's most beloved outdoor sculptures. Quoted in Ira J. Bach and Mary Lackritz Gray's *A Guide to Chicago Public Sculpture*, Calder says that it is "sort of pink and has a long neck, so I called it Flamingo." For another example of Calder's witty art, see his 1974 Universe in the lobby of the Sears Tower (233 South Wacker Drive). (Downtown)

THE FOUR SEASONS
First National Plaza
(Monroe and Dearborn Sts.)
Toward the latter stages of his career, Russian-born artist Marc Chagall developed a special relationship with the city of Chicago. Aside from the 1977 Chicago Windows, a stunning set of stained-glass windows dedicated to Mayor

ARCHITECTURAL HIGHLIGHTS

Lake Michigan

41

LAKE SHORE DR

Grant Park

JACKSON DR

Buckingham Fountain

Grant Park

COLUMBUS DR

Art Institute of Chicago

CONGRESS PLAZA DR

Chicago Cultural Center

Carson Pirie Scott

MICHIGAN AV

Auditorium Theater

Fine Arts Building

E HARRISON ST

E BALBO AV

E 8TH ST

WABASH ST

Marshall Field's and Co.

STATE ST

James R. Thompson Center

City Hall

Monadnock Building

The Rookery

DEARBORN ST

POLK ST

E WACKER DR

LA SALLE ST

LA SALLE ST

WELLS ST

Sears Tower

Chicago River

N WACKER DR

LAKE ST

RANDOLPH ST

WASHINGTON ST

MADISON ST

MONROE ST

ADAMS ST

JACKSON BLVD

VAN BUREN ST

CONGRESS PKWY

HARRISON ST

CANAL ST

CLINTON ST

JEFFERSON ST

DES PLAINES ST

DAN RYAN EXPWY

90 94

HALSTED ST

W POLK ST

University of Illinois at Chicago

LOCATION OF ARCHITECTURAL HIGHLIGHTS

MILE

KILOMETER

0

Richard J. Daley and donated to the Art Institute of Chicago, he crafted this monolithic outdoor mosaic in 1975. The breathtaking (and recently renovated) *Four Seasons* depicts in panels impressionistic scenes of Chicago in all of its seasons. It's not always easy to tell the exact geographical locations to which Chagall is paying tribute in this collage-like work, but one can clearly see the John Hancock Building. (Downtown)

LAKE SHORE DRIVE
From 5600 N. to 7100 S.

"There ain't no road quite like it, anywhere I've found." So goes the song by the Chicago-based folk-rock trio Aliota, Haynes, and Jeremiah who scored an improbable national hit in the early '70s with "Lake Shore Drive," their ode to both the most scenic stretch of road in Chicago and the hallucinogenic drug that bears Lake Shore Drive's initials. Stretching from the North Side of the city to the deep South Side, LSD is a serene serpentine drive that curves past the Near North Side and the Loop, passing virtually all of the city's major museums, all the while with great views of Lake Michigan. Near Downtown at Randolph Street, the road gives an absolutely stunning view of the Loop to the west where the ivory-white Wrigley Building lights up the city skyline. (Downtown)

MARQUETTE BUILDING
140 S. Dearborn St.

Definitely worth a stop during a walk through the Loop, this building boasts one of the most breathtaking lobbies in the city, with its bronze reliefs and resplendent mosaics. The 17-story steel-frame building was designed by Holabird and

Winter Garden at the Harold Washington Public Library, p. 109

Carolyn Crimi

Roche, and the mosaics in its lobby were designed by Tiffany. Republican candidate Bernard Epton had his offices in this building when he was running for mayor of Chicago against Harold Washington. The building is named after Pere Marquette, the first known European inhabitant of Chicago who settled here briefly in 1674. (Downtown)

MIRÓ'S CHICAGO
69 W. Washington St.

Standing right across Washington Street from Picasso's monumental sculpture in Daley Plaza, Joan Miró's whimsical 40-foot sculpture of a woman with outstretched arms and an apparent pitchfork seeming to stick out of her head almost appears to be mocking the more famous Picasso—or at least seductively beckoning it to come across the street into this more secluded outdoor setting. Unveiled on the Spanish modern master's 88th birthday in 1981, the bronze, concrete, and tile statue attracted much negative attention at first, even being subjected to a vandal's splashing of red paint upon its base. Since then, however, it has become one of the city's most beloved public artworks, a worthy companion to the Picasso. (Downtown)

MONADNOCK BUILDING
53 W. Jackson Blvd.
One of the prime examples of the Chicago school of architecture, this turn-of-the-century office building in the heart of the Loop actually comprises two buildings. The northern half of the 16-story brick building was designed in 1891 by Burnham and Root. The southern half was designed in 1893 by Holabird and Roche. Together the two buildings represent an unplanned collaboration between some of the city's most storied architects. (Downtown)

THE MONUMENT WITH STANDING BEAST
James R. Thompson Center
100 W. Randolph St.
It's difficult to imagine anything that would take attention away from Helmut Jahn's imposing, glassed-in James R. Thompson Center (formerly the State of Illinois Center), but this sculpture by Jean Dubuffet, unveiled in 1985 when the renowned French artist was 84, does a pretty good job of it. Called *The Monument with Standing Beast*, Dubuffet's sculpture is a playful construction that suggests an enormous three-dimensional doodle. (Downtown)

OLD FORT DEARBORN
Michigan Ave. and Wacker Dr.
Today there is only a plaque to mark its existence, but back in the early 19th century, even before the incorporation of Chicago as a city, this was a major military outpost. Presided over by Captain John Whistler, Fort Dearborn guarded over a major trading route. During the War of 1812 the fort was abandoned and 53 men, women, and children were ambushed and killed by Indians. The fort was demolished in 1857. (Downtown)

THE ROOKERY BUILDING
209 S. LaSalle St.
Chicago lore has it that the stunning spiral staircase in this jewel of early 19th century architecture was used as the stairway that Rhett Butler and Scarlett O'Hara ascended in the classic film *Gone with the Wind*. This story is not true, but coming into this breathtaking building, one can easily see how the mistake was made. Designed in 1886 by Burnham and Root, the Rookery is arguably the single most awe-inspiring example of the Chicago school of architecture. With its reddish-brown terracotta entryway and its gold and marble lobby (which was designed by Frank Lloyd Wright in 1905), this landmark building is definitely worth a special trip. The building takes its name from the many pigeons who used to roost here back in the 19th century. (Downtown)

SEARS TOWER SKYDECK
233 S. Wacker Dr.
773/885-9696
If standing street level at the corner of Wacker and Jackson and gazing up to the top of the Sears Tower didn't do it in the first place, the 1,454-foot elevator ride to the top will certainly convince you that this is indeed the world's tallest building outside of Malaysia. Completed in

PUBLIC ART

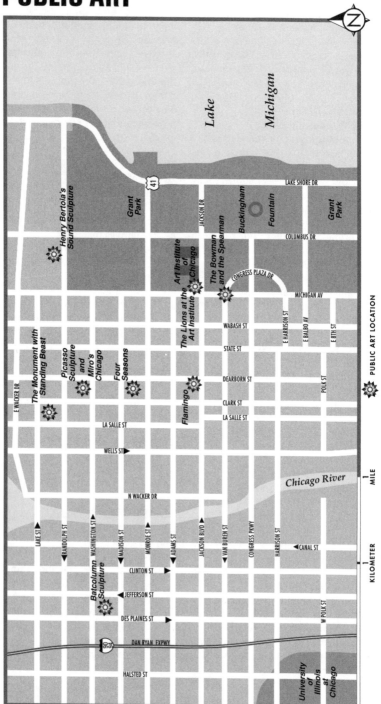

N

Lake Michigan

LAKE SHORE DR

41

Grant Park

JACKSON DR

Buckingham Fountain

Grant Park

COLUMBUS DR

Henry Bertoia's Sound Sculpture

Art Institute of Chicago

The Bowman and the Spearman

CONGRESS PLAZA DR

The Lions at the Art Institute

MICHIGAN AV

E HARRISON ST

E BALBO AV

E 8TH ST

PUBLIC ART LOCATION

WABASH ST

STATE ST

The Monument with Standing Beast

Picasso Sculpture and Miro's Chicago

Four Seasons

DEARBORN ST

POLK ST

E WACKER DR

Flamingo

CLARK ST

LA SALLE ST

LA SALLE ST

WELLS ST

Chicago River

1 MILE

N WACKER DR

LAKE ST

RANDOLPH ST

WASHINGTON ST

MADISON ST

MONROE ST

ADAMS ST

JACKSON BLVD

VAN BUREN ST

CONGRESS PKWY

HARRISON ST

CANAL ST

1 KILOMETER

Batcolumn Sculpture

CLINTON ST

JEFFERSON ST

DES PLAINES ST

W POLK ST

90 94

DAN RYAN EXPWY

University of Illinois at Chicago

HALSTED ST

0

1974 and designed by Skidmore, Owings, and Merrill, the skyscraper was originally the corporate headquarters of Sears. Located on the 103rd floor, the observation deck provides breathtaking views of not only Chicago, but also Wisconsin, Indiana, and Michigan. Observation deck open daily 9 a.m.–10 p.m. $6.75 adults, discounts for children and seniors, active military personnel free. (Downtown)

JOHN G. SHEDD AQUARIUM
1200 S. Lake Shore Dr.
312/939-2438

Since the 1991 opening of the Oceanarium, a huge (1.8 acres) addition to the original 1930 aquarium that features beluga whales and spectacular views of Lake Michigan, the Shedd has become one of the city's most popular attractions and is said to be the world's largest indoor aquarium. Though the dolphin shows and feeding demonstrations attract the most attention, the real stars remain the 600-plus species visitors can see here—from penguins to eels to tropical fish. Excellent exhibits include the Shedd's famous 90,000-gallon coral reef exhibit featuring sea turtles, sharks, and green moray eels (daily feedings are conducted at 11 a.m. and 2 p.m.); and the Asian River exhibit with its 12-foot waterfall and hundreds of fish swimming in and out of ivy and bamboo. Daily 9–6, Thu 9–9. $11 adults, $6 adults on Thu, discounts for children and seniors. (Downtown)

JAMES R. THOMPSON CENTER
(formerly State of Illinois Center)
100 W. Randolph St.

During the 1980s, German-born, Illinois Institute of Technology–trained, postmodern bad-boy architect Helmut Jahn was considered the hottest item in Chicago architecture since the early 20th century. His glass and mirrored buildings, among them sleekly elegant Xerox Centre, an addition to the Chicago Board of Trade, and the United Airlines Terminal at O'Hare Airport, are bold, arrogant, and unforgettable "prima donnas," as he has referred to them. This leviathan, which houses the governmental offices for the state of Illinois, was completed in 1986. Sadly, it was the beginning of the end for Jahn's brief stint as Chicago's reigning architect. Resembling something between a UFO and a Hyatt hotel, the enormous glass structure was one of the most controversial buildings ever to be erected in Chicago. From the outside, perhaps, it may look like a displaced monument to egoism. But take a ride up one of the building's glass elevators and look down at the atrium below and you'll see a stunning view of Jahn's unique vision. Also check out the Jean Dubuffet sculpture in front. (Downtown)

HAROLD WASHINGTON LIBRARY CENTER
400 S. State St.
312/747-4200

As far as architectural marvels go, this is far from the city's finest exemplar. A sprawling, mausoleum-like structure that is surprisingly inconvenient to navigate, the main branch of the Chicago Public Library, unveiled in 1991, invites remarks that range from passable to appalling. The somewhat grim and alienating facility was designed by Thomas Beeby of Hammond Beeby Babka, whose design was chosen over far more imaginative proposals, most notably those of Chicago architect Helmut Jahn. That said, this library does merit mention for the fact that it is the country's largest public library and the second largest library in the world. If you're here to read or research rather than to admire, you'll do quite well with the library's numerous study areas and research facilities. The great music library encompasses the Chicago Blues Archives, and the Municipal Reference Library is an excellent source for research on city politics. The library has more than 1.5 million books and nearly 13,000 periodicals. The children's library here is also excellent (For more information see Kids' Stuff). Sun 1–5; Mon 9–7; Tue, Thu 11–7; Wed, Fri, and Sat 9–5. Free. (Downtown)

NEAR NORTH

AMOCO BUILDING
200 E. Randolph St.
312/856-6111
This whitish granite skyscraper, designed by E.D. Stone/Perkins and Will in 1974, is the third tallest in the city. Eighty stories high, the Amoco Building sits on a plaza that is noteworthy for a serene, sound-producing sculpture created by Harry Bertoia over a large, rectangular reflecting pool. (Near North)

ASTOR STREET
Running north from Division Street, just west of Lake Michigan on the Gold Coast
Home to the wealthy and the influential, this north-south street on Chicago's Gold Coast is just a couple blocks west of the lake (40 East, 1200 to 1600 North) and features some of the most stunning residences in Chicago. A short walk from one end of the street to the other reveals exquisite examples of late-19th-century and early-20th-century architecture, including the Russell House (designed in 1929 by Holabird and Root) at 1444 North Astor Street, the Joseph T. Ryerson House (registered in the list of Chicago Historical and Architectural Landmarks), and the James Charnley House (designed in 1892 by Frank Lloyd Wright) at 1365 North Astor Street. (Near North)

BUGHOUSE SQUARE
Walton St. and Clark Street
Located across Walton Street from the Newberry Library (60 W. Walton St.), this one-square-block city park is usually empty. But back in the '30s and '40s this was the hub of left-wing political activity as communist soapbox orators and agitators of all stripes would gather here to speak. These days Bughouse Square comes alive only once a year, in June, for public debates paying tribute to the square's political history. Chicago legend and noted oral historian Studs Terkel usually attends. (Near North)

JOHN HANCOCK CENTER OBSERVATORY
875 N. Michigan Ave.
888/875-VIEW
Though it's been decades since the Hancock was the city's tallest building, in many ways this observation deck provides the best views of the city. Located on the 94th floor of the 1,107-foot-tall John Hancock Center (completed in 1969), the observatory is not quite as isolated from the hustle and bustle of Chicago nightlife as that of the Sears Tower, so the nightime panorama here is an ever-evolving one. A recent sky-

NEAR NORTH

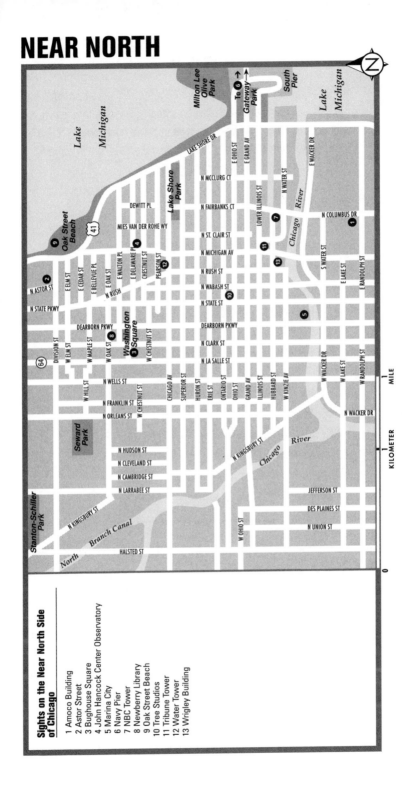

Sights on the Near North Side of Chicago

1 Amoco Building
2 Astor Street
3 Bughouse Square
4 John Hancock Center Observatory
5 Marina City
6 Navy Pier
7 NBC Tower
8 Newberry Library
9 Oak Street Beach
10 Tree Studios
11 Tribune Tower
12 Water Tower
13 Wrigley Building

ART DECO

For a short time in the 1920s and 1930s, art deco—an architectural school which borrowed from the cubists, the Bauhaus movement, and the French art nouveau style and was honed to perfection in New York City—was all the rage in Chicago. Here are 10 prominent examples of this architectural style.

1301 N. Astor St. *(Philip Maher, 1930)*

333 N. Michigan Ave. *(Holabird and Roche, 1928)*

919 N. Michigan Ave. *(Holabird and Root, 1920)*

American National Bank Building *1 N. LaSalle St. (Vitzhum and Burns, 1930)*

Carbon and Carbide Building *230 N. Michigan Ave. (Burnham Brothers, 1929)*

Chicago Board of Trade Building *Jackson Blvd. at LaSalle St. (Holabird and Root, 1930)*

Civic Opera House *20 N. Wacker Dr. (Graham, Anderson, Probst, and White, 1929)*

Frank Fisher Apartments *1209 N. State Pkwy. (Andrew Rebori, 1938)*

La Salle National Bank Building *135 S. LaSalle St. (Graham, Anderson, Probst and White, 1934)*

Two Riverside Plaza *400 W. Madison St. (Holabird and Root, 1929)*

deck renovation provides an outdoor Skywalk for the less acraphobic visitors. Talking telescopes give a basic background on Chicago history. 9 a.m. to midnight. $7 adults, discounts for children and seniors. (Near North)

MARINA CITY
300 N. State St.
Designed by Bertrand Goldberg in 1967, Marina City—with its own shopping centers, movie theaters, marina, skating rink, and bowling alley—was once the quintessential example of high-rise living. You may also remember it as the location where a car sailed through the guardrail in its parking lot and splashed into the Chicago River in the Steve McQueen film *The Hunter.* Now it's not quite the high-tech marvel that it was 30-plus years ago, but the cylindrical twin towers are still a

remarkable example of '60s high-rise architecture. Marina City now houses the House of Blues nightclub. (Near North)

NAVY PIER
600 E. Grand Ave.
312/595-7437

It's partly a shopping center. It's partly a kids' playground. It's partly an entertainment facility. It's partly a food court. With 50 acres of space, Navy Pier can be a lot of things. One of the biggest draws here is the 150-foot-tall Ferris wheel, which affords riders absolutely breathtaking views of the city. But with nine different restaurants, 11 food-court vendors, a 3-D movie theater, an outdoor stage that features live entertainment by national acts, the Crystal Gardens' indoor botanical garden with tons of flowers and silly squirting fountains, and a merry-go-round, there's more than enough to keep one occupied for an entire day. (Near North)

NBC TOWER
435 N. Cityfront Plaza Dr.

Few Chicagoans take particular pride in the fact that both *The Jenny Jones Show* and *The Jerry Springer Show* are filmed here. But those are the primary reasons that this 1989 structure, modeled after New York's Rockefeller Center and designed by Skidmore, Owings, and Merrill, is a major tourist attraction. (Near North)

NEWBERRY LIBRARY
60 W. Walton
312/943-9090

With nearly 1.5 million bound volumes and 5.5 million manuscripts and archival items, the Newberry Library is not only a prime exhibit space, but also a major research facility with collections of rare books, documents, and maps. Among the library's vast cache of holdings are the papers of such noted figures as Clarence Darrow and Ben Hecht, manuscripts concerning Lewis and Clark's expeditions, the Williamsburg 1754 edition of George Washington's journal, and a cornucopia of other arcane materials. The museum also hosts frequent fine-art exhibits, lectures, classes, and concerts. Mon,

Fountain at the Lincoln Park Conservatory, p. 116

Carolyn Crimi

Fri, Sat 8:15–5:30; Tue, Wed, Thu 8:15–7:30. Free. (Near North)

OAK STREET BEACH
600 N. Lake Shore Dr.
This is the ultimate see-and-be-seen beach in Chicago—you can smell the suntan oil from about a mile away on summer days. A paradise for sunbathers and voyeurs alike, this is Chicago's only free outdoor version of a singles club. For the less solar-inclined, just west of this beach is the Chess Pavilion where chess grandmasters and grandmasters-in-training meet every day under a stone overhang for highly contested games. (Near North)

TREE STUDIOS
4 E. Ohio St.
Designed by Parfitt Brothers in 1894, this striking U-shaped complex was funded by philanthropist Lambert Tree, who sought to create low-cost housing and studios for Chicago artists. More than a hundred years later, though frequently threatened with demolition, this landmark is still the location for many of the city's artists. It's also just down the block from the remarkable Medinah Temple. with its signature dome. The Medinah, which serves as headquarters for the Chicago branch of the Shriner's is home to the Shriner's Circus and occasional films and concerts performed by the Chicago Symphony Orchestra. (Near North)

TRIBUNE TOWER
435 N. Michigan Ave.
The winning entry in a nationwide design competition, the Gothic-style Tribune Tower has one of the more bizarre attractions of any major Chicago tourist site: A series of arti-facts from some of the more noteworthy sites around the world, including stones from the Great Pyramid and the Parthenon, are literally embedded in the building's exterior walls. The skyscaper was designed by New York's Raymond Hood and John Howells. (Near North)

WATER TOWER
806 N. Michigan Ave.
312/467-7114
Built in 1869, this is one of the few buildings that survived the Great Chicago Fire and the only one that is located right in a high-traffic area of the city. A castle-like stone structure, which looks a lot like a rook in a chess game, the Water Tower was built around a 138-foot-high water pipe. The Water Tower no longer has any particular function other than to serve as a good place to find scads of free tourist information. (The pumping station across the street is still functioning). The park around the Water Tower is an excellent spot to relax after lugging bags of goods purchased at the nearby Water Tower Place shopping mall. (Near North)

WRIGLEY BUILDING
400 N. Michigan Ave.
The legend is that Graham Anderson Probst and White in 1924 designed these headquarters of the Wrigley chewing gum company to look like a birthday cake. And though it's hard to find evidence to prove this, it certainly looks a little bit like a celebratory cake of some sort. Lighting up the night with its white terra-cotta facade, the Wrigley Building is one of Chicago's most visible architectural landmarks. (Near North)

NORTH SIDE

Lake Michigan

North Av Beach

South Lagoon

Lincoln Monument

Fullerton Beach

North Lagoon

Diversey Harbor

Belmont Harbor

Bird Sanctuary

Lincoln Park

Lincoln Park Zoo

Lincoln Park

LAKE SHORE DR

LAKEVIEW AV

SHERIDAN RD

LINCOLN PARK WEST

SEDGWICK ST

ARLINGTON PL

Oz Park

Lincoln Park Campus

W SURF ST

BRONTPON

STRATFORD

BROADWAY

HALSTED ST

CLARK ST

GEORGE ST

CLIFTON AV

CLIFTON AV

RACINE ST

SOUTHPORT AV

ASHLAND AV

HERMITAGE AV

LINCOLN AV

W WRIGHTWOOD AV

BELDEN AV

CLIFTON AV

ARMITAGE AV

CORTLAND ST

CLYBOURN AV

ELSTON AV

Graceland Cemetery

Wrigley Field

IRVING PARK RD

C&NW RR

Chicago River

DAMEN AV

Hamlin Park

DIVERSEY PKWY

FULLERTON PKWY

HERMITAGE ST

GRACE ST

ADDISON ST

LEAVITT ST

BELMONT AV

BELDEN AV

LEAVITT ST

ARMITAGE AV

NORTH AV

MILWAUKEE AV

WESTERN AV

ROSCOE ST

CAMPBELL AV

MAPLEWOOD AV

GEORGE ST

CAMPBELL AV

CALIFORNIA AV

CAMPBELL AV

California Park

Revere Park

To 5

MILES

KILOMETERS

Sights on the North Side of Chicago

1 Elks Veterans Memorial
2 Halsted Street
3 Lincoln Park Conservatory
4 Lincoln Park Totem Pole
5 Lincoln Park Zoo Rookery
6 St. Mary of the Angels Church
7 Sheridan Road
8 Wrigley Field

NORTH SIDE

ELKS VETERANS MEMORIAL
2750 N. Lakeview Ave.
773/477-2750
One of the most remarkable buildings on Chicago's North Side, this 1926 Lincoln Park landmark is owned and operated by the state's Elks Association. A rotunda resembling a Washington, D.C., government building from the outside, inside the peace memorial displays a stunningly opulent collection of American sculptures, paintings, and murals. The main reception room, with its magnificent chandeliers and Oriental rugs, is worth the trip. The building is dedicated to the memory of Elks Club members who died during World War I. Mon–Fri 9–5, weekends 10–5. Free. (North Side)

HALSTED STREET
800 W. from 2800 N. to 3600 S.
They don't call this area Boys' Town for nothing. Chicago's burgeoning gay community, which represents a substantial voting bloc, is centered around Halsted Street from Diversey Street (2800 N.) to Addison Street (3600 N.) Here you'll find gay cabarets, nightclubs including the famous Roscoe's (3356 N. Halsted St., 773/281-3355), and gay-themed restaurants and stores (check out Gay Mart, 3457 N. Halsted St., 773/929-4272). For further information about gay nightspots or organizations, pick up a copy of the free weekly *Windy City Times*, available at most stores in the area. (North Side)

LINCOLN PARK CONSERVATORY
2400 N. Stockton Dr.
312/742-7736
For those who are not quite so enthused about venturing all the way to Chicago's West Side to see stunning displays of cacti, azaleas, and other sundry forms of flora, this sprawling greenhouse provides the next best alternative. Exhibits change with the seasons and feature annual exhibits showcasing mums, Christmas flowers, and the like. This humid wonderland, built in 1892, is housed right beside the Lincoln Park Zoo (see the Kids' Stuff chapter). Daily 9–5. Free. (Near North)

LINCOLN PARK TOTEM POLE
3600 N. Lake Shore Dr.
Shooting up from the ground 40 feet into the air, this is one of the most recognizable sights as you drive along Lake Shore Drive or pedal along the lakefront bike path. Built in 1926 by Vancouver's Kwakiutl Indians, this cedar log totem pole with a majestic thunderbird standing at its top was a gift to James Kraft, founder of Kraft Incorporated. Kraft gave the totem pole to the Chicago Park District in 1929. (North Side)

The Rookery Building, p. 107

Cervin Robinson

LINCOLN PARK ZOO ROOKERY
2400 N. Stockton Dr.
312/742-7736

Though it's located right next to the Lincoln Park Conservatory (see above) and it leads into the Lincoln Park Zoo (see Kids' Stuff), this little sanctuary remains one of the best-kept secrets of Chicago's North Side. Basically a miniature nature trail that curves around a small body of water, the zoo rookery functions as a refreshing shaded oasis within one of the most congested areas of the city. Particularly in the mornings, before the crowds have descended upon the zoo, this is an excellent place to relax, stroll, and watch for some of the dozens of varieties of birds that nest here. (Near North)

ST. MARY OF THE ANGELS CHURCH
1850 N. HERMITAGE AVE.
773/278-2644

This is the largest Roman Catholic church in the state of Illinois. Located in Chicago's Bucktown neighborhood, St. Mary is capped by a dome modeled after Michelangelo's at St. Peter's Basilica in the Vatican City. Boasting 27 murals and nearly a hundred stained-glass windows, this is one of the more impressive churches in town. (North Side)

SHERIDAN ROAD

Those who criticize Chicago as being a flat city of flat streets need only to check out this road to have their minds changed. Beginning at the north end of the city, Sheridan Road follows the lakefront into the northern suburbs, which is where it begins to get interesting. Passing Cavalry Cemetery (where first Chicago White Sox owner Charles Comiskey is buried), Northwestern University and Lighthouse Beach in Evanston, and Bahai Temple in Wilmette, the road becomes a roller

---

People Who Talk and the Audiences Who Love Them

Though Phil Donahue and Morton Downey Jr. have long since packed their bags, Chicago is still something of a TV talk show capital. Tickets are hard to get, but if you call well in advance you can reserve some. For The Jenny Jones Show (filmed at NBC Tower, 435 N. Columbus Dr.), call 312/836-9485. For The Jerry Springer Show (also at NBC Tower), call 312/321-5365. For The Oprah Winfrey Show (filmed at Harpo Studios, 1058 W. Washington St.), call 312/591-9222. Though it's not a talk show, Chicago's superstation WGN also films the kids' show Bozo's Circus live at its studios at 2501 West Bradley Place. But since the wait for tickets is about 10 years, the phone number won't be of much use.

coaster of twists, turns, and swoops the further north it gets. Along its beautiful winding way with occasional glimpses of the lakefront, Sheridan passes by ravines and the most magnificent homes of the famed North Shore, including several designed by Frank Lloyd Wright. You can take Sheridan Road all the way to Wisconsin, if you so choose. (North Side)

WRIGLEY FIELD
1060 W. Addison St.
773/404-2827

The Chicago Cubs baseball team is hardly the reason to visit this Chicago landmark (see Sports and Recreation). The real reason people keep flocking here is the stunning ballpark. Built in 1914 on the grounds of what had once been the Chicago Lutheran Theological Seminary, Wrigley Field (designed by Zachary Taylor Davis) was first known as Weeghman Park before it was purchased by chewing gum magnate William Wrigley Jr. With the possible exception of Boston's Fenway Park, it is the most picturesque baseball facility in the country. (North Side)

FAR NORTH

ESSANAY STUDIOS
1333 W. Argyle St.

There's not much to see here. The only hint of this studio's former glory is the white terra-cotta facade and the Indian-head fresco on Argyle Street. But this location is significant for the role it played in the history of moviemaking. Before Hollywood became the country's cinema capital, Chicago was a major silent movie hot spot, and screen stars like Mary

Pickford, Ben Turpin, and even Charlie Chaplin filmed at Essanay. Truth be told, Chaplin filmed only one short here *(His New Job)*, but it did represent a significant step in his development before he, like everyone else, escaped the Chicago snows for the lure of Tinseltown. Gloria Swanson started her career here as a chorus girl, and Wallace Beery was an actor at Essanay as well. (Far North)

GRACELAND CEMETERY
4001 N. Clark St.
773/525-1105

Hardly the best place for an eighth-grade field trip (as my grammar-school class learned the hard way), Graceland Cemetery is still a fascinating and eerily peaceful site where many a legendary Chicago historical figure is buried. Presided over by Lorado Taft's noted statue of death, the cemetery teems with grandiose monuments commemorating the lives of Chicago's once rich and famous. Among those for whom Graceland is the final resting place are Marshall Field, Allen Pinkerton (founder of the Pinkerton Detective Agency), George Pullman, Daniel Burnham, Potter Palmer, Ludwig Mies van der Rohe, and Louis Sullivan. Sullivan is also responsible for designing the famed Getty Tomb, burial site of lumberman George Getty. Daily 8–4:30. (Far North)

ROSEHILL CEMETERY
5800 N. Ravenswood Ave.
773/561-4900

Dating back to 1859, Rosehill marks the final resting place of several hundred Civil War soldiers and, because of this, hosts an annual Civil War reenactment. Located on the

FAR NORTH

Lake Michigan

Mundelein College

Montrose-Wilson Beach

Ardmore Hollywood Beach

Foster Av Beach

Lincoln Park

LAWRENCE DR

WILSON

MONTROSE DR

LAKE SHORE DR

41

SHERIDAN RD

N WINTHROP AV

N BROADWAY

ARGYLE ST

ELMDALE AV

Senn Park

N RIDGE BLVD

N GLENWOOD AV

N BROADWAY

N RACINE AV

Graceland Cemetery

2

BRYN MAWR AV

N CLARK ST

ARGYLE ST

St. Bonifacius Cemetery

1

41

ASHLAND AV

RIDGE AV

N RAVENSWOOD AV

RAVENSWOOD AV

RAVENSWOOD AV

DAMEN AV

Rosehill Cemetery

3

DAMEN AV

GRANVILLE AV

14

FOSTER ST

Winnemac Park

ARGYLE ST

W LAWRENCE AV

LINCOLN AV

WILSON AV

MONTROSE AV

BERTEAU AV

W IRVING PARK RD

Welles Park

W DEVON AV

N WESTERN AV

MILES

2

KILOMETERS

2

PETERSON AV

ROCKWELL ST

41

ROCKWELL ST

Chicago River

Horner Park

North Branch Chicago River

Mather Park

LINCOLN AV

N CALIFORNIA ST

Ronan Park

CALIFORNIA ST

SACRAMENTO AV

SACRAMENTO AV

BRYN MAWR AV

North Shore Channel

Chicago River

River Park

N KEDZIE AV

W ARGYLE ST

Legion Park

North

19

0

Sights on the Far North Side of Chicago

1 Essanay Studios
2 Graceland Cemetery
3 Rosehill Cemetery

WEST SIDE

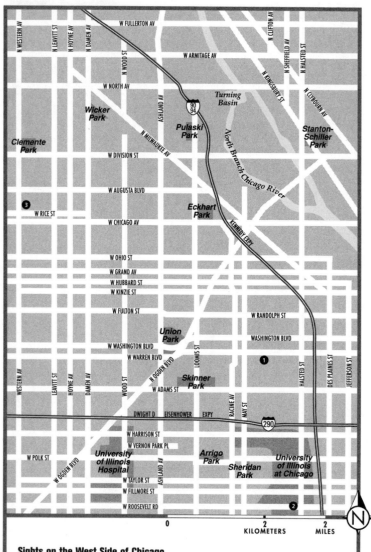

N WESTERN AV
N LEAVITT ST
N HOYNE AV
N DAMEN AV
W FULLERTON AV
N WOOD ST
W ARMITAGE AV
N CLIFTON AV
N SHEFFIELD AV
N HALSTED ST
N KINGSBURY ST
N CLYBOURN AV
W NORTH AV
Wicker Park
ASHLAND AV
90 94
Turning Basin
N MILWAUKEE AV
Pulaski Park
Stanton-Schiller Park
Clemente Park
North Branch Chicago River
W DIVISION ST
W AUGUSTA BLVD
3 W RICE ST
Eckhart Park
W CHICAGO AV
Kennedy Expy
W OHIO ST
W GRAND AV
W HUBBARD ST
W KINZIE ST
W FULTON ST
W RANDOLPH ST
Union Park
WASHINGTON BLVD
W WASHINGTON BLVD
W WARREN BLVD
LOOMIS ST
1
HALSTED ST
DES PLAINES ST
JEFFERSON ST
WESTERN AV
LEAVITT ST
HOYNE AV
DAMEN AV
WOOD ST
N OGDEN BLVD
Skinner Park
W ADAMS ST
RACINE AV
MAY ST
DWIGHT D EISENHOWER EXPY
290
W HARRISON ST
W VERNON PARK PL
University of Illinois Hospital
Arrigo Park
University of Illinois at Chicago
W POLK ST
W OGDEN BLVD
ASHLAND AV
Sheridan Park
W TAYLOR ST
W FILLMORE ST
W ROOSEVELT RD
2

0   2   2
     KILOMETERS   MILES

N

Sights on the West Side of Chicago

1 Harpo Studios
2 Maxwell Street Market
3 St. Nicholas Ukrainian
   Catholic Cathedral

city's North Side, the massive cemetery houses the graves of such departed luminaries as Julius Rosenwald (founder of the Museum of Science and Industry), John G. Shedd (founder of the Shedd Aquarium), and Frances Willard, who headed the Women's Christian Temperance Union. On a more grisly note, Bobby Franks—the victim of notorious thrill-killers Leopold and Loeb (the subjects of John Logan's play *Never the Sinner* and the Alfred Hitchcock film *Rope*)—is also buried here. Daily 8–4:30. (Far North)

WEST SIDE

HARPO STUDIOS
1058 W. Washington St.
312/633-1000
Said to be the only television and film studio owned by an African American woman, these are the headquarters of talk show host, actress, and Fortune 500 member Oprah Winfrey. Winfrey's show is taped here in what used to be a U.S. armory and a roller rink. For a reservation to see the show live (it's free), call 312/591-9222 Mon–Fri 9–5. (West Side)

MAXWELL STREET MARKET
1200 S. Halsted St. (and environs)
No matter how hard the city and the University of Illinois at Chicago has tried to do away with it, somehow the spirit of the Maxwell Street Market persists. Though it is a far cry from its former glory as a bustling marketplace of small-time hustlers, shopkeepers, and radical politicians selling everything from hubcaps to record albums in vast vacant lots, some of the shops re-

main. And the old-time street vendors still sell their wares here every Sunday morning. The days when Benny Goodman and Paul Muni used to walk these grounds may be long gone, but take a walk here on Sunday and relive the days of Chicago's most storied flea market. (West Side)

ST. NICHOLAS UKRAINIAN CATHOLIC CATHEDRAL
2338 W. Rice
773/276-4537
In the heart of Chicago's Ukrainian Village, an enclave of Ukrainian immigrants and artists of all ethnic backgrounds, stands this magnificent and overwhelming neo-Byzantine church. Built in 1913, the cathedral remains one of the cornerstones of the Ukrainian community and is an awe-inspiring architectural marvel, as well. (West Side)

NEAR SOUTH

CHICAGO DEFENDER BUILDING
2400 S. Michigan Ave.
773/225-2400
The Chicago Defender, founded in 1905 by Robert Sengstacke Abbott, was the first daily paper for the African American community in Chicago. Nearly a century later it is again the only daily paper targeted primarily at African Americans. Tours of the facility are available if you call in advance. Mon–Fri 9–5. (Near South)

CHESS RECORDS
2120 S. Michigan Ave.
There is little here to mark the history of this address, but in many ways this was where Chicago music, as we know it now, was

NEAR SOUTH

Chicago Harbor

SOLIDARITY DR

Lake Michigan

Burnham Park Yacht Harbor

LAKE SHORE DR

41

Field Museum

MCFETRIDGE DR

Soldier Field ⑤

Burnham Park

55

29TH ST

DR MARTIN LUTHER KING JR DR

CALUMET ST

Mercy Hospital and Medical Center

CALUMET

CALUMET ST

PRAIRIE AV

INDIANA AV ◀

S MICHIGAN AV ②

24TH ST
24TH PL

Dunbar Park

S WABASH AV

①

S WABASH AV

14TH ST

16TH ST

STATE ST

④

Illinois Institute of Technology

CLARK ST

S WENTWORTH AV

S WENTWORTH AV

River

NORMAL ST

Armour Square Park

CANAL ST

CERMAK RD

18TH ST

24TH ST

26TH ST

29TH ST

31ST ST

33RD BLVD

35TH ST

Chicago

WALLACE ST

90 94

HALSTED ST

2 MILES

14TH ST

MORGAN ST

Branch

McGuane Park

BLUE ISLAND RD

South Water Market

RACINE AV

2 KILOMETERS

THROOP ST

RACINE AV

ROOSEVELT RD

LOOMIS ST

Stetson Canal

33RD

THROOP ST

Addams Park

Pilsen ③

Samson Canal

Arnold Canal

ASHLAND AV

ARCHER AV

South

14TH ST

16TH ST

18TH ST

21ST PL

WOOD ST

BLUE ISLAND RD

31ST ST

33RD BLVD

Harrison Park

WOLCOTT AV

DAMEN AV

0

born. Home to the legendary record company founded by Leonard and Phil Chess, this site was the professional home for legendary artists like Muddy Waters, Etta James, Chuck Berry, and James Brown. This was also the center of Music Row, the hub of Chicago's black music recording industry where scads of artists like Gene "Duke of Earl" Chandler, Jerry "Iceman" Butler, and others cut records in the '50s and '60s when Chicago was a major capital for rhythm and blues, soul, and blues music. The Rolling Stones were so influenced by the music that came from this label that they even mention it in one of their early songs. (Near South)

PILSEN
18th St. from Halsted St. (800 W.) to Damen Ave. (2000 W.)
One of the most vibrant, up-and-coming neighborhoods in Chicago, this enclave of Latino immigrants and Chicago artists is home to many excellent restaurants, shops, theaters, and galleries. Still resisting the long-standing rumors of gentrification, the Pilsen neighborhood is home to museums like the Mexican Fine Arts Center (see Museums and Galleries) and galleries like *Calles y Sueños* (1900 S. Carpenter St.). The occasionally adventurous Blue Rider Theater (1822 S. Halsted St.) is located here as well. It's a great place for a weekend daytime walk, though if you come here after dark, be alert; the neighborhood can get somewhat dicey. (Near South)

QUINN CHAPEL
2401 S. Wabash Ave.
312/791-1846
One of the cornerstones of Chicago's

African American community, this Victorian structure, dating back to 1847, is the oldest black congregation in the city. The Quinn Chapel African Methodist Episcopal Church dates back to the days of the Underground Railroad and many national political figures spoke here, from Presidents Taft and McKinley to Martin Luther King Jr. Though it faces severe financial crises at present, it still stands as a monument to the once-thriving Black Metropolis on the Near South Side. (Near South)

SOLDIER FIELD
425 E. McFetridge Dr.
Designed by Holabird and Roche as a memorial to the victims of World War I, this 1924 national historic landmark is now the home of the Chicago Bears and large-scale rock concerts by bands like U2 and the Rolling Stones (see Sports and Recreation). (Near South)

SOUTH SIDE

CHICAGO BEE BUILDING
3600 S. State St.
One of the cornerstones of Black Metropolis, a thriving community of black businesses in the first half of the 20th century, the Chicago Bee Building was the home of the *Chicago Bee*, one of the first black-owned and -operated newspapers in the city. Funded by Anthony Overton, a prominent black business leader and founder of the Overton Hygienic Manufacturing Company, the 1925 Chicago Bee Building is striking for both its historical significance and its green terra-cotta facade. Though it has fallen into disrepair over the years, today the

SOUTH SIDE

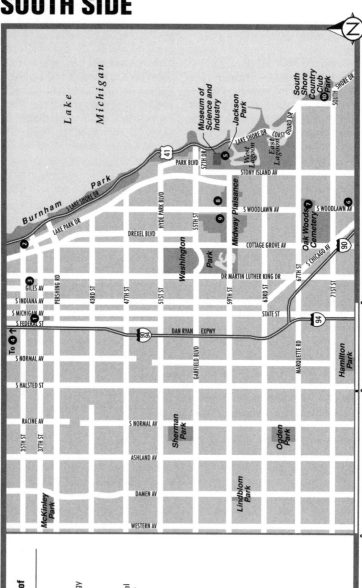

Sights on the South Side of Chicago

1 Chicago Bee Building
2 Douglas Tomb
3 Eighth Regiment Armory
4 Illinois Institute of Technology
5 Jackson Park
6 Mosque Maryam
7 Oak Woods Cemetery
8 Robie House
9 Rockefeller Memorial Chapel
10 South Shore Cultural Center

Chicago Bee is planned as the location for a new Chicago Public Library facility. (South Side)

DOUGLAS TOMB
35th St. and Cottage Grove

Designed by Leonard Volk, this impressive tomb stands on the grounds of what used to be the estate of 19th-century political leader and noted opponent of Abraham Lincoln, Stephen A. Douglas. A bronze statue of Douglas stands over the grounds of a memorial park. Below him sit four adoring women—a fitting, if somewhat too regal tribute to Lincoln's rival. (South Side)

EIGHTH REGIMENT ARMORY
3533 S. Giles Ave.

Another one of the few remaining landmarks of the once-flourishing Black Metropolis community centered on 35th and State, this armory was once home to the Eighth Regiment (serving in the Spanish American War and World War I), the first all-black-commanded regiment of the U.S. Army. The building is currently not in use. Nearby, on 35th and King Drive, is Leonard Crunelle's Victory monument, built in honor of the black soldiers who fought in World War I. Just a few blocks away, at 3763 South Wabash, stands the Wabash Avenue YMCA, which, built in 1911 and funded by Julius Rosenwald, was the first YMCA to be located in a Chicago African American community. (South Side)

ILLINOIS INSTITUTE OF TECHNOLOGY
3300 S. Federal St.
312/567-3000

The founder of a school of architecture based on the philosophy "less is more," with its straight lines and steel-and-glass, box-like structures, Ludwig Mies van der Rohe has left an indelible imprint on the cityscape. The German-born Mies van der Rohe was the major architect for this South Side college campus where architect Helmut Jahn studied and Chicago photographic pioneer Nathan Lerner taught. Check out Crown Hall (3360 S. State St.) for a quintessential example of Mies van der Rohe's design. (South Side)

JACKSON PARK
63rd St. and Stony Island Ave.

Though Frederick Law Olmsted is better known as the designer of New York's Central Park, this 500-plus-acre park that he designed in the late 1800s was one of the keystones of the famed 1893 Columbian Exposition. One of the more picturesque highlights of Hyde Park, Jackson Park, located by the Museum of Science and Industry, is lorded over by an impressive golden statue of Columbia and features an elaborate system of lagoons and the little-known but well-maintained Japanese gardens with their trickling stream and delicate footbridge. (South Side)

MOSQUE MARYAM
7351 S. Stony Island Ave.
312/324-6000

The controversial Nation of Islam faith has a powerful branch in Chicago and the national headquarters are here. The crescent moon and star you see here are a symbol of the religion that is, at present, led by Minister Louis Farrakhan, who lives in nearby Hyde Park. The Nation of Islam also publishes a newspaper called *The Final Call* and owns the Salaam Restaurant on the city's South Side. (South Side)

Top Ten Sights on Chicago's South Side

by Seannie D., Chicago deejay, lifeguard, and native Southsider

1. **The Point, 55th and the Lake** Perhaps the coolest park in the city. This grass-covered peninsula was an army installation in the 1970s. Go there on a summer day now, however, and you may see Ted Erickson, the first American to swim the English Channel, swimming laps.

2. **The Medici, 1327 East 57th St., 773/667-7394** If you're going to eat in Hyde Park, eat here. There's cool art, awesome coffee, and tables inscribed by generations of students.

3. **Bond Chapel, 1025 East 58th St., 773/702-8374, and Robie House, 5757 S. Woodlawn Ave., 773/684-1013** One is the cutest, blue-stained, glass-lit, non-denominational chapel I have ever seen. The other is a single-family home designed by Frank Lloyd Wright at the height of his Prairie School power. All of the original furniture is there, without the haul to Oak Park.

4. **Harold's Chicken, 1208 E. 53rd St., 773/752-9260** The best fried chicken in the world. Highlights include the neon sign (with the cook chasing a chicken with a moving ax) and the patented, bulletproof turn-around, used to pass chicken from the kitchen to the customer. Get sauce (mild, hot, or BBQ) on your chicken, and don't stray too far from your cardiologist.

5. **The Checkerboard Lounge, 423 E. 43rd St., 773/624-3240** Best blues bar in the city. All the greats played here (and still do). Yes, it's true that the Rolling Stones and other mega-bands show up once in a while to jam.

6. **The African Parakeets, 53rd St. and the Lake,** Yep. Big, noisy, bright green subtropical birds—lots of 'em—thriving right here in our humble Midwestern town. Rumor has it that in 1982 a pair of these critters which were being kept as pets escaped. Today they've adapted to the climate and are flourishing.

7. **House of Tiki, 1612 E. 53rd St., 773/684-1221** A wonderful place to go and have a drink late at night among other people who have had lots to drink. Atmosphere is package-shop Polynesian, and all the characters are authentic.

8. **The Cove, 1750 E. 55th St., 773/684-1013** Just steps from the Point and 57th Street beach, with all the free popcorn you can wash down, the place is a nice, dark oasis.

9. **Kenwood, bounded by 47th St. to the north, Hyde Park Blvd. to the south, Lake Park to the east, and Kimbark to the west** Here are the most impressive houses in Chicago. In the late 19th century, Chicago's industrial titans, mayor, and social elite lived here. My mom, who grew up here, told me of the time her neighbors installed a 24-karat bathtub for a visit by the Prince of Wales.

10. **The Hyde Park Art Fair, 57th St.** Many of the country's best painters, sculptors, and other artists show up on 57th Street each May to hawk their work.

For further examples of Ludwig Mies van der Rohe's architectural contributions to Chicago, check out the Federal Center Downtown (219 S. Dearborn St. between Jackson Blvd. and Adams St.), the IBM Building (330 N. Wabash St.), and the high-rise buildings at 860–900 North Lake Shore Drive.

OAK WOODS CEMETERY
1035 E. 67th St.
773/288-3800

Though not possessing the grandeur of some of Chicago's other cemeteries, this one attracts visitors from far and wide who come to visit the gravesites of many noted Chicago historical figures, including a large percentage of the city's black leaders. Mayor Harold Washington is buried here as are Jesse Owens, Ida B. Wells, and Jesse Binga, a banker who was one of the founders of Chicago's once-thriving Black Metropolis community. Also buried here are nuclear physicist Enrico Fermi, Scopes trial lawyer Clarence Darrow, and gangster Big Jim Colossimo. (South Side)

ROBIE HOUSE
5757 S. Woodlawn Ave.
773/702-8374

Available for tours, this 1909 Frank Lloyd Wright house designed for inventor Frederick Robie in the heart of Hyde Park is considered a prime exemplar of the Prairie style of architectural design and is noteworthy for its use of air conditioning and self-watering plants. Its three-car garage was also unusual for the time it was built. It is currently the headquarters of the University of Chicago Alumni Association. Daily tours at noon, $3 per person. (South Side)

ROCKEFELLER MEMORIAL CHAPEL
5850 S. Woodlawn Ave.
773/702-2100

Legend has it that legendary University of Chicago president Robert Maynard Hutchings finally had Rockefeller Chapel shut down after sundown because, as he put it, there were more souls being conceived there than saved. That means that viewers are no longer afforded the opportunity to see this stunning, 1928 Gothic-revival chapel in all its imposing, fear-inspiring glory at night. Still, even during the daytime, the Hyde Park chapel is quite an impressive spectacle for believers and nonbelievers alike with its magnificent vaulted ceiling and its splendiferous stained-glass windows. Daily 8–4. (South Side)

SOUTH SHORE CULTURAL CENTER
71st and South Shore Dr.

One of the least known architectural jewels of the city, this former country club is an opulent, palatial structure that is perhaps best known for its role in a concert scene in the film *The Blues Brothers*. Now used primarily for private parties and Chicago Park District activities including concerts, amateur theater performances, and classes, the cultural center is a striking 1906 pleasuredome of majestic

The Monument with Standing Beast,
p. 107

hallways, imposing chandeliers, and luxurious ballrooms with amazing views of Lake Michigan. It looks like something out of *The Great Gatsby*. Admission to the South Shore Cultural Center is free. (South Side)

GREATER CHICAGO

BAHA'I TEMPLE
Sheridan Rd. and Linden Ave., Wilmette
847/256-4400
Resembling something as mundane as, say, the Taj Mahal, this is one of the most architecturally striking places of worship in the Chicago area and one of the highlights of a drive down Sheridan Road (see page 117). Designed by Louise Bourgeois, the white, nine-sided temple with its ornate domed ceiling is the main local headquarters of the Baha'i faith, which was founded on a belief in the oneness of God and all religions. Daily 9–5. Free. (Greater Chicago)

CHICAGO BOTANIC GARDEN
US 41 and Lake Cook Rd., Glencoe
Boasting an oasis of flowers, trees, and nature trails, this botanical sanctuary seems to be hundreds of miles away from Chicago. Spread out over approximately 300 acres of land, the garden—with its greenhouses, formal gardens (including an exquisite English garden, a rose garden, and a Japanese garden), and nearly one million trees and flowers—has been one of the jewels of the famed north shore since it opened in 1972. The Botanic Garden is an excellent spot for a summer picnic. Tours are offered, and an orientation center features various exhibits related to botany. $5 per car. (Greater Chicago)

FRANK LLOYD WRIGHT HOME AND STUDIO
951 Chicago Ave., Oak Park
708/848-1976
Frank Lloyd Wright's homes have long been considered more admirable than livable. But this splendid home shows how the master architect himself was able to live with some of the problems his own buildings caused their residents. Keep an eye out for Wright's magnificent and innovative furnishings. Walking tours allow the viewer to check out not only Wright's own home, but also 13 other Wright-designed buildings in scenic Oak Park. Mon–Fri 11–3, Sat–Sun 11–3:30. $8 adults, discounts for children and seniors. (Greater Chicago)

GARFIELD PARK CONSERVATORY
300 N. Central Park Blvd.
773/746-5100
Though much of the city's west side has changed since it was a vibrant

melting pot for European immigrants some 50 years ago, this five-acre conservatory is one thing that has remained constant. The neighborhood can get somewhat rough, but the conservatory housed inside this 1907 glass structure with its sprawling palm trees, cacti, and the like provides a welcome tropical respite. Highlights include the Cactus House, The Fernery, and annuals shows displaying azaleas, camellias, and other flora. Daily 9–5. Free. (Greater Chicago)

HISTORIC PULLMAN DISTRICT VISITORS CENTER AND HOTEL FLORENCE
11141 S. Cottage Grove
312/785-8181
One of the most innovative experiments in city planning in the United States, the turn-of-the-century Pullman District was designed by railroad man George Pullman who sought to create self-sustaining community housing and employ workers in the same neighborhood. The Hotel Florence and the visitors center provide exhibits tracing the history of the Pullman neighborhood, and the hotel itself allows one to tour Pullman's own hotel suite. There is an ongoing exhibit entitled *Pullman: The Man, The Car, The Model Town, The Strike, The Company, The Landmark*. And that pretty much tells the whole story. This is a good starting point for a walking tour of this neighborhood which, with its 19th-century homes and arcades, is unlike any other in the city. Daily 9–5. $2 adults. (Greater Chicago)

LIGHTHOUSE BEACH
Sheridan Rd. and Central St., Evanston
This quiet, sandy beach, one of the most scenic in the city, lies on the northern edge of suburban Evanston near the Wilmette border. To the north, a small park offers access to a series of rocks beside the lake. The rocks provide a secluded feel that at night makes it seem like a private beach. Provided that the rocks are not already occupied by underage kids drinking cheap beer, there are few places more serene on the lakefront. The beach takes its name from the still-functioning Grosse Point lighthouse, which you can climb for a great view of the lakefront. (Greater Chicago)

MCDONALD'S
400 N. Lee St., Des Plaines
847/297-5022
This is where it all started. It's almost eerie to look at it now, knowing that after Ray Kroc built his hamburger stand on this site in 1955 McDonald's would become a worldwide phenomenon selling billions of burgers. The re-creation of the original McDonald's, glowing in pink neon, is open a few days a week as a museum, but even on days when it's closed it's worth gawking at to see the beginnings of a most unlikely American success story. If you get hungry there's a state-of-the-art McDonald's across the street. Wed, Fri, Sat 10–4. (Greater Chicago)

UNITY TEMPLE
875 N. Lake St., Oak Park
708/848-6225
This Unitarian-Universalist church, built in 1906, was designed by Frank Lloyd Wright and is still in use. With its remarkable stained-glass windows and bright, airy interior, Wright's temple gives a profound

sense of the eternal. Open daily 1–4. Free. (Greater Chicago)

CITY TOURS

AFRICAN AMERICAN HERITAGE TOURS
708/799-8032
The thriving South Side Black Metropolis Community of the 1920s and 1930s was the foundation for Chicago's early reputation as a home to some of the nation's greatest black businesspeople, artists, and political leaders. The heritage tours pay tribute to the city's African American history and encompass landmarks such as the homes of black historical figures, celebrities, and politicians such as the late Harold Washington, Chicago's first black mayor. $19 adults, discounts for children and seniors.

CHICAGO ARCHITECTURE FOUNDATION RIVER TOURS
875 N. Michigan Ave.
312/922-TOUR
Of all the tours offered in the city, these tours on the Chicago River are generally thought to be the best. A two-hour journey takes you through Downtown, showcasing Chicago's breathtaking architecture from an angle available nowhere else but from the river. Tours leave from underneath the bridge at Michigan and Wacker. The Architecture Foundation also offers walking and bus tours. $18 adults, discounts for children and seniors.

CHICAGO MOTOR COACH
888/DD-BUSES
"See Chicago from the top! Get off at any stop!" That's the chant you'll hear from the tour-bus hawkers promoting city tours on those familiar red double-decker buses. The tours aren't generally run by city experts; they're more the territory of college students on break who have memorized the spiels. But the view from the top does provide a good introduction to the Magnificent Mile and the Loop.

CHICAGO SUPERNATURAL GHOST TOURS
708/499-0300
Though the mysterious ghost stories offered on these tours of the Chicago River aren't particularly chilling in and of themselves, there is something decidedly creepy about boarding a boat at 11 p.m. and cruising along through the empty Downtown. Tours are led by Chicago's leading resident expert on the supernatural, Richard Crowe. $18 adults, discounts for children and seniors.

MERCURY SKYLINE CRUISES
312/332-1353
Mercury is another of the city's many cruising tours of the Chicago River and Lake Michigan. The tours offer beautiful views of the city and a are great way to cool off on a hot summer night. $12 adults, discounts for children and seniors.

NOBLE HORSE CARRIAGE RIDES
Michigan Ave. at Pearson St.
312/266-7878
It's not quite the same thing as grabbing a carriage ride in Manhattan and taking a romantic trip through a snowy Central Park. Here the horses only go as quickly as the traffic in front of them will allow. And you're more likely to smell exhaust than chestnuts roasting on an open fire. Even so, there is something charming about riding in the

Chicago in the Movies

Since the late 1970s when then-mayor Jane Byrne opened the city's doors to Hollywood filmmakers, Chicago has been one of the favorite sites for tinseltown filmmakers. So, if you're walking down the street and you have to a double-take because you think you've seen that place before, you probably have . . . at least on the silver screen. Here are where some prominent Chicago sites that have been used in major motion pictures.

1. Daley Center Plaza—*The Blues Brothers*
2. James R. Thompson Center—*Running Scared*
3. Museum of Science and Industry—*The Relic*
4. Wrigley Field—*Ferris Bueller's Day Off*
5. Marina City—*The Hunter*
6. St. Patrick's Day Parade—*The Fugitive*
7. Chicago Cultural Center—*The Untouchables*
8. Oak Street Beach—*Things Change*
9. Quimby's Bookstore—*Go Fish*
10. Lake Shore Drive—*Risky Business*
11. Phyllis' Musical Inn—*Light of Day*
12. Michigan Avenue Bridge—*Chain Reaction*
13. The Green Mill—*Thief*

back of a horse-drawn carriage up and down the Magnificent Mile, seeing the city much as one might have seen it a hundred years ago. Carriages seat four people comfortably and are usually available between 10 a.m. and midnight. $30 per half hour. (Near North)

UNTOUCHABLES GANGSTER TOURS
610 N. Clark St.
773/881-1195
Chicago has something of a love-hate relationship with its gangster past. Sure, we don't like it when Europeans approach us and say, "Oh, Chicago? You're from Chicago? Bang Bang!" We prefer to be remembered for more than Al Capone, or for Sean Connery stuffing a gun in a dead man's mouth and blowing his brains out while Kevin Costner informs a stammering witness that that's how we do business in Chicago (see Brian DePalma's *The Untouchables*). But the fact is, Chicago was a gangster town and people want to see where

Capone and Big Jim Colossimo hung out. These tours, run by a couple of fellas in gangster garb, take people from South Michigan Avenue where Al Capone used to call the shots, to the site on North Clark Street where the St. Valentine's Massacre went down, to the Biograph Theatre, where John Dillinger was gunned down by the FBI. Tours last two hours. (Near North)

WENDELLA SIGHTSEEING BOATS
312/337-1446
Leaving from the bridge below Michigan and Wacker, these hour-long boat tours down the Chicago River and onto Lake Michigan have been a long-favored staple of tourists and city dwellers who are pretending to be tourists. No great insights into Chicago history are offered here. But, on a warm summer's night, the views of Chicago are unparalleled, and there is hardly a more romantic way to spend the evening. Tour boats leave every 90 minutes. $12 adults, discounts for children and seniors. (Downtown)

Carolyn Crimi

6

MUSEUMS AND ART GALLERIES

You want museums? You've come to the right place. Covering everything from history to science to nature to fine art, Chicago is a bubbling cauldron of exhibition spaces, galleries, and cavernous cultural centers tackling an encyclopedia's worth of topics. (Is it any wonder why Encyclopedia Britannica *is based in Chicago?) Want to know about Neanderthal culture? You can check it out here. Interested in the soil composition of Mars? No problem. Care to see an Egyptian mummy? A painting by Salvador Dalí? A work by a great young artist you've never heard of? The homes and workplaces of Nobel Prize–winning authors and scientists? It's easy here. Chicago's vast array of museums parallels its vast array of cultures. For practically every ethnic and religious group, there's a museum.*

While virtually no topic remains uncovered by the dozens of museums here, Chicago is particularly strong when it comes to the world of art. With a gallery scene that rivals the ones in New York, Cologne, and London, Chicago is an explosion of contrasting styles and techniques. From Renoir to Brown, from Sargent to Sigler, from the Fauvists to Fitzpatrick, from Cassatt to Callahan, from Grooms to Gugel, from Delacroix to Darger, you can find them all here.

You say you don't know all of those names? Stick around the Chicago museum and gallery scene for few days. You will.

FINE ART MUSEUMS

ART INSTITUTE OF CHICAGO
Michigan Ave. at Adams St.
800/929-5800

Following blockbuster exhibits featuring the works of Monet and Renoir, the Art Institute continues its reputation as one of the world's finest exhibitors of impressionist paintings. But if you just go to overdose on the water lilies and the haystacks, you'll be missing a great deal of what is truly an excellent all-around art museum with impressive collections that range from the medieval to the modern. The Art Institute boasts more than 300,000 works of art in its permanent collection. The basement also holds outstanding photography exhibits. There are also a number of nifty side attractions at the Art Institute, including the restored trading floor of the Louis Sullvan–designed Chicago Stock Exchange building, collections of armor and paperweights, and a small children's museum. The museum is physically connected to the School of the Art Institute, which houses student exhibits and the Film Center of the Art Institute, one of the best screening facilities in the city for foreign films, retrospectives, and cinema classics. Open Mon, Wed, Thu, Fri 10:30–4:30, Tue 10:30–8, Sat 10–5, Sun 12–5. $7 adults, discounts for children and seniors, Tue free. (Downtown)

MEXICAN FINE ARTS CENTER AND MUSEUM
1852 W. 19th St.
312/738-1503
Appropriately located in the heart of Pilsen, Chicago's thriving Latino community just to the southwest of the Loop, this museum has been a rare success story, growing from an annual budget of $900 to $3 million in just over 15 years. Featuring rotating exhibits on everything from Aztec relics to retrospectives of modern artists to contemporary Mexican photography, MFACM is perhaps most noted for its annual exhibitions celebrating El Día de Los Muertos. Tue–Sat 12–5. Free. (Near South)

MUSEUM OF CONTEMPORARY ART
220 E. Chicago Ave.
312/280-2660
While its facade resembles that of a cheerless post-war museum in some mid-sized German city, MCA's interior is anything but. A great improvement over its tiny predecessor on nearby Ontario Street, the MCA (opened in 1996) boasts an impressive 7,000-plus-piece collection of works by modern masters (Rene Magritte, Ed Paschke, Claes Oldenburg, Andy Warhol, Max Ernst, Christo) and offers excellent retrospectives and special exhibits of other contemporary artists. Other attractions at the MCA include its cutting-edge series of performance art, dance, music, and film held in its 300-seat theater, and its annual summer solstice festival, a 24-hour celebration of art, music, and performance. Tue, Thu, Fri 11–6, Wed 11–8, Sat–Sun 10–6. $6.50 adults, discounts for seniors and students, children under 12 free. (Near North)

MUSEUM OF CONTEMPORARY PHOTOGRAPHY
600 S. Michigan Ave.
312/663-5554
Attached to Columbia College, this museum features photographs produced from 1959 to the present. Recent exhibits have featured the works of such notables as Ansel Adams and Lee Friedlander. Mon–Fri 12–5, Thu 10–8, Sat 12–5. Free. (Downtown)

RENAISSANCE SOCIETY GALLERY
Cobb Hall
5811 S. Ellis Ave.
773/702-8670
Sometimes you have to force your way through oceans of students to get to the gallery on the fourth floor of

Stanley Field Hall at the Field Museum, p. 142

Cobb Hall, but the crowds and the three flights of stairs are worth it. Founded in 1915, the Renaissance Society has long been on the forefront of contemporary art. It was one of the first galleries in the city to showcase the works of Picasso and Miró and, in the 1970s, was the first to exhibit works by Bruce Nauman and Joseph Kosuth. The society continues to push the envelope with retrospectives of modern artists and exhibits of the soon-to-be-next-best-things, and it also hosts frequent concerts, film screenings, and performance art demonstrations. Open Tue–Fri 10–4, Sat–Sun 12–4. Free. (South Side)

DAVID AND ALFRED SMART MUSEUM
5550 S. Greenwood Ave.
773/702-0200
Opened in 1974, the Smart is a relatively small but inviting museum located on the University of Chicago campus in Hyde Park and named after the founders and publishers of *Esquire* magazine. The museum provides an overview of centuries of

artistic history, ranging from artifacts from ancient civilizations (including Greece and China) to work by more modern artists Degas and Rodin and contemporary artists like Bruce Nauman. Twentieth-century furniture designed by Frank Lloyd Wright is also featured. Tue–Fri 10–4, Sat–Sun 12–6. Free. (South Side)

TERRA MUSEUM OF AMERICAN ART
666 N. Michigan Ave.
312/664-3939
Some believe that fine art doesn't exist on this side of the Atlantic Ocean. The Terra Museum, however, offers compelling evidence of a long tradition of such work on these shores. Spanning from the early history of this country in the late 18th century to the present, the museum's collection was started by noted late Republican fund-raiser Daniel Terra and includes works by Winslow Homer and Andrew Wyeth. But the true pleasures in this museum come from discovering the many relatively unknown American artists whose

works are gathered here. Tue 12–8, Wed–Sat 10–5, Sun 12–5. $4 adults, discounts for children and seniors, Tue free. (Near North)

UKRAINIAN INSTITUTE OF MODERN ART
2320 W. Chicago Ave.
773/227-5522
Located in the heart of Chicago's Ukrainian Village, a small enclave of shops, residences, and cultural centers, the institute is just down the street from the Ukrainian National Museum. It hosts a rotating series of exhibits by contemporary Ukrainian artists in a warm and airy environment. Wed, Thu, Sat, Sun 12–4. $2. (West Side)

VIETNAM VETERANS' ART MUSEUM
1801 S. Indiana
312/326-0270
One of Chicago's newest museums (founded in 1996 and housed south of the Loop in the Prairie Avenue Historic District), the Vietnam Veterans' Art Museum boasts an impressive and gripping collection of artwork by Vietnam vets. In an airy and comfortable space, the museum is the brainchild of two veterans and art collectors. By interspersing horrifying and compelling works with actual artifacts from the war itself, they have created a fascinating new museum. Tue, Thu–Sun 11–6, Wed 11–9. Free. (Near South)

MUSEUMS OF HISTORY AND CULTURE

BALZEKAS MUSEUM OF LITHUANIAN CULTURE
6500 S. Pulaski Ave.
773/582-6500

El Día de Los Muertos exhibit, Mexican Fine Arts Center, p. 134

Kathleen Culbert-Aguilar

Housed in what used to be a medical office building, this humble museum located on the mostly white ethnic Southwest Side features exhibits on the Lithuanian experience during World War II, as well as artifacts from Lithuanian history. A video screening available that gives a pretty good history of Lithuania is available. The staff here is especially friendly and knowledgeable. Sat–Thu 10–4, Fri 10–8. $4 adults, discounts for children and seniors, Mon free. (Greater Chicago)

CHICAGO HISTORICAL SOCIETY
Clark St. and North Ave.
312/642-4600
Though some of the more contemporary exhibits on neighborhoods might be a trifle arcane for out-of-town visitors, the permanent collections dedicated to Chicago and American history make this comfortable and spacious museum well worth visiting. The museum offers a good blend of education and entertainment focusing on many of the major incidents in

MUST-SEE MUSEUMS

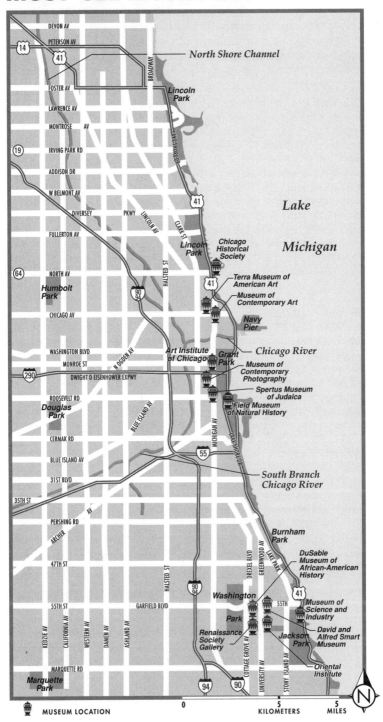

DEVON AV
PETERSON AV
14
41
BROADWAY
North Shore Channel
FOSTER AV
Lincoln Park
LAWRENCE AV
MONTROSE AV
IRVING PARK RD
19
ADDISON DR
W BELMONT AV
DIVERSEY PKWY
LINCOLN AV
FULLERTON AV
Lake Michigan
Lincoln Park
Chicago Historical Society
41
NORTH AV
64
HALSTED ST
CLARK ST
LAKESHORE DR
Terra Museum of American Art
Museum of Contemporary Art
Humboldt Park
CHICAGO AV
Navy Pier
90
WASHINGTON BLVD
N OGDEN AV
MONROE ST
290
DWIGHT D EISENHOWER EXPWY
Art Institute of Chicago
Grant Park
Chicago River
Museum of Contemporary Photography
ROOSEVELT RD
Spertus Museum of Judaica
Douglas Park
BLUE ISLAND AV
Field Museum of Natural History
CERMAK RD
BLUE ISLAND AV
MICHIGAN AV
31ST BLVD
55
35TH ST
South Branch Chicago River
PERSHING RD
ARCHER
Burnham Park
47TH ST
90 94
HALSTED ST
DREXEL BLVD
GREENWOOD AV
LAKE PARK
DuSable Museum of African-American History
41
55TH
Museum of Science and Industry
KEDZIE AV
CALIFORNIA AV
WESTERN AV
DAMEN AV
ASHLAND AV
55TH ST
GARFIELD BLVD
Washington Park
Renaissance Society Gallery
COTTAGE GROVE AV
UNIVERSITY AV
Jackson Park
David and Alfred Smart Museum
MARQUETTE RD
Oriental Institute
Marquette Park
94
90
STONY ISLAND AV

🏛 MUSEUM LOCATION

0   5   5
KILOMETERS   MILES

N

In 1967 Hungarian-born artist Christo wrapped the Museum of Contemporary Art with 8,000 square feet of tarp and rope. It was Christo's first wrapping project in the United States.

Chicago history, from its founding to the great fire to the Colombian Exposition. Among the unique features of the Chicago Historical Society are the desk on which Abraham Lincoln wrote the Emancipation Proclamation, a diorama of the Chicago Fire, demonstrations of weaving and candle-making, and George Washington's inauguration suit. The museum also holds one of the city's best public research facilities and photography archives. Mon–Sat 9:30–4:30, Sun 12–5. $3. (Near North)

DUSABLE MUSEUM OF AFRICAN AMERICAN HISTORY
740 E. 56th Pl.
773/947-0660
Founded in 1961, this small but jam-packed museum is the nation's oldest dedicated to African and African American history. Featuring original slave documents, civil rights memorabilia, and collections of African and African American artwork, DuSable stands on attractive surroundings in the South Side's Washington Park. An expansion in 1993 opened a new 25,000-square-foot wing named for Chicago's first black mayor, Harold Washington. The museum also hosts film screenings, concerts, and lectures. Mon–Sat 10–5, Sun 12–5. $3 adults, discounts for children and seniors, Thu free. (South Side)

THE ERNEST HEMINGWAY MUSEUM AND BIRTHPLACE
200 N. Oak Park Ave. and 339 N.

Oak Park Ave., Oak Park
708/848-2222
In 1899 Ernest Hemingway was born in this Victorian home in the quaint Chicago suburb of Oak Park. The house provides insight into the background of the man with a fascination for war, bullfighting, and fishing who went on to win the Nobel Prize for Literature. Just a block away from the Hemingway home is the Ernest Hemingway Museum, where the author's childhood diary, letters, and early writing are displayed and a video chronicling his career is presented. The museum and home are open Fri, Sun. 1–5, Sat 10–5. $4, discounts for children and seniors. (Greater Chicago)

HULL HOUSE MUSEUM
800 S. Halsted
312/413-5353
Opened in the Charles Hull Mansion in 1889 by legendary social and labor reformer Jane Addams (Nobel Peace Prize winner of 1931), the Hull House is now preserved on the grounds of the University of Illinois at Chicago as a tribute to Addams' work. The museum houses many of her original furnishings and contains exhibits about immigrant life in America as well as about Addams herself. Nearby, Addams' original settlement dining hall has been preserved and is now used primarily by UIC. Hull House was designated a national historic landmark in 1967. Tue–Sat 9–5. Free. (West Side)

MITCHELL AMERICAN INDIAN MUSEUM
2600 Central Park, Evanston
847/866-1395

Founded by an Evanston resident who had collected artifacts from American Indian culture ever since he was a boy, the Mitchell Museum, located on the original site of the Terra Museum of American Art, now houses more than 3,000 exhibit items, including handmade canoes, baskets, rugs, and buffalo-hide shirts. The museum is a splendid tribute to the culture that once reigned supreme in this region. (Greater Chicago)

ORIENTAL INSTITUTE
1155 E. 58th St.
773/702-9520

Located on the campus of the University of Chicago, this museum houses an impressive collection of Near Eastern artifacts. If you're into Egypt and the early history of the Middle East, you're in luck. Statues, pottery, jewelry, mummies, and the like from Assyria, Egypt, Mesopotamia, Persia, and Palestine are on display here in this eye-opening museum founded by James Henry Breasted, the first American to get his doctorate in Egyptology. Tue–Sat 10–4, Sun 12–4. Free. (South Side)

PEACE MUSEUM
314 W. Institute Pl.
312/440-1860

This cozy little space is just a mile or so west of the Magnificent Mile near Chicago's River North gallery district. Established in 1981, the Peace Museum's permanent collection features such items as one of John Lennon's guitars and manuscripts and artifacts from such noted peace-loving celebs as Joan Baez, Phil Ochs, Pete Seeger, and Country Joe McDonald. Rotating exhibits have covered such topics as Martin Luther King Jr., the AIDS quilt project, and drawings from survivors of Hiroshima and Nagasaki. Tue–Sat 11–5. $3.50, Wed free. (Near North)

POLISH MUSEUM OF AMERICA
984 N. Milwaukee Ave.
773/384-3352

The Museum of Contemporary Art, p. 134

Steve Hall/Hedrich-Blessing

Ten More Off-the-Beaten-Path Museums For the Museum Addict

Haven't been worn out by all of the museums Chicago has to offer? Here are ten more little, quirky, or little-known museums for the genuine museum-oholic.

- **Air Classics Museum of Aviation**, Aurora Municipal Airport, Sugar Grove, 630/466-0888. Features exhibits of military aircraft and other aviation-related topics.

- **Fox River Trolley Museum**, South Elgin, 847/697-4676. Features some of the oldest still-operational trolleys in the country.

- **Garfield Farm Museum**, Rte. 38 and Garfield, 630/584-8485. This perfectly preserved farm dates back to the 1840s.

- **Gladys Fox Museum**, Lockport, 815/838-0803. An exhibit of glass-ware housed in the oldest church in Illinois.

- **Illinois and Michigan Canal Museum and Pioneer Settlement**, Lockport, 816/838-5080. This fascinating historical institution chronicles Illinois history from the 1600s to the present.

- **Lithuanian Art Museum**, Lemont, 630/257-2034. Houses a rotating series of exhibits of Lithuanian artists.

- **Midwest Carvers Museum**, South Holland, 708/331-6011. Along with an exhibit of more than 1,000 carvings, the museum site also features a workshop and restored windmill.

- **Pleasant Home, Oak Park**, 708/383-2654. This 30-room mansion was designed by Prairie School architect George W. Maher in 1897. Tours are available.

- **Swedish American Museum Center**, 5211 N. Clark St., Chicago, 773/728-8111. This well-designed, airy museum and gift shop in the Andersonville neighborhood is dedicated to Swedish artists and showcases Swedish contributions to the history of Chicago.

- **Volo Antique Auto Museum**, Volo, 815/344-6062. Weekend show-case of more than 200 vintage automobiles.

Of all the museums in Chicago devoted to the experiences of various ethnic groups, this is one of the most impressive. At its present location since the early 20th century, the museum boasts an exciting collection of little-known Polish fine artists and artifacts from the Polish experience in World War II, as well as tributes to noted Poles such as Pope John Paul II, Tadeusz Koszkziusco, and various cultural figures. Free. (West Side)

PRAIRIE AVENUE HOUSE MUSEUMS
1800 S. Prairie Ave.
312/326-1480

Legend has it that only the Water Tower survived the Chicago Fire, but that's not exactly true. Still standing in the Prairie Avenue Historic District just south of the Loop is the home of Caroline and Henry Clarke, built in 1835 and bearing witness to a time when Chicago was a prairie struggling to become a city. The Clarke House stands nearby the Glessner House, built in

1887 in the Romanesque Revival style. These houses, both of which offer compelling tours, provide a rare glimpse into 19th-century Chicago, precious little of which can still be found. Wed–Sun 12–4. $5. (Near South)

SPERTUS MUSEUM OF JUDAICA
618 S. Michigan Ave.
312/322-1747

This is one of the best and most intellectually satisfying of Chicago's ethnic museums. Intelligently designed and curated, it covers Jewish history through art and culture and sponsors an excellent series of lectures and cultural events. Exhibits over the years have covered topics ranging from the history of Jewish humor to *Friedrich Adler: From Art Nouveau to Art Deco* to a retrospective of the works of a post–World War II Polish émigré. Sun–Thu 10–5, Fri 10–3. $4, free Mon. (Downtown)

VIETNAM WAR MUSEUM
954 W. Carmen
773/728-6111

The Museum of Broadcast Communications, p. 142

Museum of Broadcast Communications

Chicago Architecture Foundation boat tours

Founded by Vietnam vet Joseph Hertel, this Uptown-based museum provides a comprehensive collection of artifacts from the war including photographs, documents, magazines, artwork, and souvenirs from the war. An educational and chilling experience. (North Side)

MUSEUMS OF SCIENCE AND NATURAL HISTORY

FIELD MUSEUM OF NATURAL HISTORY
Roosevelt Rd. and Lake Shore Dr.
312/922-9410
With the discovery of the now famous "Sue" the dinosaur, this massive museum (opened in 1921) of anthropological and archeological treasures has become even more impressive. More than just a good place to kill time before the Bears game at nearby Soldier Field, this natural history museum exhibits Egyptian mummies, precious gemstones (a 5,890-carat topaz, for example), Indonesian musical instruments, American Indian arti-

facts, meteorites, reconstructed dinosaur skeletons, and more. Daily 9–5. $7 adults, discounts for children and seniors, Wed free. (Downtown)

MUSEUM OF BROADCAST COMMUNICATIONS
78 E. Washington St.
312/629-6000
Housed in the beautiful Chicago Cultural Center, MBC has an extensive collection of TV and radio programs and commercials (more than 60,000) in its archives, and hosts exhibits on the history of broadcasting. There is much memorabilia and antique broadcasting equipment on display, and the Kraft Television Center allows you the opportunity to anchor your own newscast. MBC also screens classic TV and radio programs as you wander through it and offers regular live broadcasts of local radio shows. Mon–Sat 10–4:30, Sunday 12–5. Free. (Downtown)

MUSEUM OF SCIENCE AND INDUSTRY
57th St. and Lake Shore Dr.

773/684-1414
The crown jewel of Chicago museums, the Museum of Science and Industry has long been a family favorite with its vast collections of exhibits showcasing communications technology, spacecraft, and industrial processes. Founded in 1933 during the Century of Progress world exposition by Julius Rosenwald, the former chairman of Sears, the Museum was originally the Palace of Fine Arts during the 1893 World's Fair. Highlights of the museum include the Omnimax Theater, a 3,000-square-foot model railroad, a walk-through Boeing 727, a working coal mine shaft elevator, a captured German U-505 World War II submarine, a baby chick hatchery, a walk-through human heart model made famous in the Brooke Shields movie *Endless Love*, the Apollo 8 and Aurora 7 Mercury spacecrafts, and perennial favorite Yesterday's Main Street, a picture-perfect recreation of a 19th-century Chicago street complete with a nickelodeon showing Charlie Chaplin films. Boasting more than 350,000 feet of exhibit space and more than 800 exhibits, the museum has been visited by more than 155 million people. Daily 9:30–5:30. $6 ($11 for Museum plus Omnimax) adults, discounts for children and seniors, Thu free. (South Side)

MUSEUMS OF ARCHITECTURE

CHICAGO ARCHITECTURE FOUNDATION
224 S. Michigan Ave.
312/922-3432
In addition to sponsoring some of the best tours of Chicago—including boat tours of architectural landmarks—the foundation offers compelling stationary exhibits that exemplify why the city is considered one of the architectural capitals of the world. The foundation is housed in the Santa Fe Building, a Chicago architectural landmark in its own right, designed by Daniel Burnham. Daily 8–6. Free. (Downtown)

CHICAGO ATHENAEUM MUSEUM OF ARCHITECTURE AND DESIGN
6 N. Michigan Ave.
312/251-0175
Dedicated to showcasing Chicago's history as a center for architecture and design, the Athenaeum, founded in 1988, exhibits everything from architectural drawings to examples of innovative industrial, advertising, and poster design. On display are unique clocks, radios, household appliances, cameras, and corporate logos. Tue–Sat 11–6, Sun 12–5. $3 adults, discounts for students, seniors, and children. (Downtown)

OTHER SPECIALTY MUSEUMS

AMERICAN POLICE CENTER AND MUSEUM
1717 S. State St.
312/431-0005
Not a place where you're going to get the demonstrators' side of the 1968 Hippies vs. Cops story, this still isn't a bad place to learn about the human side of a profession whose presence is often taken for granted. An electric chair is displayed here as are informative, if somewhat didactic, exhibits devoted to drugs and alcohol. There is also a photo gallery of cops who died on duty. Mon–Fri 8:30–4:30. $3.50 adults,

discounts for children and seniors. (Near South)

LIZZADRO MUSEUM OF LAPIDARY ART
220 Cottage Hill Ave., Elmhurst
630/833-1616
Billing itself as the only permanent museum devoted solely to the lapidary arts (dealing with gems and stones), this suburban collection was founded by an electrical contractor who cut stones in his spare time. Founded in 1962, the museum houses beautiful jade pieces as well as ivory, scrimshaw, and a host of other precious stones and fossils. (Greater Chicago)

MUSEUM OF HOLOGRAPHY
1134 W. Washington St.
312/226-1007
This quirky little Near West Side museum offers a fair number of tantalizing, laser-generated, three-dimensional holographic curiosities. My personal favorite is a hologram of a great white shark that would put Captain Ahab on edge. Wed–Sun 12:30–5. $2.50. (West Side)

INTERNATIONAL MUSEUM OF SURGICAL SCIENCE
1524 N. Lake Shore Dr.
312/642-6502
One of the more peculiar specialty museums in town, this Gold Coast institution housed in an early–20th century home is dedicated to chronicling the history of surgery and contains a wide array of grisly instruments ranging from an antique iron lung to a variety of implements held inside a turn-of-the-century apothecary. Open Fri–Sat 8, Sunday 4. Free. (Near North Side)

ART GALLERIES

For the art-lover, Chicago is a virtual paradise with hundreds of galleries carrying everything from Andy Warhols to the latest scribbles by the talented graduates of Chicago's School of the Art Institute. Here's a list of 15 that are worth a trip. For a more complete listing of Chicago's galleries, pick up a gallery guide (either the *Chicago Gallery Guide* or the *Art Now Gallery Guide*) at any of the galleries listed below or check out the *Chicago Reader* (free weekly available at most bookstores on Fridays).

ARC GALLERY
1040 W. Huron St.
312/733-2787
The acronym stands for Artists, Residents of Chicago. The gallery primarily features the works of women artists. (Near North)

ARTEMISIA GALLERY
700 N. Carpenter St.
312/226-7323
This excellent space showcases the works of women artists. (West Side)

BERET INTERNATIONAL
1550 N. Milwaukee Ave.
773/489-6518
This witty, counter-culture museum is part of a collective of alternative galleries known as "Uncomfortable Spaces." The Beret is often funny and almost always offbeat. (West Side)

CALLES Y SUENOS
1900 S. Carpenter St.
312/243-4243
This storefront space in the heart of Pilsen highlights the work of Latino artists. (Near South)

CARL HAMMER GALLERY
200 W. Superior St.
312/266-8512
This River North gallery is dedicated to outsider artists. (Near North)

EASTWICK ART GALLERY
245 W. North Ave.
312/440-2322
This wonderful gallery space is near the intersection of North and Wells. As large as some of Chicago's art museums, it showcases the works of emerging American and European artists. (Near North)

CATHERINE EDELMAN GALLERY
300 W. Superior St.
312/266-2350
This highly respected photography gallery is in the River North gallery district. (Near North)

GALLERY 1756
1756 N. Sedgwick St.
312/642-6900
Originally an architects' gallery, the Old Town Gallery 1756 is now devoted to showcasing the works of strong, emerging artists. (Near North)

GALLERY A
300 W. Superior St.
312/280-4500
This up-and-coming River North gallery features rising Chicago and national artists. (Near North)

IDAO GALLERY
1616 N. Damen Ave.
773/235-4724
This Wicker Park gallery features challenging, cutting-edge exhibits. (Near North)

ILLINOIS ART GALLERY
100 W. Randolph St.
Suite 2-100
312/ 814-5322
Some of the top names in Chicago and throughout the Midwest exhibit here. (Downtown)

INTUIT GALLERY
1926 N. Halsted St.
773/929-7122
This rising gallery emphasizes outsider artists. (North Side)

PHYLLIS KIND GALLERY
313 W. Superior St.
312/642-6302
This top-of-the-line River North gallery has long nurtured the works of Chicago Imagists. (Near North)

ANN NATHAN GALLERY
218 W. Superior St.
312/664-6622
This River North gallery emphasizes sculpture. (Near North)

PERIMETER GALLERY
210 W. Superior St.
312/266-9473
This all-purpose gallery places an emphasis on crafts along with paintings and sculpture. (Near North)

TEN-IN-ONE GALLERY
1542 N. Damen Ave.
773/486-5820
This excellent Wicker Park gallery showcases the works of irreverent and antiestablishment artists. It's part of the "Uncomfortable Spaces" collective. (West Side)

Kohl Children's Museum

7

KIDS' STUFF

A city with a body of water the size of Lake Michigan, miles and miles of uninterrupted beachfront, and hundreds of acres of public parkland hardly needs anything else to keep kids entertained. The beach is an immense, unending playground in and of itself where kids can hunt for precious stones, fling slimy strands of seaweed, dig bottomless holes in the sand, and float with exquisite laziness atop the pristine water. Still, if building sand castles, frolicking on teeter-totters and jungle gyms, swimming, roller-skating, and playing soccer, tennis, basketball, and baseball begins to wear thin after a few days, there are a slew of other options available to please even the most difficult child with the most idiosyncratic personality.

The rambunctious child will delight in the Chicago area's many amusement parks. There are water slides and paintball games and choo-choo trains and hair-raising rollercoaster rides which, though they may send adults into the intensive care unit, will provide hours of adrenaline-infused excitement for the PG and PG-13 set. The quiet, more introspective child has other choices at his or her disposal including concerts, story hours, and the city's incredible selection of museums, most of which have special programs for kids. Even the child already on the way to becoming a shop-oholic will find Chicago an intensely exciting spending playground, with its numerous toy stores and kids' shops. The sports fanatic an array of professional and semi-professional events to choose from. Finally, there are the places that every kid likes—the zoos, the kid-friendly restaurants, the story hours, and the puppet shows, all of which make Chicago a children's paradise.

ANIMALS AND THE GREAT OUTDOORS

BROOKFIELD ZOO
First Ave. and 31st St., Brookfield
708/485-0263

Rivaled in size in the United States only by the zoos in San Diego, Milwaukee, and Washington, this 200-acre zoo is well worth the 20-minute drive out of Chicago and the entire day it will take to view all of its exhibits. Aside from the more than 2,000 animals who inhabit this facility and the de rigeur dolphin show, one of the jewels of the zoo is its Tropic World habitat, a huge mock-up of a tropical rain forest in which uncaged apes and other species frolic freely and dart in and out of occasional rainstorms. Daily 9:30–5:30. $6 adults, $3 children 3–11 and seniors, $4 parking. (Greater Chicago)

INDIAN BOUNDARY PARK ZOO
2500 W. Lunt
312/742-7887

Tucked away near the northern edge of the city, this is hardly a world-class zoo. It houses only a few llamas, the occasional alpaca, and a couple of swans. But there is a certain quaint charm to this quiet neighborhood park with its elaborate playground and tiny animal collection. A perfect place for a picnic, a tennis match, or just a stroll along a serpentine pathway to feed the ducks in the pond, Indian Boundary is one of the city's best-kept secrets. Open daily sunrise–sundown. Free. (Far North)

LINCOLN PARK ZOO
2200 N. Cannon Dr.
312/742-2000

This free, sprawling 35-acre zoo—which claims to have the greatest annual attendance of any zoo in the

Brookfield Zoo's
Habitat Africa! *exhibit*

© Chicago Zoological Society/Jim Schulz

country—would be worth the trip even if it started charging admission. Highlights include a wonderful ape house, a refreshing outdoor seal exhibit, a children's zoo, and a "Farm-in-the-Zoo" in which kids can interact with cows and chickens up-close and personal. A special treat is the winter "Zoo Lights" festival, when the zoo turns into an evening light-sculpture extravaganza in which animals frolic beneath the glow of their luminous counterparts. One of the favorite annual events here is Caroling to the Animals, in which scads of holiday revelers bring cheer to the animals with song. The event usually happens the first week of December. Daily 9–5. Free. (North Side)

MORTON ARBORETUM
Rte. 53 and the East West
Tollway, Lisle
708/968-0074

This 1,500-acre expanse of plants, gardens, woodlands, and nature trails is only about a half hour away from

Chicago. In the summer months turtles stroll nonchalantly along the paths while other animals can be seen scampering up and down the countless varieties of trees. A visitors center features a library, restaurant, and gift shop, and loads of information about the nature trails. Daily 7–7. $7 per car. (Greater Chicago)

NORTH PARK VILLAGE NATURE CENTER
5801 N. Pulaski Rd.
312/744-5472

Even though this is still technically a part of the city, you'd hardly know it. On the grounds of what used to be one of the city's tuberculosis sanitariums sits this expanse of parkland and a nature center where kids can learn how bees make honey, how to get syrup out of maple trees, and more. Special bird-watching walks are held here, and the center sponsors night walks through its spacious grounds so visitors can try to spot owls. If you're very quiet, sometimes you can see foxes and rabbits scampering by. Daily 10–4 (Far North)

MUSEUMS AND LIBRARIES

ADLER PLANETARIUM
1300 S. Lake Shore Dr.
312/922-STAR

Though kids may lose patience quickly with the planetarium's three floors of astronomy exhibits, there are a number of attractions here that should keep them intrigued for hours. The best of these are the sky shows, which use eye-catching visuals to teach astronomy to all ages. Sky shows have included *Is There Life on Mars?*, *Solar System Vacation*, *Africa Skies*, *The Sky Tonight*, and, for young kids, *Stargazing with Meteor Mouse*. Following evening sky shows on Friday nights, the Doane Observatory transmits stunning live telescopic views of outer space to the sky show auditorium. See Museums chapter for more information. Mon–Thu 9–5, Fri 9–9, weekends 9–6. $3 adults, $2 children 4–17, free Tue. (Downtown)

ART INSTITUTE OF CHICAGO
Kraft Education Center
Michigan Ave. and Adams St.

Lincoln Park Zoo

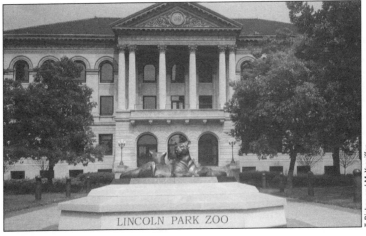

LINCOLN PARK ZOO

T. Bishop and M. Yossiffon

Things to Do with the Kids in Chicago
by John Zehren, successful businessman, publisher, and father of two girls

1. **Head to the beach either at North Avenue or at the uncrowded Montrose**. Kids love it. Arrive before 10:30 in the morning for free parking. North Avenue now has rentable chairs and umbrellas, and hot dogs, fries, and shakes from Johnny Rockets.

2. **Go to Navy Pier Children's Museum.** Make a puppet, play in the waterworks, drive an ambulance, ride the bus. There are free live music performances that invite participation from the kids, a Ferris wheel, a seasonal ice rink, and boat rides. A whole day of fun.

3. **Have dinner at Leona's on Augusta.** This is the only decent restaurant with an eat-in kids playroom. It comes equipped with video movies, pinball, a jungle gym play center, and drinks for mom and dad.

4. **Check out Lincoln Park Zoo and the petting farm.** This free zoo is a great deal. Lions, tigers, elephants, polar bears, monkeys, and more make the kids go wild. Go before 10:30 a.m. or face the crowds.

5. **Take a paddleboat ride and have lunch at Cafe Brauer next to Lincoln Park Zoo.** Great photo-op on the bridge, with the city in the background.

6. **Go to Merriville Water Park in Indiana.** It's not in Chicago, but it's only 45 minutes away and is a total riot for kids. It's an easy day trip if you have nappers that need to get home. Even our one-year-old found good fun in the toddler waterpark section.

7. **Send your kid to Apple Camp.** In summer this camp has different themes every week. Kids can try swimming, computers, tumbling, and more. Fun is scheduled for the wee ones every day in addition to the usual strenuous preschool curriculum.

8. **Go to Fullerton Library for storytime.** Here, nice kids sit and listen to good stories being read aloud by animated storytellers.

9. **Dine at Chuck E. Cheese.** It is lame and loud, but the kids like it and it's a nice change of pace from banging into the same four walls at home. Order pizza and a beer and hit the slides with your kids.

10. **Go to Shedd Aquarium.** Watch the scuba diver feed the fish in the lobby aquarium—it will give your kids goose bumps—then checkout the dolphin show for an extra four dollars.

312/443-3600

Most major museums in Chicago are pretty good about having kids' programs. But few cater as directly to children as does the Art Institute, which has a mind-boggling array of activities for children, special bi-monthly calendars dedicated solely to children's events, and even a separate center for exhibits geared to children. The Art Institute also sponsors workshops, demonstrations, and classes. Kids of all ages can go on special family tours of the museum, watch professional artists at work, learn to create art on their own, and participate in contests where they follow clues to learn about the museum's paintings. In the Medard and Elizabeth Welch Family Room, young visitors can read art picture books and books about art and artists written for early readers. During the summer and on school holidays, Sears sponsors story hours and performances. This is truly an excellent museum for the whole family. See Museums chapter for information about exhibits of interest to adults. $7 adults, $3.50 children, free Tue. Mon, Wed, Thu, Fri 10:30–4:30; Tue 10:30–8; Sat 10–5; Sun 12–5. (Downtown)

CHICAGO CHILDREN'S MUSEUM
Navy Pier
700 E. Grand Ave.
312/527-1000

With 60,000 square feet of exhibit space, this is an impressive facility and the only museum in the city that is geared specifically to kids. Highlights include an inventing lab, an indoor nature trail complete with waterfalls and a log cabin, the Climbing Schooner (a three story–high boat), and Waterways, in which raincoat-clad kids get to play with the wet stuff. Open Tue–Sun 10–5, Thu 10–8. $5, free for children under one, family night 5–8 Thu. (Near North)

FIELD MUSEUM OF NATURAL HISTORY
Roosevelt Rd. at Lake Shore Dr.
312/922-9410

If your kid's into dinosaurs (not the purple, smiling, PBS kind), this is the place. The Field Museum features very impressive reconstructions of dinosaur skeletons. A hands-on exhibit called the Place of Wonder lets kids play with animal skins, fossils, and various anthropological artifacts. See Museums

---

Chicago International Children's Film Festival

If you happen to be traveling in Chicago during the month of October, make it a special point to check out Chicago's only film festival for children (held at Facets Multimedia, 1517 W. Fullerton, 773/281-9075). Described as "Cannes for Kids," this is one of the biggest competitive film festivals for children, showcasing over 150 full-length films, shorts, and cartoons. The festival also holds workshops for children in acting and filmmaking, led by professional actors and directors.

chapter for more information. Daily 9–5. $7 adults, $4 children 3–17, free Wed. (Downtown)

THOMAS HUGHES CHILDREN'S LIBRARY
Harold Washington Library Center
400 S. State St.
312/747-4300

Many of the city's libraries do an excellent job with kids' programs, and the Harold Washington Library (the main branch, which happens to be the largest public library in the country) is no exception. Monday and Wednesday mornings the library offers "Story Time Extravaganza" for kids ages three to five. Friday mornings the same program is offered for kids ages six to eight. On Tuesday mornings the library has "Toddler Time," with special programs for children 24 to 35 months old. Special theater and story programs are held for kids ages six and up on Saturdays. Sun 1–5; Mon 9–7; Tue and Thu 11–7; Wed, Fri, and Sat 9–5. Free. (Downtown)

KOHL CHILDREN'S MUSEUM
165 Green Bay Rd., Wilmette
847/256-3000

Since it opened in 1985 this has been one of the most popular museums in the city, with tons of exhibits and events just for kids. Check out Chagall for Children, a fine art exhibit for kids; the computer center; The Construction Zone, where kids learn how to build their own homes; H2O, which is all about learning and playing with water; and the exhibits on racial prejudice. A special treat is the mock-up of a CTA subway train. The museum also sponsors special storytelling hours and sing-alongs. Tue–Sat 9–5, Sun 12–5, Mon 9–5. $5 adults and children,

free for children under age one. (Greater Chicago)

MUSEUM OF SCIENCE AND INDUSTRY
Lake Shore Dr. and 57th St.
773/684-1414

At this hands-on science museum you can tour a captured U-505 submarine, take a tour through a coal mine, or check out Colleen Moore's beautiful, enchanted fairy castle. Every holiday season an exhibit of Christmas trees from around the world is featured. The Omnimax theater, in the museum's Henry Crown Space Center, shows spectacular films that send viewers on virtual voyages on rollercoasters, into outer space, or into the depths of the ocean. The museum is open daily 9:30–5:30. $6 adults, $2.50 children 3–11, free for children under three, free Thu. (South Side)

JOHN G. SHEDD AQUARIUM
1200 S. Lake Shore Dr.
312/939-2438

Kids and adults alike find it difficult to resist this underwater paradise. See Museums chapter for more information. Fri–Wed 9–6, Thu 9–9. $11 adults, $9 children 3–11, free for children under three, reduced admission Thu. (Downtown)

PUPPETS AND FILMS

IMAX THEATER AT NAVY PIER
848 E. Grand Ave.
312/791-7437

3-D technology has improved since the days of going cross-eyed while watching *The Creature from the Black Lagoon* or *Comin' at Ya* with colored glasses at the drive-in. This state-of-the-art cinema, located in a huge shopping and entertainment mall, shows films guaranteed to make you swear that you are flying, riding on a rollercoaster, or staring down at New York City from the top of the Empire State Building. This huge-screen theater with its funky 3-D headsets provides a mind-blowing experience for kids of all ages. Call for current features and show times. (Near North)

THE PUPPET PARLOR
1922 W. Montrose Ave.
773/774-2919
Home to the National Marionette Company, the only resident marionette company in the city, the Puppet Parlor is a neighborhood 70-seat puppet theater which changes shows every couple of months. The theater makes its own marionettes and, on weekend afternoons, performs its own versions of kids' classics such as *Cinderella* and Hans Christian Andersen's *The Snow Queen*. The Puppet Parlor has been in business for more than 25 years and has been so successful that it has begun to do shows that have appeal for both children and adults including a Ziegfeld Follies–style revue and selections from operas. $6. (North Side)

CHILDREN'S THEATER

Many of the city's best theater companies offer special weekend matinée programs for kids which range from puppetry to live-action renditions of classic children's stories. These are some of the better companies around with special kids' programs:

CENTRE EAST
North Shore Center for the Performing Arts

Carolyn Crimi

Oak St. Beach, p. 193

9501 N. Skokie Blvd., Skokie
847/673-6300

ETA CREATIVE ARTS FOUNDATION
7558 S. South Chicago Ave.
773/752-3955

IVANHOE THEATER
750 W. Wellington Ave.
773/539-4211

LIFELINE THEATRE
6912 N. Glenwood St.
773/761-4477

MARRIOTT'S LINCOLNSHIRE THEATRE FOR YOUNG AUDIENCES
10 Marriot Drive, Lincolnshire
847/634-0200

PICKWICK THEATER
Touhy Ave. and Northwest Hwy., Park Ridge
773/989-0532

RAVEN THEATRE
6931 N. Clark St.
773/338-2177

VILLAGE PLAYERS THEATRE
1010 Madison St., Oak Park
708/383-9829

STORES KIDS LOVE

CHILDREN IN PARADISE
909 N. Rush St.
312/951-5437

A lot of children's bookstores these days seem to be first and foremost about selling toys, with books as a sort of afterthought. Not here. With the exception of a stuffed animal here and there, this store is almost exclusively dedicated to kids' books—from alphabet books for toddlers to adventure stories for more mature readers. Children In Paradise also offers an especially good selection of pop-up books. (Near North)

F.A.O. SCHWARZ
840 N. Michigan Ave.
312/587-5000

Without a doubt the largest and the best kids' store in the city, this is a great place to take the tots; the only problem is trying to convince them to leave. Like castaways on Pinocchio's Pleasure Island, children could spend days here exploring the floors of stuffed animals and models; jumping up and down on the foot-activated keyboard; or chatting with the bubble-blowing humans dressed as toy soldiers in front of the store. (Near North)

MAGIC INCORPORATED
5082 N. Lincoln Ave.
773/334-2855

Founded by magician Jay Marshall, who used to be a regular on the Ed Sullivan Show, this is the biggest and best magic shop in the city. With a huge mail-order catalogue, Magic Inc. affords the family's budding Harry Houdini the opportunity to learn how to master the age-old cups-and-balls trick, make a coin disappear, even pull a rabbit out of a hat. Aside from the incredible variety of tricks available here, there are also a good number of books on sale that teach the art of prestidigitation. Most of the folks working here are magicians, so chances are that if you buy something, you may get an impromptu magic show as well. (North Side)

TOYSCAPE
2911 N. Broadway
773/665-7400

This quiet oasis of toys and games (with an accent on the handmade) just may be the nicest store for kids in the entire city. Positively crammed with stuffed animals, wooden toys, and some more specialized novelty items (exquisite music boxes, kaleidoscopes, mobiles), Toyscape is a veritable oxymoron in the world of fast-paced, in-your-face merchandising: a subtle and almost intellectual old-fashioned children's store. (North Side)

Feel like sleeping a little longer, but don't want your kids watching TV? Turn on the radio Sunday mornings at 7:30 to WLIT-FM 93.9. The *Let's Read* children's story hour should keep the kids glued to the radio.

Africa *exhibit at the Field Museum, p. 151*

CHILDREN'S BOOKSTORE STORY HOURS

A lot of bookstores in the city and suburbs host special story hours for the kids. It's a great way to turn your kids on to literature while you listen along or browse through the bookstore for some choices of your own.

BARNES & NOBLE
590 E. Golf Rd., Schaumburg
847/310-0450
Friday evenings at seven, Wednesday mornings at 10:30, both for children ages two to six. (Greater Chicago)

BARNES & NOBLE
659 W. Diversey Pkwy.
773/871-9004
Thursday afternoons at two, Saturday mornings at 11 for children ages two to six. (North Side)

BORDERS BOOKS AND MUSIC
1629 Orrington Ave., Evanston
847/733-8852
Thursday and Sunday afternoons at two for children ages two to seven. (Greater Chicago)

BORDERS BOOKS AND MUSIC
3232 Lake Ave., Wilmette
847/256-3220
Thursday mornings at 10, Saturday mornings at 11 for children under age four. (Greater Chicago)

CHILDREN IN PARADISE
909 N. Rush St.
312/951-5437
Tuesday and Wednesday mornings at 10:30. (Near North)

I DREAM IN COLOR BOOKSTORE
5309 S. Hyde Park Blvd.
773/288-5437
Tuesday and Wednesday mornings at 10:30, Saturday afternoons at three. (South Side)

MAGIC TREE BOOKSTORE
141 N. Oak Park Ave., Oak Park
708/848-0770
Tuesday mornings at 10 for preschoolers. (Greater Chicago)

WOMEN AND CHILDREN FIRST
5233 N. Clark St.
773/769-9299
Wednesday mornings from 10:30 to 11 for children ages two to four. (Far North Side)

THEME PARKS AND RECREATION

KIDDIELAND
8400 W. North Ave., Melrose Park
708/343-8000
There was a time when all amusement parks looked like this. Kiddieland is a great place both for kids and nostalgic adults who want to visit an old-fashioned park. Favorite rides at the park are the miniature train, a 1925 carousel, antique cars, and the watercoaster (part rollercoaster and part water slide). Arcade games, including skeeball, are also offered. Summer daily 10:30 a.m.–10 p.m. (but call in advance because the hours tend to change often). $3 adults and children over 36" tall, free for children under 36", $6.50 seniors. (Greater Chicago)

NOVELTY GOLF
3650 W. Devon Ave.
847/679-9434
A long-time neighborhood staple, this is the best miniature golf course in the city. Novelty's nine holes and two courses require you to shoot balls through windmills, over little pools of water, onto a rotating roulette wheel, up ramps, and through doors that slide shut just at the wrong moment. A popular spot for children's birthday parties, this place hasn't changed since the '60s. After golf there are opportunities for more innocent fun, including a video arcade and a batting cage which allows kids to hit everything from major league fastballs to slowly pitched softballs. (Far North)

RAINBO ROLLER RINK
4836 N. Clark St.
773/271-6200
Locals who grew up in the '60s remember this as an ice-skating rink where the Chicago Black Hawks would practice from time to time. Now the Rainbo is the biggest roller rink in the city. Things can get a little rough around here, particularly in the evenings, but if you stick to the daytime this is a good place to try out that new pair of skates. (North Side)

SIX FLAGS GREAT AMERICA
I-94 and Rte. 132, Gurnee
847/249-1776
Six Flags is fun for the whole family—except for those with a fear of heights. The park is filled with rides and rollercoasters of every shape, size, speed, and fear level. There are rollercoasters that turn upside down, rollercoasters that creep up then shoot down at 90-degree angles to the ground, water slides, and rides that spin around and around until you lose your lunch. A favorite of families and bored sailors, Great America also has rides for the less daring including a beautiful, old-fashioned merry-go-round. The park is populated by strolling Warner Brothers cartoon characters like Bugs Bunny and Foghorn Leghorn. You can take pictures of your kids with the Looney Toons crowd. Don't try to talk to them, though, for the park management does not allow the characters to speak. May–September 10–9. $32. (Greater Chicago)

Marshall Field's

8

SHOPPING

While shopping as we now know it began on State Street, Chicago commerce today spreads out in all directions from the Loop and reaches to the furthest edges of the city and beyond. Though many mom-and-pop department stores have left town to make way for the big chains of the world, Chicago still maintains a good mix of the local and the national. Quirky and burgeoning neighborhoods explode with eclectic ethnic shops and old-time businesses while high-priced touristy areas positively bulge with every major department store or designer outlet that you could possibly imagine. Bargain-conscious strip mall lovers, antique hunters, and well-heeled, exclusive shoppers searching for the latest fashion all will find something in Chicago to satisfy their tastes.

SHOPPING DISTRICTS

THE LOOP

It's been some time since the Loop could be called the shopping mecca of Chicago. With the meteoric growth of the Magnificent Mile shopping district and similar development in the suburbs and the North Side, the Loop, despite a period of slow growth since the crippling '70s, remains a bastion primarily of bargain stores and sometimes-cheesy chains, fast-food restaurants, and drugstores. Still, with the presence of Carson Pirie Scott and Marshall Field's, the city's two most magnificent department stores, one could hardly call the Loop an unexciting shopping locale. After all, State Street is still known as "That Great Street."

CARL FISCHER AND CO. MUSIC
312 S. Wabash Ave.
312/427-6652

Few stores like this one exist anymore. This music store—Chicago's oldest and most comprehensive—

features a mind-boggling array of sheet music. Here you can find everything from the most obscure show tune from No, No Nannette to the latest pop hits to an excellent selection of classical music scores. (Downtown)

CARSON PIRIE SCOTT
1 S. State St.
312/641-7000

It seems hardly fair. In most any other city, Carson's would probably be the jewel in the department store crown. But with the presence of Marshall Field & Co., this magnificent giant must take a respectable yet still distant second place. Designed by Louis Sullivan at the turn of the century, Carson's resembles Field's in size and selection, if not always in quality. On the plus side, this is a better spot to go if you're looking for bargains on designer clothing and sports clothing or trying to avoid the crowds. The annual Christmas window displays based on Tchaikovsky's *Nutcracker Suite* are a highlight of the holiday season. The store is listed in the National Register of Historic Places. (Downtown)

CENTRAL CAMERA
232 S. Wabash Ave.
312/427-5580

Somewhere in the world there may be a more impressive or better-stocked camera store than this one, but if so, I haven't seen it and it probably isn't as memorable as this turn-of-the-century jewel. A cavernous emporium of cameras, equipment, and supplies, Central Camera, with its picturesque neon sign on Wabash Avenue, looks as if it was frozen in time the moment it opened in 1899. (Downtown)

EDDIE BAUER
123 N. Wabash Ave.
312/263-6005

Given that Chicago is not exactly an outdoorsperson's paradise, it's not entirely surprising that this nationwide chain was started not here but in Seattle. Even so, this is a very well-stocked and reasonably priced headquarters for the hunter, camper, skier, or yachtsperson that lies beneath even the most staid of Loop businessfolk. It's an excellent place to find the sweaters so useful in Chicago winters, or the backpacks for those much needed winter trips out of town. (Downtown)

MARSHALL FIELD'S
111 N. State St.
312/781-1000

Chicago has had its share of fine department stores, but few have ever bred as loyal a following as this one, the gem of the city's shopping world. In fact, Field's is arguably the finest department store in the country, if not the world (proponents of Harrod's or Printemps might want to interject at this point). What makes Field's different from any other department store? Perhaps it's the architectural history: Designed by D.H. Burnham & Co., the store has been a staple of the Loop since the turn of the century and features a spectacular dome designed by Tiffany. Perhaps it's the tradition: Every Christmas families line up for hours to enjoy lunch or dinner under the massive tree in the Walnut Room dining room, which looks out onto the Skate-on-State ice-skating rink; and every Easter an equal number of patient guests wait to have brunch with the Easter Bunny. Perhaps it's the excellent array of restaurants, which include Hinky

Dink Kenna's pub. Perhaps it's the Christmas windows, lovingly designed every year with a different storybook motif. Or perhaps it's the shopping—10 floors of stores cover an entire square block in the heart of the Loop. Maybe it's the famous eight-ton clock on State Street, or the Frangos, the signature chocolate candies that have been a hallmark of Field's for eons. Field's also has a decent but nowhere near as impressive or historical branch in the Water Tower Place on the Near North Side (312/335-7700), and 23 other stores throughout the Chicago area. (Downtown)

THE MAGNIFICENT MILE

They call Michigan Avenue the "Magnificent Mile," and the name fits, especially where the shopper is concerned. Acres upon acres of malls, department stores, and specialty shops catering to every budget can be found along this street or a block or two to the east or west. If there's a store you've heard of, it's very likely you'll find it on the Mag Mile. Literally hundreds of stores can be found here, including everything from fancy shops like Burberry's and Brooks Brothers to exciting gizmo heavens like Hammacher-Schlemmer to intriguing little oddities like the Garrett Popcorn Shop, home to probably the best caramel popcorn in the city.

BANANA REPUBLIC
734 N. Michigan Ave.
312/642-7667
Though it may not be the mysterious safari outfitter that its name implies, Banana Republic does offer an impressive four floors of men's and women's casual clothing at relatively reasonable prices. There is also a smaller Banana Republic outlet nearby at Water Tower Place. (Near North)

BANG & OLUFSEN
15 E. Oak St.
312/787-6006
If there weren't price tags on the merchandise here, you might think that you had walked into a museum of design rather than an actual store. In fact, when you get a closer look at these prices, you might decide to treat the place like a museum anyway. No one ever said that buying the sleekest, most elegant CD racks, stereo equipment, televisions, telephones, and telephone answering machines available in the Western Hemisphere would be a cheap proposition. The eye-popping displays are definitely worth a look. (Near North)

TIP

If you're planning a weeklong stay in Chicago, do yourself a favor and save your Magnificent Mile shopping until after the weekend is over, especially during prime-time holiday season. Though many stores try to lure the hordes with one-day weekend sales, the crowds and headaches you'll avoid by postponing your purchases to a Monday might well be worth the 15 percent you have saved on that lovely Ann Taylor chemise.

BLOOMINGDALE'S (AND 900 N. MICHIGAN SHOPS)
900 N. Michigan
312/440-4460

Located in the 900 N. Michigan shopping mall (which features a movie theater, a tinkly piano player, several decent restaurants, and about 75 stores (including Coopersmith's Book Store, Galt Toys, J. Crew, and the Museum Store of the Art Institute), the Chicago branch of Bloomingdale's is probably the city's best department store after the Loop's Marshall Field & Co. It features six vast floors of designer wear, house-

hold items, office products, home furnishings, and about anything else you could possibly want. It's not the best place to find cheap items, but the men's and women's clothing here is certainly no more expensive than average. (Near North)

BRUDNO ART SUPPLY
610 N. State St.
312/751-7980

Located in the historic Tree Studios, which was built to supply affordable residences and work spaces for artists, Brudno's remains one of the best stores for professional and

---

The Ten Best Places to Shop

by Kay Martinovich, renowned Chicago theater director and shopper

1. **Gallimaufry Gallery**, 3345 N. Halsted St., 773/348-8090
   A fabulous handcrafted treasure and gift shop!

2. **He Who Eats Mud**, 3247 N. Broadway, 773/525-0616
   Great cards and other stuff, too.

3. **Fourth World Artisans**, 3440 N. Southport Ave., 773/404-5200
   All kinds of cool stuff from all over world.

4. **The Pink Frog**, 857 W. Belmont Ave., 773/525-2680
   Funky women's apparel.

5. **Hubba-Hubba**, 3338 N. Clark St., 773/477-1414
   Funky new and vintage women's apparel.

6. **Transitions Bookstore**, 1000 W. North Ave, 312/951-7323
   Great alternative bookstore.

7. **Rand McNally**, 444 N. Michigan Ave., 312/321-1751
   Lots of maps!

8. **Chicago Blooms**, 1149 N. State St., 312/951-1688
   Flowers, flowers, flowers.

9. **Dinkel's Bakery**, 3329 N. Lincoln Ave., 773/281-7300
   Fabulous!

10. **WTTW Store of Knowledge**, Water Tower Place, 312/642-6826
    All kinds of cool PBS stuff.

budding artists. Brudno's offers excellent selections of brushes, acrylics, and watercolors as well as sketchpads and everything else that an artist could need. Staff members here are especially friendly and helpful. (Near North)

FILENE'S BASEMENT
830 N. Michigan Ave.
312/482-8918
Somewhere between the elegance of Neiman Marcus and the slapdash bargain-basement atmosphere of a Woolworth's lies this bargain hunter's department store. With shopping bags trumpeting "I Just Got a Bargain," and signs declaring "Never Pay Full Price Again" and "Bargains are Our Business," Filene's offers racks and bins of designer clothing at discount prices. The store is located in the new Plaza Escada shopping mall, which also features an F.A.O. Schwarz, Victoria's Secret, Structure, and Borders Books. (Near North)

NAVY PIER
600 E. Grand Ave.
312/595-7437
You don't come to Navy Pier to shop at any one particular store. You come to walk the entire length of the facility and poke in and out of more than a hundred shops. Somewhere between a carnival and a shopping mall, Navy Pier offers gifts at countless stores and kiosks. Available here are books, T-shirts, toys, train sets, and basically everything else you could possibly imagine. There is a lot of junk here, too, but if you're shopping for gag gifts, this is one of the best places to do it. (Near North)

NEIMAN MARCUS
737 N. Michigan Ave.
312/642-5900

So you say that elegance counts more than price? You've come to the right place. The Chicago branch of this Texas-based department store offers a fine selection of high-end designer wear for men and women as well as excellent gift items and even pastries and candies. If you've come looking for bins of cut-rate merchandise, you're better off elsewhere as this tony, understated department store with its tastefully designed displays has an atmosphere of subtlety and sobriety to match its sumptuous tastes. (Near North)

NIKETOWN
669 N. Michigan Ave.
312/642-6363
There was a time that the Sears Tower and the Rock 'n' Roll McDonalds could have called themselves the city's most popular tourist attractions. Now, with the absolute worldwide explosion of the Chicago Bulls and Michael Jordan, this Nike superstore has become a very close contender. Though it is technically just a sporting goods store, the majestic atmosphere, harrowing slogans ("Just Do It," "Go Ballistic"), abundance of Nike swooshes, and imposing sculptures make it almost akin to a religious shrine dedicated to the pursuit of competition and bodily health in the 21st century. Icons here include Michael Jordan, Terrell Davis, Suzy Hamilton, and a frighteningly shirtless Scottie Pippen. You can buy shoes here, too. (Near North)

THE POTTERY BARN
734 N. Michigan Ave.
312/587-9602
The gardening motif (there are flowers and watering cans on sale as you enter) of the Pottery Barn makes for a pleasant and airy oasis for the city

Urban Outfitters

T. Bishop and M. Yossiffon

traveler. Most of what's for sale here consists of excellent last-minute ideas for the wedding or shower shopper. Featuring attractive displays of glassware, picture frames, and vases, the Pottery Barn can be a reasonably priced alternative to the often overcrowded Crate & Barrel just down the street. (Near North)

URBAN OUTFITTERS
935 N. Rush St.
312/640-1919
Walking a thin line between the daringly alternative and middle-of-the-road, this store gains a good deal more attention for its funky atmosphere and strange selection of kooky gift items than for its reasonably priced casual clothing. The scent of incense, the hard-driving Patti Smith music, the special-interest books (for example, *Sex Tips for Straight Women from a Gay Man*), and the collections of pastas and candies in the shapes of various body parts might send the timid shopper scurrying elsewhere. But much of the rest of what's on sale here wouldn't look unusual on anyone

who did most of their shopping at the Gap. Urban Outfitters also has a North Side branch on 2352 North Clark Street. (Near North)

WATER TOWER PLACE
835 N. Michigan Ave.
312/440-3166
With more than a hundred shops, plus movie theaters, and restaurants, and directly connected to the Ritz-Carlton Hotel, this marble-tiled building is probably the most impressive mall in the city. Containing both seven-floor branches of Marshall Field's and Lord & Taylor, and numerous gift shops and excellent specialty stores (including Godiva Chocolatier, Victoria's Secret, Aunt Diana's Fudge, and Alfred Dunhill cigars), Water Tower Place also has a number of stores that are worth a trip in and of themselves. (Near North)

CRABTREE & EVELYN
835 N. Michigan Ave. (fifth floor)
312/787-0188
What may best be regarded as the next stop following a purchase at Vic-

toria's Secret, the eternally classy Crabtree & Evelyn has an air about it that calms and soothes even before one has applied any of its products. Dedicated to spiritual and bodily health, the store offers a selection of soaps, oils, votive candles, bath gels, and other such items in a variety of scents. It's not a bad place to pick up a bathrobe either. (Near North)

CRANE & CO. PAPER MAKERS
835 N. Michigan Ave.
312/397-1936

From a distance, the stationery and fine paper sold here look like well-packaged, 100-percent cotton, French cuff shirts. And, though a closer glimpse reveals the truth, the initial impression does say a good deal about how seriously Crane & Co. takes their paper products. Featuring tastefully designed stationery as well as diaries, embossed invitations, and address books, the 1801 company is clearly not the place to purchase a cheap ream of loose-leaf. It is, however, an excellent locale to impress someone with an eloquent love letter or poem. (Near North)

EXPRESS
835 N. Michigan Ave.
312/943-0344

Offering a good selection of women's casual clothing at reasonable prices, this store has a youthful and carefree feel to it, as may be suggested by the propulsive dance-club music that resounds through it. The store hosts frequent sales and is a favorite of the funky teenage crowd. (Near North)

THE NORTH FACE
875 N. Michigan Ave.
312/337-7200

The location of this store on the first floor of the 1,100-foot John Hancock

Building is well-chosen. If there were any chance you could find equipment to climb up to the observation deck from down here, most likely you could buy it at The North Face. Boasting the slogan "I am not alive in an office!" and proudly proclaiming that it is located at 87.624 degrees longitude and 41.898 degrees latitude, this store offers an excellent line of alpine equipment, climbing gear, tents, expedition wear, and the like. This is clearly one of the better outlets for the outdoorsman or outdoorswoman in town. (Near North)

RIZZOLI BOOKSTORE
835 N. Michigan Ave. (third floor)
312/642-3500

While it's not really the place to go if you want to find the latest John Grisham novel or a cute calendar with a picture of Garfield on it, this is probably the most understated and classy bookstore in town, especially since Waterstone's left its Near North facility for an O'Hare Airport kiosk. Featuring an excellent selection of children's books, as well as a decent number of classical CDs upstairs, Rizzoli is probably best known for its comprehensive selection of art books, which run the gamut from Egon Schiele to Maurice Sendak. Many of the art and architecture books are also surprisingly affordable and a good deal may be found on sale. (Near North)

THE SHARPER IMAGE
835 N. Michigan Ave.
312/335-1600

If there is a heaven for the gizmo-lover, this surely must be it. Once known in Chicago as only a catalog outlet, this branch (as well as the one Downtown) allows the would-be James Bond in all of us to inspect a vast variety of titillating devices.

Though much of what's for sale here is quite pricey, who could say no to a home lie detector? A pair of night-vision military binoculars? A remote control Mercedes? A mock-up of a 1950s radio? Neon sculptures? Lava lamps? Watches? Robots? Wind chimes? Jukeboxes? Ultra-high-tech massage equipment? The world's most comfortable TV chair? If this is your thing, you could probably spend a day in here. (Near North)

WARNER BROS. STUDIO STORE
835 N. Michigan Ave.
(second and third floors)
312/664-9440

From a store dedicated to the multitude of stars from Looney Toons cartoons, you'd expect perhaps some Bugs Bunny T-shirts and maybe a Daffy Duck sweatshirt or two. This shop, however, boggles the mind with its wide array of Warner Brothers cartoon merchandise. You want a smock with Sylvester on it? Maybe a mug with Tom and Jerry? Pepe Le Pew on a cookie jar? How about a soap dispenser with the Tasmanian Devil on it, baby clothes with a picture of Tweety Bird, or even a framed original print of any of the Warner Bros. family? It's all here. (Near North)

WTTW STORE OF KNOWLEDGE
835 N. Michigan Ave.
(seventh floor)
312/642-6826

WTTW—Chicago's one major public television station—is the inspiration for this vast collection of brainy gifts. Resembling a museum store without the museum attached to it, the Store of Knowledge offers great stuff for the kids (3-D puzzles, scientific models, glow-in-the-dark globes, and solar system mobiles, as well as a good deal of Tickle Me Elmo mer-

chandise) as well as things that might go over well with the older set (much PBS programming is available on video here including George Eliot's *Middlemarch* and the complete set of classic P.G. Wodehouse *Jeeves and Wooster* programs). Who might be interested in a game called "Alien Autopsy," I do not care to speculate. (Near North)

SAKS FIFTH AVENUE (AND CHICAGO PLACE)
700 N. Michigan Ave.
312/944-6500

With Neiman Marcus, Bloomingdale's, Lord & Taylor, and Marshall Field & Co. all within easy walking distance, Saks tends to get overlooked. That's a shame, because this excellent seven-floor department store features if not everything from A to Z, at least everything from A to Y (Ann Taylor to Yves St. Laurent). The advantage is that Saks, which also has its own beauty salon, is often less crowded than its more imposing nearby competitors. Saks also benefits from being located in the Chicago Place shopping center, which boasts a food court and the slogan "8 Floors, 50 Stores." Among the more noteworthy of these are The Body Shop (first floor), Talbots (first floor), Ann Taylor (second floor), Florsheim Shoes (second floor), Williams Sonoma (second floor), and Room & Board (fifth through seventh floors). (Near North)

RAND MCNALLY MAP AND TRAVEL STORE
444 N. Michigan Ave.
312/321-1751

It's hard to get lost in this city, especially if you wind up in this store, home of the city's widest selection of maps. Books, charts, globes—every-

The Oak Street Shuffle: Ten More Stores That Will Impress Your Friends

Oak Street, just off the Magnificent Mile, could probably merit a shopping chapter in and of itself. Within just one block you can find apparel by dozens of the world's most famous and exclusive designers in chic stores and boutiques. So, if you haven't had enough of the high-fashion on the Magnificent Mile, here are 10 other stores that are worth checking out if you step onto Oak.

1. **Barney's of New York**, 25 E. Oak St., 312/587-1700
2. **Gianni Versace**. 101 E. Oak St., 312/337-1111
3. **Giorgio Armani,** 111 E. Oak St., 312/751-2244
4. **Hermés of Paris,** 110 E. Oak St., 312/787-8175
5. **Jil Sander,** 48 E. Oak St., 312/335-0006
6. **Sonia Rykiel,** 106 E. Oak St., 312/951-0800
7. **Stephane Kelian**, 121 E. Oak St., 312/951-2868
8. **Sugar Magnolia,** 34 E. Oak St., 312/944-0885
9. **Sulka,** 55 E. Oak St., 312/951-9500
10. **Ultimate Bride,** 106 E. Oak St., 312/337-6300

thing for the professional or amateur photographer or lost Chicago tourist can be found here. (Near North)

ULTIMO
114 E. Oak St.
312/787-0906
Hardly the place to go for a bargain, this is pretty much the top of the line when it comes to shopping for women's and some men's fashions. Exclusivity is the watchword here. Many world-famous designers' clothing may be purchased in Ultimo's quiet and elegant surroundings. Just don't come in looking for the bargain racks. (Near North)

BELMONT AVENUE ANTIQUE DISTRICT

Chicago has never been particularly known for its antique shopping—some of the best bargains can be found way out of the city in small towns like Sandwich. But the great thing about the city's antique shops is that most of them are located within easy walking distance of each other. For antique bargains, try starting at the corner of Belmont and Lincoln. Poke around there for a little bit, then walk due west on Belmont into the city's up-and-coming Roscoe Village neighborhood.

20TH CENTURY REVUE ANTIQUES
1903 W. Belmont Ave.
773/472-8890

Of the many antique stores in the Roscoe Village neighborhood, this is no doubt one of the classiest and the funkiest. Everything here looks as if it stepped out of a 1950s kitchen or dining room or an Edward Hopper painting. Attractively displayed couches, tables, kitchens, and dining room furniture all can be found here. This is not a place to go if you're after a cheap bargain. If you're looking to outfit your home with a charming retro feel, on the other hand, this is the place that you can do it. (North Side)

BETTY'S RESALE SHOP
3439 N. Lincoln Ave.
773/929-6143

Betty's has never been accused of being anything much to look at. You'd be hard-pressed to find a more chaotic collection of dusty furniture items, old appliances, and God knows what else. But amid the musty mess, you may find excellent bargains on wonderful vintage chairs, couches, and dinner tables. While it's not for the squeamish or the snooty, Betty's is a scavenger's delight. (North Side)

PHIL'S ANTIQUE FACTORY
2042 W. Belmont Ave.
773/528-8549

Not everything for sale here is an antique in the technical sense, but there sure are enough of them. Like a rummage sale that goes on every day of the week, Phil's offers tremendous finds in housewares, furniture, and assorted doodads and memorabilia in and among the dusty collections of useless stuff. It's a fun place to go hunting. (North Side)

CLARK STREET CORRIDOR

Cutting a swath from the toniest areas of Lincoln Park to the more rugged areas of Wrigleyville, Lakeview, and Andersonville, Clark Street provides an excellent cross-section of shopping opportunities from well-respected chain stores like The Gap, The Limited, Tower Records, Borders Books, and Urban Outfitters to more specialized and individualized outposts for second-hand clothing, Asian gift items, and music. A short walk down nearby Broadway or Halsted leads shoppers from the well-known chains to other stores that cater largely to Chicago's gay population. (North Side)

THE ALLEY
858 W. Belmont Ave.
773/883-1800

Perhaps not as hard-edged and "alternative" as it used to be, and now catering as much to kids up from the suburbs as young toughs and would-be greasers, this is still a prime outfitter for the punk and wanna-be punks of Chicago. Located nearby Punkin' Donuts (the name affectionately given to the parking-lot hangout adjacent to Dunkin' Donuts at Clark and Belmont), the Alley is a T-shirt and leather paradise specializing in police jackets and motorcycle gear. (North Side)

CENTURY MALL
2828 N. Clark St.

If you could cross a disco with an indoor shopping mall, you might come up with something like the Century, home to hip, trendy outlet stores that cater to both straight and gay neighborhood yuppies and hipsters. You'll find dozens of clothing and specialty shops, a food court, and a Bally's

Health Club on the top floor. The Limited occupies the mall's prime retail space on the first floor. (North Side)

HANIG'S SLIPPER BOX
2754 N. Clark St.
773/248-1977
Located at the bustling intersection of Clark and Diversey, Hanig's offers one of the widest selections of shoes in town. Catering to all the different sorts of folks who live in this neighborhood—from conservative yuppies to funky rock 'n' rollers—Hanig's carries full lines of designer footwear including Doc Martens, Birkenstocks, and Rockports, as well as designs by Kenneth Cole, Timberland, and Johnston & Murphy. There is another Hanig's on the Magnificent Mile (660 N. Michigan Ave., 312/642-5330). (North Side)

SATURDAY AUDIO EXCHANGE
2919 N. Clark St.
773/935-8733
When they say Saturday, they mean

Water Tower Place, p. 162

Water Tower Place

Saturday. This stereo store—offering good deals on used merchandise, overstocks, and slightly damaged equipment—is open all day every Saturday. This is the key stop in Chicago for the audiophile and the incredibly knowledgeable staff has a daunting way with the stereophonic lexicon. Closed every other day of the week except Thursday evenings, this is the key spot in Chicago for stereo bargains. (North Side)

SECOND HAND TUNES
2604 N. Clark St.
773/929-6325
There are a surprising number of second-hand music stores on this stretch of Clark Street. But for selection in CD, cassette, and vinyl formats, this one's the best. If you're willing to burrow through the stacks of old creased record albums and the racks of slightly damaged items in the cutout bin, you're likely to come up with some great finds. Second Hand Tunes also has outlets in Evanston, 847/491-1690, and in Hyde Park, 773/684-3375. (North Side)

TOWER RECORDS
2301 N. Clark St.
773/477-5994
For music lovers and those who have tired of the café scene, Tower is fast becoming one of the city's biggest hangouts, particularly between 10 p.m. and midnight. Its immense collection and vast space make it the largest and best record store in town. (North Side)

CLYBOURN CORRIDOR

Clybourn Avenue—knifing diagonally from the Near North Side of the city toward the northwest—is one of the fastest growing shopping districts around. Located in a gentrifying area that once housed factories and vacant lots, the Clybourn Corridor is now home to numerous pockets of shopping malls containing everything from bookstores to outdoor-goods shops to excellent groceries to specialty pastry shops, as well as restaurants and movie theaters.

FACETS VIDEO
1517 W. Fullerton Ave.
773/281-9075
Facets has the best selection of videos in town. Attached to Facets Multimedia, one of the city's premier art cinemas, Facets Video has thousands upon thousands of videos in stock with a special accent on the obscure, the foreign, and the out-of-print. You might not find *Titanic* or *Jurassic Park* here, but you're more than likely to find most anything else. (North Side)

KRASNY & COMPANY
2829 N. Clybourn Ave.
773/477-5504
If you want to turn your home into your very own restaurant, check out this place, one of the best restaurant-supply houses in town offering kitchen and dining supplies at low prices. You'll find everything from menus to restaurant candles to cookware and glassware. The store may not look like much—it resembles a huge, cluttered warehouse—but great bargains abound. (North Side)

PIER ONE IMPORTS
2112 N. Clybourn Ave.
773/871-6610
An excellent place to find home furnishings or last-minute wedding gifts, this is one of several Pier One outposts in the city. There are frequent sales here and good bargains may be had on rugs, lampshades, glassware, and other sundry household items and decorations. (North Side)

SAM'S WINE AND LIQUORS
1720 N. Marcey St.
312/664-4394
A guy I know calls this place "Tower Records for the dipsomaniac," and he's not completely off-base. Most grocery stores don't devote as much space to all of their stock as Sam's does to wine. You'll find everything from the cheapest bottles of plunk to the rarest Australian table wines here. It's the perfect place to find something to impress your dinner host. (Near North)

TREASURE ISLAND
2121 N. Clybourn Ave.
773/880-8880
For international cuisine at reasonable prices, it's difficult to beat this excellent supermarket chain, which also has a number of other outlets in the city. With an array of unusual produce and food items from around the world, Treasure Island has a distinctly global feel. The hand-rolled sushi here is quite good. (North Side)

WHOLE FOODS
1000 W. North Ave.
312/587-0648
They say it's only a food shop, but with the natural food health craze upon us it's more like a way of life. Though quite expensive, this is one of the premier natural foods groceries in the city with an excellent juice bar, elaborate displays of premade dinners (which change daily), and one of the best salad bars in town. (North Side)

DEVON AVENUE (6200 N.)

Chicago's reputation as a very seg-regated city is not particularly ac-curate when it comes to this neighborhood, which is one of the most diverse, multicultural bazaars you'll find anywhere in the world. Here in this Far North Side neigh-borhood, for about two miles of Devon Avenue, you can see Jewish bookstores beside Indian groceries, Russian delis beside Greek grocers, and sari shops and food from Jerusalem, Bombay, Istanbul, Bei-jing, and everywhere in between.

INDIA SARI PALACE
2536 W. Devon Ave.
773/338-2127
This neighborhood—the main head-quarters for Indian and Pakistani shopping in Chicago—draws people from throughout the Midwest in search of goods from groceries to clothing. This sari emporium has the most dazzling selection of fabrics on a street chock full of Indian clothing options, and the license plates out in front from Iowa, Missouri, Indiana, and Michigan attest to it. (Far North)

ROSENBLUM'S WORLD OF JUDAICA
2906 W. Devon Ave.
773/262-1700
For Jewish literature, toys, and reli-gious items, it's tough to find a store that is more comprehensive than Rosenblum's. Here you can find racks of books dealing with Jewish holi-days as well as Judaism itself, and a wide selection of Jewish and klezmer music on cassette and CD. More tra-ditional supplies relating to Judaism can be found here as well, such as menorahs, prayer books, yarmulkes, and prayer shawls. (Far North)

Marshall Field's

The eight-ton clock at Marshall Field's, p. 158

OTHER NOTABLE STORES

ALCALA'S WESTERN WEAR
1733 W. Chicago Ave.
773/226-0152
The rumor is that Bulls star and au-tomobile pitchman Scottie Pippen does a lot of his shopping here. But if that isn't enough to get you to come to Alcala's, maybe the 10,000 pairs of boots they offer will con-vince you to make the trip. Acala's offers the best selection of cowboy boots, 10-gallon hats, and all else that calls the West to mind this side of Dallas. (West Side)

ALLISON LA PARISIENNE
8834 S. Cottage Grove
312/994-8975
No outfit is complete without a hat to make just the right bold and self-con-fident statement. This South Side spot, located in the quiet, middle-class Chatham enclave, is a women's clothing shop which specializes in just this sort of apparel—hats for

Top Ten Bookstores

by Paula Kamen, world-renowned Chicago feminist author whose books include _Feminist Fatale_.

1. **57th Street Bookstore, 1301 East 57th St.**
   Billed as "where serious readers go for fun," this nook-filled, winding store boasts some of the most provocative author programming in the city.

2. **Seminary Cooperative Bookstore, 5757 S. University Ave.**
   The dank, perilously narrow, and labyrinthine corridors of this intellectual and cloistered basement of a real-life seminary contain the best selection of academic books in the country, offering comfort only to the most antisocial and unmaterialistic die-hard book lovers.

3. **Barbara's Bookstore, 1350 N. Wells St.**
   The pinnacle of independent bookstore charm and comfort.

4. **Women and Children First, 5233 N. Clark St.**
   One of the top feminist bookstores in the country, with progressive children's books, gay and lesbian literature, and an interesting array of women's 'zines.

5. **Quimby's Bookstore, 1854 W. North Ave.**
   The ultimate store for lovers of the quirky and homemade, Quimby's offers the best selection of offbeat and independently made 'zines and small-press publications in town. Featured in the 1994 film _Go Fish_.

6. **Unabridged, 3251 N. Broadway**
   Unabridged reflects the specialized interests of the neighborhood's large gay population. However, both gay and straight book lovers will find comfort here.

7, 8. **Powell's, in Hyde Park at 1501 E. 57th St., and the North Side at 2850 N. Lincoln Ave.**
   These two vast stores are treasure troves of used books and discounted remainders, replete with musty smells and towering bookshelves. Be careful accessing that especially alluring but weighty Marxist tome on the creaky ladders.

9. **Newberry Library's AC McClurg Bookstore, 60 W. Walton St.**
   Operated by the Seminary Co-op Bookstores, this small store stands out for its selection of fine literature and art books.

10. **Borders, 830 N. Michigan Ave.**
   I tried to stick to the more respectable and unique independents, but I couldn't resist listing one of the most truly enjoyable bookstore visits —the hegemonic media corporate monopoly be damned. This vast, four-level, still glisteningly new store is a media lover's dream.

church, hats for weddings, and hats for a night on the town. Designer clothing is also available here. (South Side)

ANCIENT ECHOES
1003 W. Armitage Ave.
773/880-1003
The accent here is on the handmade. Using traditional artists and those who work in traditional styles, Ancient Echoes offers one-of-a-kind holiday ornaments and handcrafted jewelry. (North Side)

AROMA WORKSHOP
2050 N. Halsted St.
773/871-1985
Though the phrase "you are what you eat" is a popular one, here it doesn't apply; at the Aroma Workshop you are what you smell. With a mind-boggling array of scents, the Aroma Workshop crafts its own therapeutic oils, lotions, soaps, and gels. They will even use your input to create brand new aromatherapeutic scents. (North Side)

BIGBSY & KRUTHERS
1750 N. Clark St.
312/440-1750
So you want to get dressed up to look like Chicago Bulls coach Phil Jackson? You can't be blamed. With the possible exception of slickmeister Pat Riley, Jackson does set the standard for dressing for success in the NBA, and this men's clothing store, which outfits many of Chicago athletes and celebs, is one of the reasons. Featuring an excellent array of both business and casual attire, B & K, not surprisingly, caters especially to the big-and-tall crowd. (Near North)

CELESTE TURNER
Fremont and Armitage Ave.
773/549-3390
The most world-renowned designers aren't what usually show up in this trendy and sophisticated women's clothing shop. Here the accent is on Chicago designers and Celeste Turner herself. The store offers an excellent selection of suits, dresses, and sweaters in a refreshingly unpretentious atmosphere. (North Side)

CHERNIN'S
606 W. Roosevelt Rd.
312/922-4545
There may be stores with a wider selection of shoes, but if there are, I haven't seen them. A veritable warehouse of footwear at reasonable and often discounted prices, Chernin's is located near the old Maxwell Street market neighborhood which is still a key stop for many a thrifty shopper. (Downtown)

CHINATOWN
Wentworth Ave. (between 22nd and 25th Sts.)
There is no one store to go to in Chinatown. It pretty much functions as a mall several blocks long filled with herbs, foods, and gift items. Located just a couple of miles south of the Loop, Chicago's Chinatown cannot compete in size or variety with those in New York or San Francisco. But if you're looking for bargains on woks, bulk fortune cookies, Asian cookware, ginseng, tea, or funky gift items, you're liable to find everything in this dense and lively area. (Near South)

CONTE DI SAVOIA
1438 W. Taylor St.
312/666-3471
This may be the best Italian grocery and deli in town. Here you will find pastas of all shapes and sizes, racks of spices and Italian desserts, freez-

Saturday's Child, p. 173

that matter, any time of year when you're in search of a costume or novelty item. Located in the Swedish Andersonville neighborhood, The Drum is a veritable warehouse of fabrics, beads, masks, costumes, and other such paraphernalia. (Far North)

FLASHY TRASH
3524 N. Halsted St.
773/327-6900

As far as vintage and second-hand clothes shopping goes, this is pretty much the top of the line. Many urban models are outfitted for their fashion shoots here. There are some new items on sale here as well, but the funky old fashions are what attracts attention. (North Side)

ers full of Conte Di Savoia's homemade sauces, ravioli, lasagna, and many other Italian delicacies. The store is located in Chicago's Little Italy, a neighborhood stretching for a mile or so in and around Taylor Street. (West Side)

D'AMATO'S BAKERY
112 W. Grand Ave.
312/733-6219

Tucked away amid the dwellings of a small enclave of Italian families, D'Amato's is probably the city's best Italian bakery. Not surprisingly, D'Amato's carries an excellent selection of breads and desserts (including, of course, cannoli and tiramisu). Specialties include tasty and crunchy sesame sticks as well as slices of pizza made with D'Amato's own dough. (Near North)

THE DRUM SHOP
5216 N. Clark St.
773/769-5551

This is the perfect spot for shopping during the Halloween season or, for

JAZZ RECORD MART
444 N. Wabash Ave.
312/222-1467

In search of a long out-of-print Miles Davis album? Maybe you just want to shop for some old 78-rpm records to put on the antique phonograph in your swinging bachelor pad. For the jazz aficionado, this is pretty much the one and only choice in Chicago. Chock-full of new releases and rare oldies, the Jazz Record Mart is a virtual encyclopedia of the history of jazz and blues music. It's also a great place to quiz the staff and fellow shoppers about their considerable jazz knowledge. (Near North)

KALE UNIFORM
555 W. Roosevelt Rd.
312/563-0022

Wanna get dressed up like a Chicago cop? Maybe a member of the Illinois sheriff's police or the U.S. postal service? This is where government officials go to get outfitted. Here you can find Chicago police officers' leather jackets, firefighters' shirts, postal service uniforms, and everything you might need to look like a city official. They won't sell you the official patches here (that would be against the law), but you can find everything else from the hats to the shoes at low prices. (Downtown)

MERZ APOTHECARY
4716 N. Lincoln Ave.
773/989-0900

This may very well be Chicago's oldest business and it is also one of its most unusual. Located in the largely German neighborhood of Lincoln Square, Merz has been around since 1875 and is the city's best outlet for homeopathic medicines and herbal treatments. Housed in a strangely serene location, the store also sells a good selection of soaps and oils. (Far North)

METRO GOLDEN MEMORIES
5425 W. Addison St.
773/736-4133

Paradise for the nostalgia buff. This Northwest Side store, tucked away in an unassuming storefront, boasts a jaw-dropping selection of TV, radio, and movie memorabilia. Here you can find stills of all your favorite stars from the days of the silents up to the present, original movie posters from thousands of films, old copies of *Life* magazine, and other screen fanzines. MGM also has by far the city's widest selection of recordings of old radio shows including everything from *Amos 'n Andy* and the *Jack Benny Show* to the classic thrillers *Suspense* and *Lights Out.* (North Side)

OLD TOWN SCHOOL OF FOLK MUSIC
4536 N. Lincoln Ave.
773/728-6000

A relic of the '60s and '70s, when Chicago was one of the country's folk music capitals, the Old Town School is an excellent choice if you're shopping for sheet music or a guitar, harmonica, or ukelele. It carries a wide variety of music accessories and holds frequent classes for beginner musicians. (Far North)

PAPER SOURCE
232 W. Chicago Ave.
312/337-0798

The name pretty much tells the whole story here. But apart from a wide variety of elegant and occasionally daring paper stocks, Paper Source also has a great selection of wrapping papers which range from the most conservative and elegant to the silliest children's birthday paper. Perfect for wrapping the gift you purchased on the Mag Mile. (Near North)

RECKLESS RECORDS
3157 N. Broadway
773/404-5080

An effective antidote to some of the more staid and predictable chain music stores in the city, Reckless remains one of the best outlets for industrial, alternative, and imported-rock music. Bolstered by a highly knowledgeable staff, Reckless is not the place to find old Kansas or Nazareth LPs. But if it's hip, twisted, or underground, you're likely to find a copy of it here. (North Side)

SATURDAY'S CHILD
2146 N. Halsted St.
773/773/525-8697

Stuffed in between bars, yuppie hangouts, and restaurants sits one of the city's best stores for kids. Not only featuring the usual and none-too-surprising collections of kiddie books and stuffed animals, Saturday's Child has an intriguing selection of gizmos, games, and models. Especially cool are the vast bins of superballs, juggling toys, and toy animals, all of which are perfectly suitable for children of every age. (North Side)

SPORTMART
620 N. LaSalle Dr.
312/337-6151
The "Wall of Fame" is what initially attracts attention to this massive sporting goods store. Outside you can compare your hand size with those printed in stone by some of Chicago's greatest athletes including Michael Jordan, Ryne Sandberg, and Ernie Banks. Inside, the store itself has the city's largest selection of sporting goods and team merchandise including floor upon floor of uniforms, camping equipment, running shoes, and everything else the pro or amateur athlete could possibly need. (Near North)

SPY SHOP
1156 N. Dearborn
773/664-SPYS
It's doubtful how practical most of the stuff for sale at this store is. But if you're looking for a place to browse around or just feel like pretending you're James Bond for a while, there may not be a better place. Calling itself a "discreet electronics and security shop," Spy Shop has everything you need to begin your career as a private eye or a secret agent, including all the latest innovations in surveillance and monitoring equipment. (Near North)

UNCLE DAN'S
2440 N. Lincoln Ave.
773/477-1918
Though it may not be as well-known as its nationally famous competitors

such as Erehwon or The North Face, this one-time army-navy surplus store is also quite a good outdoors store. Uncle Dan's, offering everything from tents to bandannas to just about anything in flannel, is a perfect place to stop before that drive into the Wisconsin North Woods. (North Side)

VOGUE FABRICS
621 W. Roosevelt Rd.
312/829-2505
Making one's own dresses may not have quite the same snob appeal as buying them at Nordstrom, but if you're looking to buy material for clothes, sheets, or anything else, this is by far the best location in Chicago. Stacked wall to wall with rolls of fabrics of every size, shape, or pattern (all of which may be had at incredibly low prices), this is a fantastic wholesale outlet for the professional or amateur tailor or seamstress. Designer fabrics by the likes of Calvin Klein and Liz Claiborne are available for way-cheap prices. (Near South)

SHOPPING IN THE SUBURBS

So you've had it with Chicago shopping? Or, for some reason, you're still looking for more? No problem. Though the city may end at certain prescribed borders, shopping doesn't have to end there. Chicago's suburbs also feature some excellent shops and absolutely huge malls where you should be able to find everything you need. (North Side)

GURNEE MILLS
6170 W. Grand Ave., Gurnee, IL
847/263-7500

Even with so many great stores in the city, some people still find it necessary to drive 45 minutes north of Chicago on I-94 to go shopping. But then again, this is Gurnee Mills, and stories are plentiful of people who have flown in from across the Atlantic just to get a few bargains at this gigantic shopping mall. They say the money they saved on clothing more than made up for the airfare. Featuring literally hundreds of bargain-priced outlet stores, Gurnee Mills includes a Lord & Taylor Clearance Center, a JC Penny Outlet, Spiegel Outlet Store, TJ Maxx, Marshalls, Saks Fifth Avenue Outlet Store, The Gap Outlet, Bugle Boy Outlet, Bigsby & Kruthers Clearance Store, and many more in a noisy and somewhat hectic setting. (Greater Chicago)

NikeTown, p. 161

T. Bishop and M. Yossiffon

OLD ORCHARD SHOPPING CENTER
Old Orchard Rd. and Skokie Blvd., Skokie 847/674-7070

This was one of the Chicago area's first outdoor shopping malls and it just keeps getting larger. Now containing nearly 150 stores—and continually expanding—Old Orchard can be a nightmare to navigate (especially during weekends and the holiday season). But, for those who want to hit all of the major department stores in a short amount of time, this is tough to beat. Here you can find spacious branches of Marshall Field's, Saks Fifth Avenue, Nordstrom, and Barnes & Noble, as well as a great assortment of restaurants and a multiplex movie theater. (Greater Chicago)

WOODFIELD MALL
Woodfield Rd. at Rte. 53 S.,

Woodfield
847/330-1537

Located 40 minutes northwest of the Loop in Schaumburg, the Woodfield Mall isn't exactly convenient. The 285 stores in this mall, however, make the trip worthwhile. Stores include Nordstrom, Marshall Field's, JC Penny, and Lord & Taylor. (Greater Chicago)

NOTABLE BOOKSTORES AND NEWSSTANDS

ACT ONE
2540 N. Lincoln Ave.
773/348-6757

It may seem surprising that a city with such a rich theatrical culture has only one theater bookstore, but this one is so comprehensive that a second isn't really necessary. Stacked full of play scripts, career guides, how-tos, and books about the theater and film industries, this is the major literary headquarters for Chicago's thespians. If you're looking for any play old or new, you'll be hard-pressed not to find it here. And, if you don't see it, they'll special-order it for you. (North Side)

AFROCENTRIC BOOKSTORE
234 S. Wabash Ave.
312/929-1956
This is probably the best place to find books relating to the city's considerable African American heritage as well as books by African American authors often overlooked by the major chain stores. The store's motto is "Seeing the world through an Afrikan point of view." (Downtown)

B. DALTON BOOKSELLERS
175 W. Jackson Blvd.
312/922-5219
and
129 N. Wabash Ave.
312/236-7515
One of the last remaining booksellers in the Loop, B. Dalton is a good spot for purchasing new releases, best sellers, and gift items. The store also contains a decent collection of literature and a number of well-thumbed periodicals. (Downtown)

BARNES & NOBLE BOOKSELLERS
659 W. Diversey Ave.
773/871-9003
and
1441 W. Webster Ave.
773/871-3619
Though this is a chain bookstore, it is one of the most comfortable and elegant. With its subdued lighting, Barnes & Noble more closely resembles a library than its bright and noisy competitor Borders. Packed with books on every subject imaginable, Barnes & Noble also offers ample café space, an excellent selection of periodicals, and occasional author readings. (North Side)

BOOKSELLERS ROW
408 S. Michigan Ave.
312/427-4242
Next to the Fine Arts movie theaters in the Fine Arts Building, this used-books store is a good place to stop and browse through paperbacks before catching a new hit French film. The store has a great selection of used books about Chicago. (Near South)

BORDERS BOOKS & MUSIC
2817 N. Clark St.
773/935-3909
and
830 N. Michigan Ave.
312/573-0564
Some people like their bookstores quiet and reserved; Borders Books & Music is anything but. Crammed wall-to-wall with several floors of books, Borders is the intellectual singles bar of the 21st century. With an excellent collection of sale books and literature, Borders is a bustling spot where people spend hours exchanging phone numbers, sipping coffee, and sometimes reading books. (North Side and Near North)

EUROPA BOOKS
832 N. State St.
312/335-9677
Just in and hoping to catch up on the news in Paris, London, or Spain? Hoping to read something in a language other than English? Europa Books (which also has an outpost in the Wrigleyville area) is the city's premier stocker of foreign books, magazines, and newspapers. Europa specializes in Europe and the romance languages with excellent collections of French, German, and Spanish books and newspapers. (Downtown)

POWELL'S BOOKSTORES
1501 E. 57th St.
773/955-7780
and
2850 N. Lincoln Ave.
773/248-1444

If you had a grandfather who was a professor and he had an immense basement, it might have looked something like this. Slightly musty but none the worse for wear, Powell's boasts an excellent collection of used books from every discipline imaginable. Filled with nooks and crannies where you may discover long-sought-after, out-of-print volumes, this is a book-lover's paradise. (South and North Sides)

SEMINARY CO-OP BOOKSTORE
5757 S. University Ave.
773/752-4381

This is where many University of Chicago students shop for their texts, so sometimes it can get pretty crowded in this maze-like bookstore that recalls a scene out of a Jorge Luis Borges short story. But the store's selection of scholarly and literary works is amazing and one could spend days here exploring all the nooks and crannies. The Seminary also runs 57th Street Books in Hyde Park (1301 E. 57th St., 773/684-1300) and AC McClurg Bookstore at Newberry Library (60 W. Walton St., 312/235-3520). (South Side)

Chicago Park District

9

SPORTS AND RECREATION

Here's the first thing you need to know about this city: Chicago is a sports town. This city lives, drinks, breathes, sleeps, dreams, and even plays sports sometimes. There are two sports-talk radio stations in Chicago and even more sports-talk radio shows. Chicago has two professional baseball teams here. It's also home to the most storied franchise in the history of the National Football League, one of the original six members of the National Hockey League, and the greatest dynasty in the history of the National Basketball Association (Boston Celtics fans are entitled to insert their comments here). And, on top of that, there's professional soccer, minor league hockey and baseball, and a slew of college and high school teams drawing huge crowds at every game they play.

Now if that weren't enough to make this a town bursting at the seams with sports, then you have the people of the city. And though they may love to watch the Bears, the Hawks, the Cubs, the Northwestern Wildcats, and the DePaul Blue Demons fight it out, they love to play sports even more. No matter what the weather might be, they are out there. In the 100-plus-degree heat with 100-percent humidity, they are there in the parks, sweating it out playing pick-up basketball, 16-inch softball, fast-pitch, soccer, and tennis, or maybe just casually biking through the parks or strolling along a nature trail. And, when the temperatures dip way below zero and you can almost see your breath forming frost on the air, they are still out there, ice-skating in the city's rinks, jogging through the snow along the lakefront, warming their hands over a garbage-can fire as they drop their fishing lines into holes in the frozen lake. And if they're not there, most likely they're inside in the fieldhouses and the fitness clubs, pretending it's summer and that they're sweating in the hot August sun.

TRIVIA

The first professional baseball all-star game was held in Chicago at old Comiskey Park in 1933. The American League defeated the National League 4–2 and, not surprisingly, a Babe Ruth home run was the decisive factor in the A.L.'s victory.

PROFESSIONAL SPORTS

Baseball

A city rivaled in baseball futility only by Boston, Chicago is home to broken dreams and desperate hopes which spring eternal . . . or at least until October when the Cubs and the White Sox are usually watching the World Series on big-screen TVs from the comfort of their luxurious sofas.

The **Chicago Cubs**, whose last World Series appearance came in 1945, play in the nation's most picturesque baseball park: **Wrigley Field** (1060 W. Addison). With its ivy-covered brick outfield walls, manually operated scoreboard, its predilection for daytime baseball, and its proximity to the hopping Lakeview neighborhood, Wrigley is a fantastic tourist sight no matter what the score is or what place the Cubs manage to find themselves. Despite the 1998 passing of legendary broadcaster Harry Caray, it is difficult to beat a warm summer day in the Wrigley Field bleachers with its legendary "bleacher bums" and the emergence of outfielder Sammy Sosa as a bonafide superstar. And, though there was much civic outcry in 1988 when the Cubs finally acquired lights, abandoning their long-standing tradition of day-only baseball, even purists have to admit that there are few sights more stunning than Wrigley Field at night. Wrigley Field is just a few short steps away from the Addison El stop on the Engelwood-Howard line. Tickets may be purchased at the box office or by calling either 312/831-CUBS in Illinois or 800/347-CUBS from out of state.

The new **Comiskey Park** (333 W. 35th St.), home to the **Chicago White Sox,** who last won the American League pennant in 1959, is not quite so picturesque and, even with the presence of future Hall of Fame slugger Frank Thomas, it has been difficult to lure fans to this somewhat soulless baseball facility on the South Side. Nevertheless, if you avoid the acrophobiac's nightmare of the upper-deck seats and don't have a problem with the White Sox management's tendency to hire damaged rent-a-players as bargain-basement stopgaps, it is difficult to go wrong with the intimacy of the lower deck and the stadium's elaborate concessions, which offer everything from traditional ballpark hot dogs to deli sandwiches to *churros* to excellent bratwurst. The exploding scoreboard, which erupts with fireworks whenever a hometown slugger lofts a home run, was the brainchild of Bill Veeck, the baseball pioneer who owned the Sox in the 1970s. The scoreboard also has a Diamondvision instant replay and video display feature which often seems to get more attention than the action on the field. The stadium is readily accessible by the El. Tickets are almost always available at the box office or in advance by calling 312/831-1769.

For more affordable family-style baseball entertainment, the **Kane County Cougars** minor league baseball team has proven to be a hot ticket as well.

Basketball

The imminent departure of basketball's greatest player of all-time, Michael Jordan, may be a cause for immense civic distress. But it will also mean that tickets will be easier to get. Ever since the **Chicago Bulls** began their six-time championship run in 1991, every game has sold out and scalpers and ticket brokers usually can get at least $75 a head even for standing-room tickets. Good seats at the **United Center** (1901 W. Madison Street) can easily equal the price of a night in a presidential suite at one of Chicago's luxury hotels. If you're feeling lucky, though, you can try calling Ticketmaster at 312/559-1212. But you're better off trying to find a slovenly individual on the street with a couple of seats that he's selling on the sly. Scalping, may we remind you, is illegal. But what's the chance of spending the night in the clink with a hefty fine when compared to the chance to see "Da Bulls" in action. It's probably best to drive or take a taxi here, but if you feel like taking public transportation through some rather seedy sections of town, try the #20 Madison Street bus. Or, if you're less of a risk taker, step aboard the #19 Stadium Express bus which goes back and forth from Michigan and Chicago Avenues on the Magnificent Mile to the United Center when the Bulls are playing.

If you're a basketball fan and not just a Bulls fan, you might have better luck and actually a better time checking out the college basketball

The Cubs at Wrigley Field

T. Bishop and M. Yossiffon

scene. Tickets for **DePaul Blue Demons** (Rosemont Horizon, 773/362-8000), the **Loyola Ramblers** (6525 N. Sheridan Rd., 773/508-2560), **Northwestern University Wildcats** (1705 Ashland Ave., Evanston, 847/491-7887), and the **UIC Flames** (1150 W. Harrison St., 312/413-5700) games are all easier and cheaper to obtain.

Football

Michael McCaskey, CEO of the **Chicago Bears**, has been threatening for years to move his storied NFL franchise founded by the legendary George Halas and take it to the northwest suburbs or Gary, Indiana, where he can get a better deal than at the Chicago Park District's **Soldier Field** (425 E. McFetridge Dr.). But until he does, there is nothing like the experience of sitting all bundled up in this brutally cold 1924 stadium with the winds whipping off a frozen Lake Michigan. True, it is tough to find a more bone-chilling

---

Chicago Bears in the Hall of Fame

The Chicago Bears, winners of Super Bowl XX in 1986 (a 46–10 victory over the New England Patriots), have long been a team of legends. The Bears have more long-time team members in the Pro Football Hall of Fame than does any other team in the National Football League. These members include:

George Halas	Sid Luckman
Jimmy Conzelman	Clyde "Bulldog" Turner
John "Paddy" Driscoll	George McAfee
Guy Chamberlin	George Blanda
George Trafton	Bobby Layne
Ed Healy	George Connor
Red Grange	Bill George
Bronko Nagurski	Doug Atkins
Bill Hewitt	Gale Sayers
Roy "Link" Lyman	Dick Butkus
George Musso	Mike Ditka
Walt Kiesling	Walter Payton
Dan Fortmann	Mike Singletary
Joe Stydahar	

---

experience than watching the Bears take on the Tampa Bay Buccaneers in mid-December. But this is football after all, and Chicago has produced more than a few tough guys over the years from Mike Ditka to Dick Butkus to Bronko Nagurski to Walter Payton to Bob Avellini. A bit of the tough veneer may have worn off the Bears over the past 10 years or so since "Da Coach" Ditka was fired and replaced by the far less charismatic Dave Wannstedt. But the fans are as hard-nosed and committed as always and all of them still have fresh in their minds the Bears' 1986 Super Bowl drubbing of the New England Patriots to keep a warm glow about them. Soldier Field is a relatively easy mile-and-a-half walk from the Loop and is also accessible via the #146 State Street bus. Tickets are usually only available via scalpers or ticket brokering services, but if the Bears' mediocrity continues on into the next millennium, you might try scooping up some tickets from the box office.

A cheaper and more subdued football choice is the **Northwestern University** team which, though it has finally attained a certain level of respectability, can still be a relatively easy ticket. The **Wildcats** play at Ryan Field (1501 Central Ave.). For ticket information, call 847/491-7503.

Hockey

The **Chicago Black Hawks** do play in the same facility as the Chicago Bulls, but that's where the similarities end. Though the Bulls have attracted an increasingly corporate crowd as clients are wooed in plush skyboxes or near center court, the Black Hawks remain a more blue-collar (if still somewhat expensive) form of entertainment. Though a far cry from the days of the Chicago Stadium, which used to be clouded by a nearly impenetrable fog of cigarette smoke and eau-de-Stroh's by third period, the **United Center** (1901 W. Madison St., 312/455-7000) still is a rather raucous facility when the Hawks are playing, particularly when their arch-rival Detroit Red Wings are in town. A storied franchise which still hasn't been able to escape the stigma of having let Bobby Hull ("The Golden Jet")—one of the greatest players of all time—jump to Winnipeg of the World Hockey Association, the Black Hawks have not won a championship since 1961. And, owner Bill Wirtz, who still refuses to broadcast home games on TV, is far from the most popular figure in town. But the boisterous faithful still turn out in droves to cheer on Tony Amonte and the next generation of Hawks. As with the Chicago Bulls, to get here you can just get on the #19 Stadium Express bus which goes back and forth from Michigan and Chicago Avenues on the Magnificent Mile to the United Center when the Hawks are playing.

A cheaper hockey option may be had with the relatively new **Chicago Wolves** minor league hockey team in the International Hockey League. The team plays at the **Rosemont Horizon** (6920 N. Mannheim Rd., 847/635-6601).

Horse Racing

The announced closing in 1998 of **Arlington International Racecourse** cast a dim glow on the future of one of the more storied aspects of Chicago life.

TRIVIA

Though their name might suggest otherwise, the Harlem Globetrotters actually began life not far from Chicago in Hinckley, Illinois. They were founded here by Chicago native Abe Saperstein in 1927.

Arlington was arguably the most luxurious and popular racecourse in town and its closing leaves the Chicago area with three major horse-racing facilities. These are the **Hawthorn Race Course** (3501 S. Laramie Ave., 708/780-3700), which offers both harness and thoroughbed racing; **Maywood Park** (North and 5th Aves., 630/343-4800); and **Sportsman's Park** (708/652-2812), which presents thoroughbred racing in the summer. If you don't have time to get to these facilities, you can still put down a bet at one of the city's off-track betting parlors (233 W. Jackson Blvd., 312/427-2300; or 177 N. State St., 312/419-8787) Downtown in the Loop.

Soccer

Though everybody keeps saying that soccer will be the sport of the 21st century, Chicago has been slow to catch on. The 1994 World Cup did bring sell-out crowds to Chicago's **Soldier Field**, but there was little crossover into general interest in the sport. There have been a number of attempts to bring both indoor and outdoor professional soccer into Chicago, most notably with the Chicago Sting who were a relatively hot ticket during the heyday of the National American Soccer League in the early 1980s. The current pro soccer franchise is the **Chicago Fire** who play at Soldier Field. But truth be told, the best soccer is not being played on the professional level. By far, the most exciting games are played on weekends in the summer on the soccer fields near **Montrose Beach** (4600 N. Lake Shore Dr.). Here, Spanish is the only language spoken and a furiously competitive but sportsmanlike atmosphere pervades as dozens of amateur teams square off against each other for world-class soccer matches. The sidelines swarm with vendors selling nachos and cheese with jalapeño peppers and deliciously refreshing fruit bars, of which mango and coconut are the two best flavors. It's a truly exciting and entertaining multicultural experience.

RECREATION

Basketball

Anyone who's seen the movie *Hoop Dreams*, the great Chicago-made documentary about inner-city high school students trying to succeed in hoops, knows that pickup basketball games are part and parcel of the city's urban atmosphere. Helped by a generous donation from the Chicago Bulls organization, the city is now teeming with basketball courts and anyone with a basketball and some guts can get up a game. Some of the most highly contested games usually can be found near the housing projects, most notably **Cabrini Green** (418 W. Oak St.), but this is far from a safe neighborhood and, though the competition and the camaraderie are great on the court, the risks of walking around here might not be worth it. Safer choices include **Green Briar Park** (6501 N. Peterson Ave.), the schoolyard at **Gordon Technical High School** (3633 N. California Ave.), and the courts at **Warren Park** (6621 N. Washtenaw Ave.). But these choices only scratch feebly at the surface of an overwhelming basketball scene that is one of the most enjoyable aspects of a Chicago summer. Note also that every summer the city holds a three-on-three basketball tournament at **Grant Park** on Columbus Drive.

Batting Cages

Though to some it may seem like a rather sophomoric form of entertainment, lots of Chicagoans of all ages still limber up to step into the city's batting cages to practice their baseball swings as a machine hurls ball after ball at varying speeds into their strike zones. The best batting cages in the city can be found at **Novelty Golf** (3650 W. Devon Ave., Lincolnwood, 847/679-9434). Another and more convenient choice is **Wrigleyville's Sluggers** (3540 N. Clark St., 773/248-0055), which boasts a middle-of-the-road singles bar on the first floor and a second floor filled with arcade games and indoor batting cages. Here you will find twenty-somethings—sometimes sober, sometimes not—swinging away either at major-league fastballs or easier-to-hit, floating softballs.

Biking

Bike-riding in the city is far from a placid activity. Unless you're a professional bike messenger, it's likely that you'll find weaving your way in and out of bike-hostile traffic to be a hair-raising experience akin to a daredevil stunt performed by Evil Kneivel. The one exception within the city is the unfortunately crowded, yet still highly picturesque 15-mile-plus **Lakefront Bike Trail.** It's not difficult to find. Just head for the lake and follow the yellow lines either south to the Museum of Science and Industry or north to the end of Lake Shore Drive. From here you can continue your journey north by following the signs all the way into Evanston and the northern suburbs. If, on the other hand, you were hoping to get out of the city and do some biking on more rugged terrain or at least with some trees around you, the **North Branch Bike Trail** is another good option. Starting on the northwest side of Chicago at Caldwell Woods (Devon and Caldwell, 800/870-3666), this beautiful 20-mile trail will take you all the way to the exquisite Chicago Botanic Garden (U.S. 41 and Lake Cook Rd.). The ride is wonderfully leisurely and the trail is somewhat less crowded than Chicago's lakefront. One of the more challenging rides around is the 8 1/2-mile **Fox River Trail** (708/232-5980), beginning in Elgin, Illinois. This one swoops by rivers, marshes and a waterfall before it gets to Illinois Highway 64. To the south of the city is a new 12-mile-long route: The **Old Plank Road Trail** goes from Logan Park in Park

Forest all the way to Will County's Hickory Creek Junction Forest Preserve along the path of what was once an abandoned railroad. The 11-mile-long **Busse Woods Bicycle Trail**, beginning at the Ned Brown Preserve (847/366-9420), is another option. If you didn't have the forethought to bring a bike with you, you can always rent one at **Turin Bicycle** (1027 Davis St., 847/864-7660), which has locations in Evanston and at North Pier (312/923-0100); or you can pop by at various locations on the bicycle trail along the lakefront and rent one from **Bike Chicago** (312/944-2337).

Billiards and Pool

Martin Scorsese didn't shoot *The Color of Money* (sequel to the 1960s classic *The Hustler*) in Chicago by accident. He knew, like all Chicagoans do, that this is a pool-playing kind of town. In a city known for its cons, hustles, and swindles, pool is a game of choice. Chicagoans don't speak softly and carry a big stick; they speak loudly and they carry a pool cue. And there are a number of places where they wield them. One of the best is **Chris' Billiards** (4637 N. Milwaukee Ave., 773/286-4714). It has 45 pool tables, plus tables for billiards and snooker, and holds many weekly competitions. Part of *The Color of Money* was shot here. Another great and atmospheric pool hall is **Marie's Golden Cue** (3241 W. Montrose Ave., 773/478-2555). A fun location for some excellent competitive pool playing is **St. Paul Billiards** (1415 W. Fullerton Ave., 773/472-9494), where *The Color of Money* was also shot. Of course, if you need some other distractions, there are many fine taverns in the city where you can get a shot and a beer along with your pool game. For this sort of pool playing (especially since archaic licensing laws prohibit the sale of alcohol in billiard parlors), check out the **Gingerman Tavern** (3740 N. Clark St., 773/549-2050) or the **Red Line Tap** (7000 N. Glenwood Ave., 773/465-8005).

Bowling

Though it may not be high up on the list of tourist attractions in any city (Milwaukee might provide a notable exception), Chicago does certainly offer a variety of options for the bowling addict. There are dozens of lanes open at all hours in Chicago. Among the more atmospheric options are **Waveland Bowl** (3700 N. Western Ave., 773/472-5900), a raucous North Side establishment where bowlers of every race, creed, and color imaginable gather until the wee hours of the morning (Waveland is open 24 hours). Late-night bowling is also available at **Diversey River Bowl** (2211 W. Diversey Ave., 773/227-5800), a favorite choice of many local rock 'n' rollers. For more old-fashioned bowling entertainment, check out **Southport Lanes** (3325 N. Southport Ave., 773/472-1601), the only bowling facility in town which still employs pin boys.

Casinos

No matter what you may have heard or what movies you may have seen, gambling is pretty much illegal in Chicago with the exception of the occasional off-track betting parlor. Though there have long been rumors of attempts to reconfigure antigambling legislation to allow gambling boats to

Tennis on Chicago's public courts, p.194

Chicago Park District

dock close to Navy Pier, or at least somewhere within the city limits, you still have to drive quite a ways out of town if you want to shoot craps, play blackjack, or try your luck at the roulette wheel. Pity the poor hydrophobic gambler, because pretty much the only options you have are aboard riverboats. The **Hollywood Casino Aurora** (800/888-7777) has made one of the biggest splashes on the relatively new casino scene, offering Las Vegas–style entertainment featuring national comedians (i.e., Don Rickles) as well as opportunities to meet celebrity athletes while playing the slots, blackjack, and the like. **Empress River Casino** (Joliet, 888/4-EMPRESS) offers tons of slot machines and card games as it cruises around scenic Joliet, home to both the notorious Stateville Correctional Center and White Fence Farm, a long-time country-style dining favorite with the best corn fritters in town. And, finally, just over the Indiana border, there is another gambling mecca of sorts, the **Majestic Star** (E. Chicago, Indiana, 800/746-9262).

Day Hikes

For some, walking from the Mag Mile to the Loop and back with armloads of shopping bags is enough of a hike; and if you make the wrong turn in Downtown Chicago and start running you may indeed have experienced sufficient exertion. However, if your idea of hiking involves nature trails, forests full of pine, and small woodland animals scampering past you, you'll have to venture a little bit outside the city limits. In Barrington at the **Crabtree Nature Center** (Palatine Road a half-mile east of Algonquin, 847/381-6592), there are three short nature trails that curve their way over, around, and through marshes and ponds. If you're quiet, you might see a fox or a frog or two. Way to the north of the city, almost by the Wisconsin border, is **Illinois Beach State Park** (Sheridan and Wadsworth Rds., 847/662-4811), a scenic location that will hopefully continue to improve with the recent closing of the nuclear power plant in Zion, Illinois. With its sand dunes, immense varieties of birds, and occasional cactus, the state park offers several different trails that range from a simple half-mile jaunt to rugged trails through forests and beside the lakefront. Though it's perhaps not the most exciting of the trails, the one that wins points for the best name is the 1 1/2-mile "Dead River Trail." Also to the north of the city, but not quite as much of a trek, is the **Ryerson Conservation Area** (21950 N. Riverwoods Rd., 847/948-7750) in suburban Deerfield. On the site of what were once Indian trails, Ryerson offers not-particularly-taxing, but still-scenic hikes along the Des Plaines River and beside forests of maple trees. Another northerly choice may be found at the **Chicago Botanic Garden** (U.S. 41 and Lake Cook Rd.), which offers a 2 1/2-mile trail through its immaculate gardens. There are also excellent short trails through the stunning 1,500-acre **Morton Arboretum** (Route 53 and the East West Tollway, 708/968-0074) in Lisle, Illinois, about 45 minutes west of downtown Chicago. See Kids' Stuff for more information about the arboretum.

Fast-Pitch

Who says that to play baseball you need nine guys on a side? That's not the Chicago way to play. The game here is called "Fast-Pitch" and all you need is two people, a bat, a mitt, a rubber ball, and a brick wall with a strike zone painted on it. The latter can be found on many a Chicago public school building (you can even paint your own, though this is against the law). Though the game might not be as popular as it was in the '70s and '80s, there is still a contingent of die-hard fast-pitch players that gathers every summer weekend on the schoolyards for games. Just remember that a line drive past the pitcher is a single, a considerable distance further is a double, just in front of the fence is a triple, and over the fence and out onto the street is a home run. You can make any place into your own fast-pitch field, but two popular spots are the school-yards of the **Daniel Boone Elementary School** (6701 N. California) and **Dewitt Clinton Elementary School** (6110 N. Fairfield St.).

Fishing in Chicago

Chicago Park District

Fishing

One doesn't generally go into a restaurant and hear a waiter waxing eloquently about the quality of Lake Michigan fish. But that doesn't mean that there's not a lot of fishing to be done in the Chicago area. In fact, Lake Michigan and the city's rivers are teeming with fish. Even Lake Michigan on its own, all 976,000 acres of it in the state of Illinois, can be a great place to catch brown trout, chinook and coho salmon, lake and rainbow trout, smallmouth bass, smelt, and yellow perch. The Chicago Park District lagoons are fairly well stocked with catfish. Some of these include **Riis Park** (6100 W. Fullerton Ave.), Lincoln Park (2045 N. Lincoln Park West), **Gompers Park** (4224 W. Foster Ave.), and **Jackson Park** (6401 S. Stony Island Ave.). Outside of the city, but still in Cook County, there's a fair amount of carp, catfish, walleye, and small and largemouth bass to be had. For a more complete list or information on any of these fishing spots, stop by any bait shop in Chicago and pick up a copy of *Illinois Fishing Information,* a very comprehensive free guide to fishing in the state put out by the Illinois Department of Natural Resources. One of the best bait and fishing supply shops in the city area can be found in Bridgeport at **Henry's Sports & Bait Shop** (3130 S. Canal St., 312/225-FISH).

In Lake Michigan, some people just drop their lines at **Diversey Harbor** (2800 N. and Lake Michigan), but if you want to try your luck out on the stormy Lake Michigan waters, there are a decent number of charter boats, including **Captain Bob's Charters** (888/829-FISH), which offers sportfishing for salmon and trout. A more complete list of these sorts of charters can be obtained from the **Chicago Sportfishing Association** (312/922-1100).

One of the most popular times of year for fishing in the city is in the early spring from March 1 to April 30. You may wonder why when you drive by the lake at night during these times that you see bursts of starry light and fires blazing. These are the haunts of the smelters who gather by the lake to ensnare the silvery fish that are such a popular Midwest delicacy, particularly when they're breaded and fried. The most popular locations range from **Montrose** (4600 North) and Lake Michigan all the way south to **22nd Street** (2200 South) and Lake Michigan. Just look for the lights and the fires. Unfortunately, even for the smelt, you need a license. For more information on how to get one call 800/ASK-FISH.

Fitness Clubs

Most of the major hotels in Chicago offer their own health-club facilities or make arrangements with nearby athletic facilities to give their guests temporary memberships. If this isn't the case where you're staying, you can try getting a short-term guest membership at some of the better clubs in the city. Try either of the excellent **Lakeshore Athletic Clubs** (441 N. Wabash Ave. in Downtown Chicago, 312/644-4880; or 1320 W. Fullerton Ave. on the North Side, 773/477-9888), or go to the pricey see-and-be-seen **East Bank Club** (500 N. Kingsbury St., 312/527-5800), which is where Chicago's rich, famous, and wanna-be-influential work out.

Golf

Since the Chicago area is home to the Western Open, you'd expect to find some good golfing options within and outside of the city limits. And you'd be right. The Chicago Park district has very affordable golfing facilities, including one 18-hole course and five nine-hole courses. **Jackson Park** on the city's South Side (Hayes Dr., just west of Lake Shore Dr.) has an 18-hole, par-69 course measuring 5,538 yards. The 11th hole is the most challenging of them all with its trees and water hazards. A driving range is located adjacent to the course. Greens fees here range from $14.50 to $15.50. The nine-hole **Columbus Golf Course** (5700 W. Jackson Blvd.) is located on the West Side. Greens fees here are $10. To the south, the 3,333-yard **Marquette Golf Course** (Kedzie Ave. and Marquette Rd.) wins points for its lush fairways and greens. Fees here are $10.50 to $12.00. **Robert A. Black Golf Course** on the Far North Side (Pratt and Western Ave.) is the newest park district course. This 2,600-yard course is immaculate and pristine, and is located by the always-hopping Warren Park. Greens fees here are $10.00 to $12.50. The most visible of the city's courses is the **Sidney R. Marovitz Golf Course**, located on the North Side just to the east of scenic Lake Shore Drive (Lake Shore Dr. and Irving Park Rd.). Greens fees are $13.00 to $14.50. On the South Side near the beautifully restored **South Shore Cultural Center** (71st St. and South Shore) is the South Shore Country Club. Greens fees are $10.00 to $11.50. If you just feel like hitting a bucket of balls, there is a very popular driving range near **Diversey Harbor** (2800 N. Lake Shore Dr.). For reservations or information about tee times at the Chicago Park District golf courses, call 312/245-0909.

Outside the city there are a huge number of golfing options available ranging from **Cantigny** (27W270 Mack Rd., Wheaton, 630/668-3323) to **Kemper Lakes** (Old McHenry Rd., Long Grove, 847/320-3450) to literally hundreds of others. For more information contact **Chicagoland Golf** (630/719-1000); or turn to the center section in your copy of the Yellow Pages, which has a surprisingly in-depth roundup of all of the major golf courses in and around the Chicago area.

On the other hand, if your idea of golf involves small clubs, turning windmills, and amusing statuary, you might try a couple of the better miniature golf establishments around town. The best of these are **Novelty Golf** (3650 W. Devon Ave., Lincolnwood, 847/679-9434) and, about 40 minutes to the north of the city, **Par-King Skill Golf** (6700 W. Dempster St., Morton Grove, 847/965-3333).

Kites

Why bother coming to the windy city if you're not going to take advantage of the wind. Actually, sometimes the wind whips off Lake Michigan with so much force that even the most experienced of kite operators will turn into hapless Charlie Browns. Still, if you wish to try your luck with the fickle winds of the city, there are several places to do it. About all you need is a kite, a clear and not-too-still day, and a good expanse of open space. One of the most popular spots for kite flying in the city is **Cricket Hill**, a small hill just beyond the soccer field by **Montrose Beach** (4600 N. Lake Shore Dr.). More good open space can be found to the northwest at **Caldwell Woods** (Devon Ave. and Caldwell Sts.). During the week, when there isn't some huge summer festival going on, you might

Carolyn Crimi

Novelty Golf

even try your luck with **Grant Park** (251 S. Columbus Dr.), where you can sail your kite against the backdrop of the city's tallest skyscrapers. If you didn't plan ahead and forgot to pack a kite in your suitcase, no need to cry. There are several good places to choose from a huge selection of kites, most notably **Stanton Hobby Shop** (4718 N. Milwaukee Ave., 773/283-6446) or **A Kite Harbor** at North Pier (435 E. Illinois St., 312/321-5483).

Sailing

Lake Michigan is one of the more unpredictable bodies of water around and even on clear, windless days the white caps can make sailing surprisingly choppy. Still, this is a wonderful place to sail and if you're interested in renting a boat, you can do it at the **Chicago Sailing Club at Belmont Harbor** (3200 N. and the lake) or you can take a couple of lessons at **Fairwind Sail Charters at Burnham Harbor** near Adler Planetarium (1300 S. Lake Shore Dr.).

Skating

When the city has trouble leasing a large plot of land, that's bad news for business, but it's good news for ice-skaters. At least that's the case with the **Loop's Skate on State** (State St. between Washington and Randolph Sts., 312/744-3315). Here, a long-vacant city block has been converted into the city's most popular ice-skating rink. Weather permitting, during the winter, you can skate here for two hours at a time just for a dollar; skate rentals are reasonable, too. There is also outdoor wintertime skating at **Daley Bicentennial Plaza** (337 E. Randolph St., 312/742-7650), which offers both a pristine rink and great views of the city from 10 in the morning to 10 at night for just two bucks a throw. In Hyde Park you can skate at the mile-long **Midway Plaisance** (near 57th and Woodlawn). If you happen to be closer to O'Hare Airport, there is ice-skating available at the **Franklin Park District's** (9711 W. Waveland Ave., 847/671-4755) ice rink. Indoor skating is possible at **McFetridge Sports Center** (3845 N. California Ave., 312/ 742-7585).

For rollerskating or in-line skating, check out **Rainbo** (4836 N. Clark St., 773/251-5668), the major indoor rink in town. In-line skaters also tend to favor the lakefront bike trail (see Biking, above). If you are particularly adept at in-line skating, you might want to try and get in on a game of roller hockey—played at an amateur level in the parking lot by **Diversey Harbor** (2800 N. Lake Shore Dr.)—where skaters demonstrate their stick-handling skills while trying to shoot a ball between a pair of garbage cans.

TRIVIA

America's first auto race was held in Chicago, beginning at Jackson Park on the South Side. Held on Thanksgiving Day in 1895, the race was a 90-mile round-trip between Jackson Park and Waukegan, Illinois. The winning vehicle was a Duryea, and drivers Frank and Charles Duryea, who boasted a whopping 7½-miles-per-hour average speed, took home $2,000 in prize money for their victory.

Skiing

Downhill skiing is a tall and difficult order in the city limits. And if you don't feel like driving toward Michigan or Wisconsin, it might be tough to satisfy your need. That said, cross-country skiing is a possibility. Once in a while you might see some optimistic soul with cross-country skis sliding his or her way along the **Lincoln Park** bike trail after a particularly brutal snow, but this is far from the best place in town for cross-country skiing. The best choices, especially the **Herrick Lake Forest Preserves** in Wheaton and **Waterfall Glen Trails** in Darien, are located in DuPage County.

Softball

Four inches might not seem to be a big thing, but when it comes to softball, it means the difference between Chicago and everywhere else in the country. While softball is played nearly everywhere with a 12-inch ball and a mitt, here Chicagoans pride themselves on playing with a 16-inch softball and catching it bare-handed. Outsiders might look peculiarly upon that seemingly giant sailing ball, but for Chicagoans that 16-incher is every bit as much a part of the city's fabric as hot dogs, deep-dish pizza, and voter fraud. The games are usually well organized with hundreds of teams and leagues throughout the city, but if you want to watch or try your hand, some of your best bets are at **Riis Park** (6100 W. Fullerton Ave.), **Peterson Park** (5601 N. Pulaski St.), the southern tip of **Grant Park** (Jackson Blvd. and Columbus Dr.), or the southern end of **Lincoln Park** (2045 N. Lincoln Park West), where dozens of softball squads play every weekend in the summer.

Swimming

So the lake's not big enough for you and you're looking for somewhere else to swim. Actually, that's not a bad idea considering that even on some of the summer's warmest days, the lake temperature barely rises above 60 degrees. And though there is certainly more than enough space to swim in Lake Michigan, the lifeguards are pretty vigilant about keeping people within rather confined boundaries given the unpredictability and the strong currents of the lake.

Fortunately, if you feel like swimming and your hotel pool is either too small, too crowded, or non-existent, there are still options available; the best of these are at the **Chicago Park District fieldhouses**. Here you'll find spacious swimming pools that are surprisingly empty on weekdays. And the price (free of charge) is unbeatable. Some Chicago Park District natatorium choices include **Curie Park** (4949 S. Archer St., 312/747-6098), **Gill Park** (825 W. Sheridan Rd., 312/742-7802), **Welles Park** (2333 W. Sunnyside, 312/742-7515), **Independence Park** (3945 N. Springfield Ave., 312/742-7590), **Portage Park** (4101 N. Central Ave., 312/742-7612), **Eckhart Park** (1330 W. Chicago Ave., 312/746-5490), and **Kosciuszko Park** (2732 N. Avers Ave., 312/746-5316).

If it's a beautiful summer day and you prefer to swim at the beach, the further north or south you are from the Magnificent Mile the better off you're going to be in terms of crowds. To the north, the beaches at **Montrose Avenue** (4600 N. Lake Shore Dr.) are usually going to be far less crowded than **Oak Street Beach**. To the south, try **Promontory Point** (5941 N. Lake Shore Dr., 312/747-6620), one of the most scenic swimming areas in the city.

If you are more of a hotel pool kind of person and make your lodging decisions on the basis of swimming facilities, the best hotel swimming pool can be found at the **Hotel Inter-Continental Chicago** (505 N. Michigan Ave., 312/944-4100 or 800/327-0200).

Where Are the Best Beaches?

Chicago's lakefront offers sunning, swimming, strolling, and more. Here are some of the city's best beaches:

North Avenue Beach (1800 N.)
Volleyball central, with decent food provided at an outdoor branch of Ed Debevic's diner.

Oak Street Beach (600 N.)
Chess matches held outside everyday beneath overhang just off Lake Shore Drive.

South Shore Country Club Beach (7100 S.)
Great view of the skyline and the occasional horse (this is where the Chicago Police Department holds its horses.)

Montrose Beach (4400 N.)
One of the least crowded stretches of the lakefront. Good areas for kite-flying, and soccer fields are nearby.

Lunt Avenue Beach (7000 N.)
Excellent people watching and good snacks provided by the Heartland Café.

Lighthouse Beach (Evanston)
Located at the northern border of Evanston near Wilmette. One of the most secluded sections of lakefront for sunbathing or lazing on rocks underneath a wooded area.

Tennis

Those who tend to think of tennis as a rather elitist sport played largely by the upper crust of New England (and old England, for that matter) will be in for quite a surprise when they get to Chicago. With more than six hundred tennis courts in the city itself, there is free tennis available to everyone in every neighborhood. Though there are a few courts Downtown that charge a nominal fee for playing, most notably **Daley Bicentennial Plaza** (337 E. Randolph St., 312/742-7650) and **Lake Shore Park** (808 N. Lake Shore Dr., 312/742-7891), there are equally good courts around that don't cost a dime and provide more of a neighborhood feel. Three of the best-maintained courts are located at **Indian Boundary Park** (2500 W. Lunt Ave., 312/742-7887). Nearby there are three more courts at **Rogers School** (7435 N. Washtenaw Ave.). These are almost always available, but if you take your tennis seriously, the cracks in the cement might put you off your game. The courts at **Warren Park** (6621 N. Washtenaw Ave.) are better. If you drive around the city you're likely to find a great opportunity to try out your tennis wherever you find a spacious park or a decent-sized high school.

Tobogganing

Noteworthy as one of the flattest cities around, Chicago doesn't exactly make for a winter downhill-sports paradise. But if you have a sled, a toboggan, or even an oversized frisbee or cardboard box, you can take advantage of a few hills in and around the Chicago area for some winter fun. **Mount Trashmore** in Evanston (Dodge and Oakton Sts.)—so named for allegedly being built atop a trashheap—won't impress any alpine skiers with its rather modest height. But that doesn't stop Northsiders from taking advantage of the steep, slick inclines. To the south of the city in Palos Park lies **Swallow Cliff Woods** (Hwy. 83 and LaGrange Rd., 708/366-9420), which provides a somewhat hair-raising ride through chutes 90 feet high. Toboggans are available for rental here for three dollars. Within the city limits at **Warren Park** (6621 N. Washtenaw Ave.) is a not-too-tall, not-particularly-challenging hill perfect for youngsters.

Civic Opera House—Tony Romano/Lyric Opera of Chicago

10

THE PERFORMING ARTS

With the exception of New York, Chicago has the most vibrant performing arts scene in the country. Bursting with old, respected theater companies and fresh-faced young troupes determined to make an impression on the scene, Chicago abounds with talent. And, unlike its competitor on the East Coast, the arts are very affordable here. Sure, you can pay $50 a head to see some of the great touring shows at the city's prestigious Downtown theaters, but veer just a little off the beaten path and you can see excellent theater, dance, and classical music performances for as little as five to ten bucks.

Chicago's arts scene exists on a level for every interest and budget. In the mainstream world, the city offers an orchestra generally recognized as one of the finest—if not the finest—in the world; a venerable opera company that attracts all the international stars; and some of the world's most highly respected dance and theater companies. But that only represents a tiny sliver of the sometimes overwhelming arts scene.

On any given weekend, Chicago residents and visitors can choose from more than a hundred plays, from familiar classics to more obscure new works, plus hundreds of concerts, performance art exhibitions, concerts, and dance recitals. Whether you're a fan of old-fashioned Broadway musicals or you're looking for the latest underground thing, you're certain to find what you're looking for here. Sure, much of the greatest talent in the country usually tends to wind up in New York or Hollywood, but Chicago's where they start out and hone their craft. Home to the Chicago Symphony Orchestra, the Lyric Opera, the Goodman Theatre, the Steppenwolf Theatre Company, Second City, the Joffrey Ballet, and Hubbard Street Dance; and having given birth to household names like David Mamet, Elaine May, Mike Nichols, John Malkovich, John Belushi, Laurie Metcalf, Joan Allen, and countless others, Chicago is an explosion of talent, entertainment, and excitement.

What's Going On?

Want to find out what's going on in Chicago in the performing arts scene? The Chicago Sun-Times *and* Chicago Tribune *provide adequate arts coverage, particularly in their Friday sections. But for the most comprehensive and up-to-the-minute listings, especially for off-the-beaten-path events, pick up the* Chicago Reader *(available on Thursday evenings), the city's best free alternative weekly newspaper. The* Reader *provides a lowdown on absolutely everything going down every week. You'll find it in most bookstores, cafés, libraries, and record stores, and on selected streetcorners Downtown and Near North in yellow newspaper boxes.* New City *(available every Wednesday evening), Chicago's other major alternative weekly, is also an excellent entertainment source, though its listings tend to be less reliable.*

MAJOR PERFORMING ARTS VENUES

ARIE CROWN THEATRE
McCormick Place
2301 S. Lake Shore Dr.
312/791-6000
Throughout its history as a theater, dance, and concert hall, Arie Crown has played host to everything from *The King And I*, starring Yul Brynner, to rock acts like Humble Pie and Bob Dylan. The newly redesigned theater, located in the midst of this impossibly huge convention center (home to the annual housewares' convention and the American Booksellers Convention), seats nearly five thousand. It's not much to look at, but it's a fine enough facility should the performers be of interest. (Near South)

APOLLO THEATRE
2540 N. Lincoln Ave.
773/935-6860
A mid-sized but comfortable facility, the Apollo (located not far from De-Paul University on bustling Lincoln Avenue) usually hosts touring productions of national or Off-Broadway musical hits. Recent shows here have included *Always Patsy Cline* and *Ray Davies: Twentieth Century Man.* (North Side)

ATHENAEUM THEATRE
2936 N. Southport Ave.
773/935-6869
Called a temporary home by many of the city's homeless theater companies and dance troupes, the Athenaeum, located in one of the more impressive Chicago churches, has two theater spaces. The larger space, which recalls a 1950s school auditorium, has presented everything here from programs of African dances to productions by Chicago's

esteemed Lookingglass Theatre Company. The smaller studio space is rented to a wide variety of low-budget city theater companies. (North Side)

AUDITORIUM THEATRE
50 E. Congress
312/902-1500

If this isn't the best place in the city to see a concert, dance performance, or musical theater production, it certainly is the most beautiful. Acoustically perfect with excellent sightlines, the Auditorium was designed by Louis Sullivan and Dankmar Adler in 1899 and it is nothing short of stunning. Chicago's most opulent performing arts facility, the Auditorium is worth a tour even when nothing is playing, but that isn't often as the theater has a very packed schedule from major Broadway musicals like *Phantom of the Opera* and *Miss Saigon*, to concert recitals by the world's greatest classical musicians, to dance performances by touring companies. (Downtown)

BRIAR STREET THEATRE
3133 N. Halsted St.
773/348-4000

Owned by Chicago's prestigious Topel family and run by Fox Theatricals, a professional theater production company, Briar Street is a warm and comfortable mid-sized theater which hosts professional touring productions that aren't quite lavish enough to fit into the huge surroundings of the city's downtown theaters. Briar Street has played host to such acts as Jackie Mason and Blue Man Group and has presented such theatrical fare as Alfred Uhry's *Driving Miss Daisy* and Steve Martin's *Picasso at the Lapin Agile*. (North Side)

CHICAGO CULTURAL CENTER
Randolph and Michigan Aves.
312/744-6630

Everything from classical music concerts and theater performances by Chicago's esteemed City Lit Theatre to dance performances by a fair number of city troupes are held at this beautiful landmark location in downtown Chicago. Most notable are the free Wednesday Dame Myra Hess Memorial Concerts, a long-running series of lunchtime classical music concerts. (Downtown)

CHICAGO THEATRE
175 N. State St.
312/902-1500

Once a motion picture and vaudeville house that played host to performers such as Frank Sinatra, Jack Benny, and Danny Kaye, Chicago's most beautiful movie palace fell into disrepair in the 1970s and '80s. Today, however, it's been restored as a luxurious home for popular music concerts and stage shows like the musical *Beauty and the Beast*. The 1921 facility is a spectacle no matter what happens to be playing on its stage. Currently it is leased by Walt Disney. (Downtown)

IVANHOE THEATRE
750 W. Wellington Ave.
773/975-7171

Architecturally speaking, this is a rather peculiar facility, recalling something between a medieval fortress and a Bavarian bierstube. But inside is home to one of the nicest mid-sized stages in the city and a smaller studio theater. A number of theater groups—including the very popular Free Associates, who improvise full-length plays based on the works of authors like Brian Friel and Tennessee Williams and the

Literary Chicago

Many of the great American works of literature of the 20th century were written by Chicago authors. Here are some of them:

Nelson Algren, *The Man with the Golden Arm*

L. Frank Baum, *The Wizard of Oz*

Saul Bellow, *The Adventures of Augie March*

Ray Bradbury, *The Martian Chronicles*

Gwendolyn Brooks, *A Street in Bronzeville*

Edgar Rice Burroughs, *Tarzan of the Apes*

John Dos Passos, *USA*

Theodore Dreiser, *An American Tragedy*

Stuart Dybek, *The Coast of Chicago*

Ben Hecht, *Child of the Century*

Ring Lardner, *You Know Me Al*

Willard Motley, *Knock On Any Door*

Frank Norris, *The Pit*

Mike Royko, *Boss*

Upton Sinclair, *The Jungle*

Carl Sandburg, *Chicago Poems*

Richard Wright, *Native Son*

producers of *Hellcab*—share this facility. Look for the annual Christmas performances of City Lit Theater Company's delightful adaptations of P.G. Wodehouse's Jeeves and Wooster stories. (North Side)

LINK'S HALL
3435 N. Sheffield
773/281-0824
An alternative venue just south of Wrigley Field, this facility hosts many of the city's more avant-garde

dance and performance troupes. Performances include everything from the highly acclaimed group Doorika to the wholly original and challenging Curious Theatre Branch. (North Side)

MANDEL HALL
1131 E. 57th St.
312/702-8068
Opened in 1903, Mandel Hall is the major concert facility on the Hyde Park campus of the University of

Chicago. It features everything from folk music to pop. The hall also presents a chamber music series and a program of early classical music, and features occasional performances by the Contemporary Chamber players. (South Side)

NORTH SHORE CENTER FOR THE PERFORMING ARTS
9501 Skokie Blvd., Skokie
847/673-6300
The newest performing arts facility on Chicago's North Shore is nothing special, boasting two auditoriums that resemble high school performance facilities. But the NSCPA does have the distinction of being the permanent home of Northlight Theatre, one of the Chicago area's oldest and most respected theater companies. A number of national acts who appeal to the older suburban crowd have also played here (i.e., Lainie Kazan). (Greater Chicago)

PETRILLO MUSIC SHELL
Grant Park
251 S. Columbus Dr.
312/742-7638
This is arguably the best location in the country for free concerts. During the summer, the very talented Grant Park Symphony Orchestra offers an intriguing series of classical music concerts. When the symphony is not performing the music shell is home to many of the city's great music festivals including Blues Fest, Gospel Fest, the Country Music Fest, Viva Chicago, the Jazz Fest, and Taste of Chicago. Everyone from Buddy Guy to the Chicago Symphony to Miles Davis to John Hiatt to Jethro Tull has played here over the years, and it's never cost a dime. (Downtown)

PICK-STAIGER CONCERT HALL
1977 S. Campus Dr., Evanston
847-491-5441
A beautiful facility located on Northwestern's campus right beside Lake Michigan in Evanston, Pick-Staiger is home to many university ensembles, such as Northwestern's chorus, symphony orchestra, wind ensemble, and jazz ensemble. Many illustrious, nationally acclaimed musicians appear here as well. (Greater Chicago)

RAVINIA FESTIVAL
Green Bay and Lake Cook Rds., Highland Park
312/728-4642
Every summer, this beautiful north shore concert facility and park is packed with picnickers enjoying the weather and performances by the Chicago Symphony Orchestra, jazz musicians, and many mainstream light-pop musicians like Gordon Lightfoot, Poi Dog Pondering, and Harry Belafonte. This is one of the

Twyla Tharp's I Remember Clifford *at Hubbard Street Dance, p. 212*

Ruedi Hofmann

TOP TOP TOP TOP TOP TOP TOP TOP TOP TOP TOP

Top Ten Movies About Chicago
by Penelope Mesic, film critic for *Chicago Magazine*

His Girl Friday, starring Cary Grant and Rosalind Russell, directed by Howard Hawks

Scarface, starring Paul Muni

Some Like It Hot, starring Marilyn Monroe, Tony Curtis and Jack Lemmon

The Sting, starring Robert Redford and Paul Newman

Eight Men Out, directed by John Sayles

Medium Cool, directed by Haskell Wexler, filmed on location at the 1968 Democratic National Convention

Blues Brothers, directed by John Landis, starring John Belushi and Dan Ackroyd

Compulsion, starring Orson Welles

A League of Their Own, starring Madonna and Geena Davis

Ferris Bueller's Day Off, starring Matthew Broderick, directed by John Hughes

best places to see (or at least listen to) a concert in the Chicago area. (Greater Chicago)

ROSEMONT HORIZON
6920 N. Mannheim Rd.
847/635-6601
and
ROSEMONT THEATRE
5400 N. River Rd., Rosemont
800/859-7469
Convenient to little else besides O'Hare Airport and the airport hotels, these facilities often host major national acts. The Horizon—a cavernous stadium that features everything from major rock acts to circuses to DePaul University basket-

ball games—is the bigger of the two facilities. The more intimate Rosemont Theatre hosts somewhat smaller concerts and theatrical events like the national Irish dancing and music extravaganza Riverdance. (Greater Chicago)

SHUBERT THEATRE
22 W. Monroe St.
312/902-1500
This early–20th century theater is one of the few remaining legitimate theaters left in the Loop. Playing host to a season of imported national hit musicals and plays, the Shubert has the feel of a theater on New York's Great White Way. Pro-

ductions here have included the Tony Award–winning *Rent* and Peter Shaffer's *Lettice and Lovage*. (Downtown)

SYMPHONY CENTER
220 S. Michigan Ave.
312/435-8122

Having recently undergone a major face-lift, Orchestra Hall (home to the world-renowned Chicago Symphony Orchestra and location for many classical music and, occasionally, pop music events) has acquired a new image and a new name. Now it's not just a state-of-the-art concert facility with superb acoustics. Symphony Center, as it's now known, has its own restaurant, a newly redesigned stage, and an atrium. Throughout the year, a number of free concert events are held here. Symphony Center is also home to Chicago Sinfonietta, a chamber orchestra led by Paul Freeman. (Downtown)

THEATER BUILDING
1225 W. Belmont Ave.
773/327-5252

A theater complex on the north side of the city, the Theater Building is home to a variety of theater companies who rotate performances here throughout the year, utilizing the building's three mid-sized spaces. Quality of productions depends on which theater company is renting, but the New Tuners Theater's production of an original musical based on Hans Brinker is a perennial holiday hit. (North Side)

WORLD MUSIC THEATRE
19100 Ridgeland Ave., Tinley Park
708/614-1616

There is one of these on the outskirts of every major city, but it's the place to go if the band you want to

Herbert Migdoll/Joffrey Ballet

Valerie Madonia and Daniel Baudendistel performing with the Joffrey Ballet (p. 212) in Gerald Arpino's Round of Angels

see is playing here. A rudimentary outdoor stadium with a roofed main area and cheaper seats available on the grass, this is where many of the major touring rock acts perform during the summer. The sound isn't great and the theater is pretty much in the middle of nowhere, but acts from Aerosmith to Bob Dylan to Neil Young have played here. (Greater Chicago)

THEATER

A RED ORCHID THEATRE
1531 N. Wells St.
312/943-8722

One of the more interesting and intellectually challenging young theater

Aside from being a trailblazer in the worlds of film and theater, Chicago also played a major role in the history of television. In the 1940s *Kukla, Fran and Ollie* started at Chicago's NBC branch. Other shows that came from Chicago included *Studs' Place* (which introduced the country to Chicago broadcast legend Studs Terkel) and *Garroway at Large*, where future *Today Show* host Dave Garroway first began to attract attention.

companies in the city, the Old Town–based Red Orchid, housed in a well-designed and pristine but tiny little space, specializes in productions of overlooked European masterpieces and American classics. Some of the best unknown actors in the city can be seen here as they tear into tough roles written by the likes of Ionesco and Durrenmatt. (Near North)

AMERICAN THEATER COMPANY
3855 N. Lincoln Ave.
773/929-1031

An overriding sense of professionalism pervades this theater, which has dedicated itself to a style of performance that personifies Chicago—tough, hard-working, and respectable. Located in an unassuming North Side neighborhood, this is one of the larger theaters in the city. It has won praise for its productions of American classics *(Bus Stop, Stalag 17)*, adaptations of novels, and new works. Despite limited funds, productions here are always exquisitely designed and exceedingly well acted. (North Side)

ANNOYANCE THEATRE
3747 N. Clark St.
773/929-6200

Headed by fearless leader Mick Napier, this is the city's darker answer to the mainstream comedy success of Second City. Performing irreverent and often crass plays with names like *Co-Ed Prison Sluts* and *I'm Not Rappaport; I'm Captain Asshole,* Annoyance achieved national attention some years back for their dead-on performances of Brady Bunch TV scripts. With a well-reputed improv school and a series of successful shows to their credit that keep packing in the faithful, Annoyance continues to push the envelope to what defines good comedy and good taste. Bring your own beer. (North Side)

APPLE TREE THEATRE
595 Elm Pl., Highland Park
847/432-4335

One of the most respected of the theater companies outside the city limits, this company, located on the city's north shore, offers generally quite good productions of challenging new American plays. Recent productions have included *Blade to the Heat, Nine Armenians,* and *Kindertransport.* (Greater Chicago)

BAILIWICK THEATRE
1229 W. Belmont Ave.
773/883-1090

This is one of the busiest and most adventurous theater companies in town. The accent here is often on gay-themed theater, but this only constitutes part of the considerable activity going on here. With its large mainstage space and cozy studio, Bailiwick produces more plays per year than most any other theater company in town; these works range from exciting new plays to musicals to new spins on classics (recent examples include productions of Peter Shaffer's *Equus* and Thornton Wilder's *Our Town* with casts of both hearing and hearing-impaired actors). Bailiwick also plays host to an annual "Pride Series" of gay-themed plays as well as to a director's festival, which showcases some of the city's untapped talent. (North Side)

COURT THEATRE
5535 S. Ellis Ave.
773/753-4472
Located in Hyde Park on the campus of the University of Chicago, Court Theatre is the one theater company in the city that focuses exclusively on the classics. A very respectful and respectable company, Court offers seasons of plays that satisfy its regular crowd of professors and neighborhood intellectuals. These range from Moliere to Shaw to more modern masters like Caryl Churchill. Some of the city's finest actors work here. (South Side)

ETA CREATIVE ARTS FOUNDATION
7558 S. Chicago Ave.
773/752-3955
There are not very many black-owned and -operated theater companies in the city, but this one is one of the best. Located on the far South Side in a rather bleak but safe neighborhood, ETA offers productions of challenging new plays, revues, and overlooked classics in its mid-sized theater space. Though the quality of scripts can vary from time to time, the acting here is always top-notch. The building where the theater is housed also contains a nice, spacious art gallery that showcases African American artists. (Greater Chicago)

EUROPEAN REPERTORY THEATRE
Wellington Avenue United Church Of Christ
615 W. Wellington Ave.
773/248-0577

The Notebooks of Leonardo da Vinci *at the Goodman Theatre, p. 204*

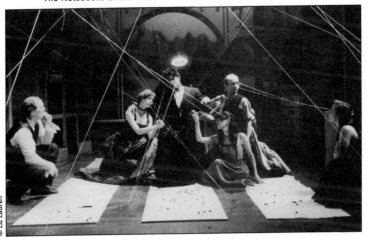

© Liz Lauren

As the name might suggest, the accent here is on the work of European playwrights. Run by a pair of Chicago transplants from Russia and Great Britain, ERC offers forcefully acted and intelligently directed productions of works by playwrights frequently unknown to American audiences. Several plays have received their English language premieres here. Though the surroundings may not look like much (ERC is located on the second floor of a North Side church), the productions here are almost always fascinating, expertly designed, and deftly performed by hardworking casts of Chicago actors. (North Side)

FACTORY THEATRE
1257 W. Loyola
773/274-1345
This may not be traditional theater in the sense that they taught you about in your college English class, but this plucky young Rogers Park theater company keeps packing in the crowds with their irreverent and often crude productions of new plays in a shabbily charming bring-your-own-beer surrounding. Covering everything from parodies of prison movies and Tarantino flicks to tributes to cheesy '70s bands to autobiographical one-person shows to loud, boisterous, and crass new scripts about young adults in Chicago, Factory has a raucous and unpretentious frat-party atmosphere. But the shows here are almost always entertaining, short, and cheap. (Far North)

GOODMAN THEATRE
200 S. Columbus Dr.
312/443-3800
For decades the Goodman has been the top theater company in the city pulling in audiences year after year

with its top-notch productions of new scripts and old classics featuring some of the best talent in the city and the country at large. Everyone from Karl Malden to Harvey Keitel to Sigourney Weaver to Roscoe Lee Browne has performed here. Having attracted national attention for helping to launch and propel the careers of playwrights like August Wilson, David Mamet, and Keith Reddin; entertainers like the Flying Karamazov Brothers; and solo artists like Eric Bogosian, David Cale, Paula Killen, and Spalding Gray, the Goodman remains an exciting blend of the up-and-coming and the old-and-established. Each year offers seasons of beautifully designed and performed works in its main theater space (probably the best designed and most comfortable in the city), and programs of more avant-garde work in its studio space. (Downtown)

GRIFFIN THEATRE COMPANY
5404 N. Clark St.
773/769-2228
Located in what was once an old movie palace in the North Side Andersonville neighborhood, Griffin has managed to stay afloat with its lack of pretension and its dedication to performing new scripts with companies of young and enthusiastic actors. Though the productions here vary from excellent to average, Griffin provides a good opportunity to see raw talent for low prices in a comfortable setting. (Far North)

IMPROVOLYMPIC
3541 N. Clark St.
773/769-2228
Chicago is known worldwide as the birthplace of improvisational comedy. One of its founders, Del Close (who has taught everyone from John

Ray Bradbury's Farenheit 451 *at Bailiwick Theatre, p. 202*

Bailiwick Theatre

Belushi to Gilda Radner), still works here. The Del Close Theatre, located in this two-theater bar and entertainment complex in Wrigleyville, offers constantly changing entertainment with everything from improvised musicals to plays to competitions to revues. Both a theater and a training facility for young actors, Improvolympic packs in the crowds for the high-energy, wacky performances by its many resident improv teams. With entertainment that can vary wildly from brilliant to dreadful in a matter of moments, this is still a great place to see the future stars of *Saturday Night Live* and Second City. (North Side)

LIFELINE THEATRE
6912 N. Glenwood St.
773/761-4477

You wouldn't know it to look at it, especially in its rather dumpy East Rogers Park neighborhood, but this is one of the most reliable theater companies in town. With an accent on adaptations of classic works of literature (Gogol's *The Overcoat*, Bronte's *Jane Eyre*, Tolkien's *Lord of the Rings*), Lifeline offers excellently designed and acted productions that are almost always viscerally and intellectually challenging. (Far North)

LIVE BAIT THEATRE
3914 N. Clark St.
773/871-1212

Don't let the somewhat dark and deserted neighborhood or the miles of cemetery across the street fool you; this is still a pretty happening and usually roomy theater. Live Bait is one of the few companies in town that maintains a certain dedication to Chicago artists, and the focus here is solely on new plays by local authors. The 70-seat theater offers three world premieres a year and has premiered the works of authors like Paul Peditto, Sharon Evans, John Ragir, and yours truly. There is a bar next door to the theater which is a hangout for actors and theater types when it's open. (North Side)

LOOKINGGLASS THEATER
773/477-9257

Not every theater company in

Ten Best Places in Which to See a Show

by Lawrence Bommer, noted theater critic for the *Chicago Reader, Chicago Tribune*, and *Windy City Times*.

1. **Black Ensemble Theater** in Uptown Center Hull House: Great sight-lines let you see everything on stage unobstructed as well as watch the audience's reactions. (Lincoln Park's Apollo Theater, Hyde Park's Court Theatre, and Skokie's Northlight Theatre have similar setups.)

2. **Steppenwolf Studio Theater:** Complete silence (no street noise), good acoustics, and a constantly changing seat configuration keep things concentrated and varied.

3. **Shattered Globe Theater:** The seating is cramped (with no arm rests) but the ingenious, in-the-round use of this postage-stamp playing area inspires intriguing blocking and subliminal sets.

4. **About Face Theater** in Lakeview Hull House: Nothing remarkable about the space except the memories. In the 1960s, under Bob Sickinger, it was the birthplace of Off-Loop theater and, as Steppenwolf's first Chicago home, saw John Malkovich, Joan Allen, Gary Sinise, Terry Kinney, and Laurie Metcalf learn their trade. After that, Bailiwick Repertory and Famous Door Theater presented some eye-popping spectacles, and now a gay theater has taken over.

5. **Ruth Page Theater:** A bit cozy inside and the side seats suck, but the lobby is inviting and there are enough bathroom stalls for even the most irregular of audiences.

6. **Live Bait Theater:** Its dull black-box interior always motivates designers to make the sets—and often the lobby—as expression-istic and flamboyant as possible.

7. **Goodman Theater:** Its huge underground theaters make great air-raid shelters.

8. **Drury Lane Oakbrook Terrace:** Highly recommended for fans of the Victorian Steamboat School of Beaux-Arts Decor. The chandeliers alone could bail out a Third World country. Add some deck chairs and you can pretend you're on the Titanic.

9. **Victory Gardens Theater** in Lincoln Park: Nothing remarkable about any particular auditorium, just the fact that there are four of them in one building and you can feel the cumulative energy.

10. **Chicago Theatre:** The common man has his palace and it's often more glorious than anything on stage. And as for memories . . .

Chicago has a permanent address. A lot of them are nomadic, bouncing from one theater space to another as funding permits. One of the city's finest peripatetic crews is this highly athletic group of graduates of Northwestern University whose blending of both physical and mental gymnastics has made them a unique and exciting company. Having won acclaim for their very physical productions of plays like Upton Sinclair's *The Jungle*, *The Arabian Nights*, and Joe Orton's *Up Against It,* Lookingglass is worth checking out if they happen to be performing while you're in town. David Schwimmer of *Friends* fame is a company member.

MARRIOTT'S
LINCOLNSHIRE THEATRE
Route 21, Lincolnshire
847/634-0200

It's hardly convenient to Downtown Chicago, but the 45-minute ride north of the city to get here is probably worth it if you're a fan of Broadway musicals. Housed in a spacious and elegant theater, the Lincolnshire offers both premieres and revivals of musicals performed by the most talented members of Chicago's musical theater community. (Greater Chicago)

MARY-ARRCHIE THEATRE
731 W. Sheridan Rd.
773/871-0442

Owned and operated by one of the Chicago theater scene's most recognizable characters (the tripped-out actor-pharmacist-gadfly-hippie Richard Cotovsky), Mary-Arrchie is an unpredictable and exciting theater company offering everything from stolid productions of new scripts to impossibly huge and ambitious productions of overlooked masterpieces. A dingy space located up a flight of stairs over a grocery, Mary-Arrchie exemplifies the grittiness, resourcefulness, and raw talent that has given Chicago theater its considerable reputation. (North Side)

NEO-FUTURARIUM
5153 N. Ashland Ave.
773/275-5255

The smart and quirky neo-futurists with their theater space located above a funeral home are notable for their irreverent and dadaistic take on theater. They have won acclaim for their decidedly unconventional adaptations of Dostoevsky's *Crime and Punishment* and Kafka's *The Trial*. But they are probably most known for their long-running show *Too Much Light Makes The Baby Go Blind*, an evening of 30 short plays performed in one hour every Friday and Saturday night at 11:30. (Far North)

NEXT THEATRE COMPANY
927 Noyes St., Evanston
847/475-1875

In any other city, Next—a very professional, resourceful, and talented theater company performing seasons of new and classic works—would be a rarity. Located in a cultural arts center in Evanston, Next has had success for more than 15 years producing consistently smart, effective, and well-acted works which have ranged from plays by relatively new authors like Constance Congdon and Donald Margulies to adaptations of works by Hemingway and cyberpunk author William Gibson to Shakespeare. (Greater Chicago)

ORGANIC TOUCHSTONE THEATRE
2851 N. Halsted St.
773/404-4700

Here's another one. A theater company in Chicago that takes full advantage of the city's boundless acting talent with seasons of excellent scripts. Not the most adventurous company in the city, Organic Touchstone (located at the site of the old Steppenwolf Theatre space) presents Chicago premieres of works that have had considerable success elsewhere. Examples include plays by the likes of modern European masters like Brian Friel, David Hare, and Ronald Harwood. (North Side)

RAVEN THEATRE
6931 N. Clark St.
773/338-2177
The way North Side location and the choice of plays might fool you into thinking that this was an amateur community theater, but you'd be wrong. Though Raven does present the sorts of American classics favored by the usual park districts and summer camp troupes, the theater also presents bang-up, wonderfully acted revivals of works by the likes of Tennessee Williams, Edward Albee, and Arthur Miller. It's a perfect neighborhood location to see the shows that formed American theater. (Far North)

ROADWORKS PRODUCTIONS
773/489-7623
Another one of the city's nomadic tribes of actors, Roadworks is definitely worth checking out when they're performing in various places at various times throughout the year. Like Lookingglass, this is a group made up of primarily Northwestern graduates and they have won national acclaim for their incredibly strong ensemble performances, most notably in productions of Patrick Marber's *Dealer's Choice*, Mike Leigh's *Ecstasy*, and James Finney Boylan's *The Planets*.

SECOND CITY
1616 N. Wells St.
312/337-3992
This is where it all started. Begun above a Chinese laundry, Second City has become a nationwide phenomenon and industry, influencing generations of American comedians. It seems that everyone who has ever been on *Saturday Night Live* or *Second City Television* got their start here: Bill Murray, John Belushi, Gilda Radner, Alan Arkin, George Wendt . . . the list goes on and on. Still providing the launching pad for comedians' careers, Second City's ever-changing shows of scripted skits as well as straight improv are still the measuring stick by which all comedy in the country is judged. Many of the famed comedians who came out of Second City still pop by on occasion to watch or participate in this legendary comedic theater showplace. (North Side)

SHAKESPEARE REPERTORY
1016 N. Dearborn St.
312/642-2273
The city's only exclusively Shakespearean company, Shakespeare Rep presents several of the Bard's works every year, slowly working its way back and forth through the Shakespearean canon. While the venue is not the most comfortable place to see a play, this is nevertheless a highly talented company which provides expert and respectful revivals that should please all Shakespeare lovers. (Near North)

SHATTERED GLOBE THEATRE
2856 N. Halsted St.
773/404-1237
The Shattered Globe Theatre, a respected ensemble company, performs seasons of new work and American classics. It's located across

from the Steppenwolf Theatre Company and next door to the Gaslight Corner, one of the city's best bars. (North Side)

STAGE LEFT
3408 N. Sheffield Ave.
773/883-8830
One of the older and more established low-budget companies in town, Stage Left offers seasons of new works and adaptations performed by ensemble members and up-and-coming members of the Chicago theater community. Seasons are usually eclectic; recent shows have included an adaptation of a work by science fiction writer Philip K. Dick, and a one-woman show about struggling to survive in Sarajevo. (North Side)

STEPPENWOLF THEATRE
1650 N. Halsted St.
312/335-1650
Twenty years ago it was just another sprightly little company tucked in the

Top Ten Dance Companies to Catch When You're in Town
by Laura Molzahn, dance critic for the *Chicago Reader*

1. **River North Dance Company:** Taps Chicago's best jazz-dance choreographers; silky dancing.

2. **Joffrey Ballet of Chicago:** A recent transplant with great dancers, so-so choreography.

3. **XSight! Performance Group:** A genuinely exciting collaborative dance-performance group; into nudity.

4. **Jellyeye Drum Theatre:** An exhilaratingly loud, innovative drum-dance ensemble

5. **Jan Erkert and Dancers:** Features modern choreographer who tackles heavy subjects with sensitivity and sophistication.

6. **Bob Eisen:** Veteran modern-dance choreographer who's never anyone but himself, and he's one of a kind.

7. **Mordine and Company Dance Theatre**: Ditto for Shirley Mordine.

8. **Muntu Dance Theatre of Chicago:** The city's best African and African American dance company.

9. **Trinity Irish Dance Company:** Award-winning step dancers made famous by their appearance on *The Tonight Show*.

10. **Hubbard Street Dance Chicago:** Internationally known company with fabulous dancers and the best choreography money can buy.

basement of a north suburban church. Now the Steppenwolf is nationally hailed as one of the best (if not the best) theater companies in the country. Having founded a tough, gritty Chicago-theater style based on ferocious acting and minimal sets, Steppenwolf jump-started the careers of ensemble members John Malkovich, Gary Sinise, Laurie Metcalf, K. Todd Freeman, John Mahoney, and a slew of others. Now boasting seasons of new and classic work along with a more adventurous studio and performance series, Steppenwolf still defines the cutting edge of theater while maintaining an aura of respectability. Many of the Steppenwolf crowd who have gone on to fame and fortune come back every year to perform. (North Side)

STRAWDOG THEATRE
3829 N. Broadway
773/528-9696
One of the best little theater companies in town, Strawdog offers productions of great new plays, many of which are premieres. Despite its unremarkable surroundings, Strawdog overcomes budgetary constraints by delivering top-notch acting and direction in often unfamiliar scripts. Terry Johnson's *Imagine Drowning*, John Patrick Shanley's *The Big Funk*, and Alan Ayckbourn's *Absent Friends* are some of the plays that Strawdog has produced. (North Side)

TRAP DOOR THEATRE
1655 W. Cortland St.
773/384-0494
One of the more daring little companies in town, Trap Door has won acclaim for their productions of original works as well as works by internationally acclaimed but generally unproduced artists like R.W. Fassbinder. The dingy setting adds to the rough-and-tumble nature of Trap Door's shows. (West Side)

VICTORY GARDENS THEATER
2257 N. Lincoln Ave.
773/871-3000
A veteran of the absolute explosion of Chicago theater in the 1970s, Victory Gardens offers world and Chicago premieres of mainstream plays by its resident playwrights including Claudia Allen and Jeffrey Sweet. Appealing to a more conservative theater audience than some of Chicago's more daring theaters, Victory Gardens frequently premieres plays that go onto national success, most notably James Sherman's international hit *Beau Jest*, concerning a Jewish woman who hires a non-Jewish actor to play her Jewish boyfriend to please her parents. (North Side)

CLASSICAL MUSIC AND OPERA

CHICAGO SYMPHONY ORCHESTRA
Symphony Center
220 S. Michigan Ave.
312/294-3000
Long known as one of the finest symphonies in the world, the CSO grew to international prominence under the leadership of the late Sir Georg Solti. The symphony began life in 1891. In its one hundred-plus-year history, it has recorded more than nine hundred albums and has won 53 Grammy Awards from the National Academy of Recording Arts and Sciences. Currently under the leadership of Daniel Barenboim, the

Buying Tickets

HOT TIXX
108 N. State St.
312/977-1755
Located in a small booth on State Street, this service offers half-price same-day tickets to a huge variety of theater and music performances in the city.

TICKETMASTER
312/559-1212
The major source for tickets for almost all major venue events in Chicago, Ticketmaster has outlets in many of the city's department stores and record stores.

CSO continues to hold onto its considerable reputation, performing both at Symphony Center and, in the summer, at the Ravinia Festival. (Downtown)

LYRIC OPERA OF CHICAGO
Civic Opera House
20 N. Wacker Dr.
312/332-2244
Located in an opera house that was opened in 1929, the Lyric Opera has the only seats in the city that might be tougher to reserve than those at a Bulls game. Every year, the estimable opera company brings in some of the world's finest opera talent (previous years have seen performances by Samuel Ramey, Jesse Norman, Kiri Te Kanawa, Mirela Freni, Placido Domingo, and virtually every other major opera star) in lavishly designed productions overseen by directors of world-class stature including Robert Altman, Harold Prince, Sir Peter Hall, Peter Sellars, and Robert Wilson. Presenting an annual series of familiar warhorses with controversial world premieres, the Lyric Opera, under the direction of Bruno Bartoletti, is well worth the steep ticket prices. (Downtown)

LIGHT OPERA WORKS
Cahn Auditorium
Northwestern University
847/869-6300
As its title suggests, LOW deals in the more fluffy operatic fodder that does not have quite the same sort of snob appeal as the fare at the Lyric. Nevertheless, this is a well-respected company that has performed operettas by Kurt Weill and Gilbert and Sullivan, as well as musicals like and *The Fantastiks*. (Greater Chicago)

DANCE

CHICAGO MOVING COMPANY
3035 N. Hoyne
773/880-5402
A veteran of the Chicago dance scene for more than 25 years, Chicago Moving company is a fascinating and intellectually stimulating company led by mystic-choreographer-dancer-guru Nana Shineflug. Incorporating elements of jazz and improvisation with its evocative and sometimes politically charged dance numbers, CMC performs at a variety of Chicago venues.

HUBBARD STREET DANCE
218 S. Wabash Ave.
312/663-0853

One of the most successful companies in the Chicago dance scene and one of the few that can afford to pay its dancers full-time wages, Hubbard Street began humbly in a studio on Hubbard Street in 1977. Now, under the direction of Lou Conte, the company is one of the nation's most recognized jazz troupes and has attracted internationally acclaimed choreographers like Twyla Tharp.

THE JOFFREY BALLET
OF CHICAGO
70 E. Lake St.
312/739-0120

Chicago scored a major coup when the Joffrey decided to move its headquarters here from New York City. Performing the works of artistic director Gerald Arpino as well as other luminaries like founder Robert Joffrey and Agnes DeMille, the 40-plus-year-old company is one of the most highly reputed in the country with its ever-increasing repertoire of modern ballets.

MORDINE AND COMPANY
DANCE THEATER
4730 N. Sheridan Rd.
773/989-3310

Led by Shirley Mordine and housed in the Dance Center of Columbia College, Mordine and Company is one of the most reputable and venerable dance institutions in the city. The eclectic and always fascinating Mordine has fashioned experimental dances using puppets and live performers to music by Kurt Weill and J.S. Bach. It's always worth a look.

Kate Hoddinott—Buddy Guy's Legends

11

NIGHTLIFE

Chicago is the home of the blues. Muddy Waters, Junior Wells, Koko Taylor, Howlin' Wolf, and Buddy Guy have all called the city home. It's one of the world's greatest jazz capitals as well. Since the Great Migration of the early 20th century, when southern black musicians road the rails to the north, greats from Louis Armstrong to Kahlil El Zabar have made Chicago their headquarters. All styles of jazz are offered here, from mainstream jazz performed by noted Chicagoan Von Freeman to avant-gardists like the world-famous AACM, the New Horizons Ensemble, and Eight Bold Souls.

Chicago is also a burgeoning rock music capital having given birth to bands such as Chicago, The Buckinghams, The Ides Of March, American Breed, and The Cryan' Shames in the 1960s; Styx, REO Speedwagon, and Survivor in the '70s; Material Issue and Cheap Trick in the '80s; and Liz Phair, Urge Overkill, Shellac, Veruca Salt, Poi Dog Pondering, and Smashing Pumpkins in the '90s. Even now Chicago has an exploding rock scene featuring everyone from national acts like Smoking Popes, Triple Fast Action, Figdish, Catherine, Tortoise, and Gastr Del Sol to lesser-known up-and-comers like The Bells. Industrial music was partially founded here with the rise of bands in the '80s like Ministry, Pigface, and the Revolting Cocks, and the international dance phenomenon of house music was started on Chicago's South Side.

All of this means that it's not exactly hard to find some sort of late-night entertainment in Chicago. In fact, you'd have to be agoraphobic not to. Every sort of entertainment imaginable is available in bulk in Chicago, from dance to music to comedy to film. Whatever late-night taste is here, Chicago certainly has something to fit your palate.

DANCE CLUBS

BERLIN
954 W. Belmont Ave.
773/348-4975
Though it's primarily known as a gay bar, this disco brings in a fair number of straight customers as well, especially women who don't feel like being bugged by frat house guys who frequent many of the city's other dance clubs. Video screens are a popular attraction here, as are the club's disco nights, in which you'll swear that Donna Summer, The Village People, and Frankie Goes To Hollywood never went out of fashion. (North Side)

CLUB 950
950 W. Wrightwood Ave.
773/929-8955
Immortalized in song by Iggy Pop of all people, this cheap and somewhat dingy club brings in the left-but-not-too-left-of-center crowd of punks and recent DePaul grads (plus some students with good fake IDs) who identify themselves as "alternative." It's a healthy antidote to some of the slicker and more expensive clubs in town with good mixes of industrial and techno music. (North Side)

CROBAR
1543 N. Kingsbury St.
312/413-7000
Shortly before he opened the supremely tacky nightclub Illusions (157 E. Ontario), Chicago Bulls star Dennis Rodman made this his stomping grounds. The hip crowd of black-clad fashion models, clubbers, and scenesters remain here at Crobar, a pulsating mélange of hard-driving dance music, thrashing dance, and strobe-light mayhem. A classic. (Near North)

DELILAH'S
2771 N. Lincoln Ave.
773/472-4771
For years, when it was known as Crash Palace, this was the stomping ground for many members of the city's rock 'n' roll and industrial music cliques. Today Delilah's excellent deejays—who occasionally include members of Smashing Pumpkins and Urge Overkill, as well as Chris Connelley (former frontman for Ministry and The Revolting Cocks, and currently with The Bells)—continue to attract a funky crowd as they spin a good mix of garage, punk, and ska. (North Side)

THE DOME ROOM
632 ½ N. Dearborn St.
312/266-2114
Though located in the same building as the mainstream disco Excalibur, the crowds that come here couldn't be more different. With its programs of heavy metal, industrial, and dance bands, this dark club attracts young punks, goths, and metalheads. Bondage nights are occasionally held here. (Near North)

EXCALIBUR
632 ½ N. Dearborn St.
312/266-1944
Known as The Limelight back in the eighties, the Excalibur is an impossibly huge disco which attracts a crowd that's a little too touristy and suburban for many Chicagoans. Boasting a restaurant, pool tables, video games, and several dance floors, Excalibur lies somewhere in the nether region between a hip discotheque and your nephew's Bar Mitzvah. Though everyone who goes here seems to be having a great time, few of them seem to come from within the city limits. The building

DOWNTOWN

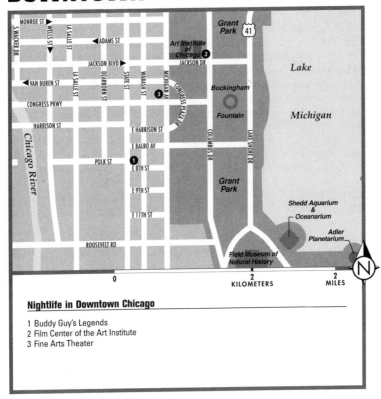

MONROE ST
S WACKER DR
WELLS ST
LA SALLE ST
ADAMS ST
JACKSON BLVD
LA SALLE ST
DEARBORN ST
STATE ST
WABASH ST
MICHIGAN AV
VAN BUREN ST
CONGRESS PKWY
HARRISON ST
POLK ST
ROOSEVELT RD
Chicago River

Art Institute of Chicago ❷
JACKSON DR
❸
CONGRESS PLAZA DR
E HARRISON ST
E BALBO AV
❶
E 8TH ST
E 9TH ST
E 11TH ST

Grant Park 41
Lake Michigan
Buckingham Fountain
COLUMBUS DR
LAKE SHORE DR
Grant Park
Shedd Aquarium & Oceanarium
Adler Planetarium
Field Museum of Natural History

0   2 KILOMETERS   2 MILES

N

Nightlife in Downtown Chicago

1 Buddy Guy's Legends
2 Film Center of the Art Institute
3 Fine Arts Theater

---

itself, a Chicago landmark and one of the few to survive the Chicago Fire, is worth a look on its own. (Near North)

NEO
2350 N. Clark St.
773/528-2622

Impressive if only for its staying power, this has been a key spot for the hipster crowd ever since the '70s. A rather mainstream crowd comes on weekends to enjoy the dance music spun by the deejays, but things tend to get harder-edged on Neo's popular Mondays and Tuesdays. (North Side)

OCTAGON
2483 N. Clark St.
773/549-1132

Octagon is known to get so crowded with frisky twenty-some-things on weekend nights that local wags have taken to calling it "Oc-topus." That said, however, it's a fun—if somewhat mainstream—neighborhood dance club which allows Lincoln Parkers to drink, mingle, and sing along to Top 40 "alternative" hits. In past years, New Year's Eve at Octagon has known to become somewhat un-friendly. (North Side)

RED DOG
1958 W. North Ave.
773/278-1009

Red Dog offers funk, hip-hop, acid jazz, and dance music in an almost cathedral-like setting. This was the hottest place in the city when Wicker Park became the center of Chicago's groove scene. And even now that Wicker Park has mainstreamed itself with excessive gentrification, Red Dog still pulls in the hipster crowd until four o'clock in the morning on weekends. (West Side)

SMART BAR
3730 N. Clark St.
773/549-4140

Located beneath Cabaret Metro, this is one of the key dance spots in the city—not really for the wannabe crowd, but for those looking for an outlet in the tough, urban jungle. A favorite spot of the city's artists and actors, the Smart Bar has a great, dungeon-like atmosphere and a slew of talented deejays. Sundays, however, belong to deejay Jesse de la Peña, the city's premier acid jazz deejay and the leader of Chicago's finest acid jazz outfit, Liquid Soul. (North Side)

JAZZ CLUBS

ANDY'S
11 E. Hubbard St.
312/642-6805

Though it's located in a rather touristy section of town and is usually populated by power-lunching (or dinnering) businesspeople, that doesn't keep Andy's from being one of the best traditional jazz spots in town. The club hosts some of Chicago's and the nation's best jazz talent including the legendary Franz Jackson, who performs here regularly. Andy's is especially popular with the working crowd for its lunchtime and after-work jazz sets, though top-notch late-evening entertainment is offered as well. (Near North)

THE COTTON CLUB
1710 S. Michigan Ave.
312/341-9787

One of the classiest music clubs in the city, The Cotton Club caters to a middle- to upper-middle-class, largely African American crowd. The club offers a variety of jazz, cabaret, and, occasionally, comedy performers in a slick atmosphere. Appropriate attire is required. (Near South Side)

THE GREEN MILL
4812 N. Broadway
773/878-5552

Word on the street is that Al Capone hung out here in the 1920s. The other urban legend has it that Charlie Chaplin, Mary Pickford, and Douglas Fairbanks Jr. used to drink to excess here after a hard day's shooting at Essanay Studios. It's tougher these days to find a celebrity or a world-renowned mobster, but that doesn't stop Chicagoans of all stripes from coming here to see some of the world's best jazz performers. Sunday evenings provide a diversion of a sort as the Green Mill and Chicago poet Marc Smith host the famed Uptown Poetry Slam, a fiercely contested and always entertaining weekly poetry competition. (Far North)

GREEN DOLPHIN STREET
2200 N. Ashland Ave.
773/395-0066

Cashing in on 1960s nostalgia and the supper club craze, this slick club has

NEAR NORTH

Nightlife on the Near North Side of Chicago

1 600 N. Michigan Movie Theater
2 Andy's
3 Blue Chicago
4 Crobar
5 The Dome Room
6 Esquire
7 Excalibur
8 House of Blues
9 The Jazz Showcase
10 Second City
9 Tony and Tina's Wedding
11 Zanies

become one of the hottest spots in the city on weekends for swinging singers, cigar-chomping scenesters, and jazz aficionados. Green Dolphin's attractions include a jazz ballroom, a restaurant, and a popular outdoor garden area. Some of the city's best jazz, salsa, and acid jazz groups perform here. (West Side)

THE JAZZ SHOWCASE
59 W. Grand Ave.
312/670-2473

This is the most serious outlet for jazz in the city. It isn't about drinks; it's about the music. All the top names in jazz—from Clark Terry to Dewey Redman to Pharoah Sanders to Johnny Griffin—play here. Run by Chicago jazz impresario Joe Segal, The Jazz Showcase moved here from its long-time headquarters in the Blackstone Hotel. Here, jazz is treated as a high art form and the crowds that come are as respectful and attentive as audiences listening to the Chicago Symphony Orchestra at Symphony Center. This is clearly the best jazz club in town. (Near North)

THE NEW APARTMENT LOUNGE
504 E. 75th St.
773/483-7728

Six nights a week, this is just like any other unremarkable bar on the South Side of Chicago, although with its New Year's Eve party decor it may be a little tackier than most. But that changes on Tuesdays when the New Apartment Lounge hosts Von Freeman, perhaps the city's best and most highly reputed saxophonist. Freeman is often joined by some of the city's best jazz talents who come just for the opportunity to jam with him. The neighborhood is a little rough, but there's plenty of parking

---

The Sad Fate of Division Street

Those familiar with Chicago may notice a curious absence of bars located in the Rush Street and Division Street area. Though for many years this was one of the hot spots in the singles scene, having been immortalized in the Rob Lowe and Jim Belushi vehicle About Last Night *(based loosely on David Mamet's* Sexual Perversity In Chicago*), the nightlife scene here has gotten more than a little cheesy and overpopulated by kids with fake IDs, wayward sailors, and folks up from the suburbs. Still, if you're looking for the sleazier, frat-boy drinking, get-into-a-bar-fight side of life, you can still check out Chicago's answer to New Orleans' Bourbon Street minus the transvestite bars. Some old favorites here include* **Butch McGuires** *(20 W. Division St., 312/337-9080),* **Mother's** *(26 W. Division St., 312/642-7251), and* **The Lodge** *(21 W. Division St., 312/642-4406). Enjoy.*

nearby; and, inside, the club is perfectly safe and friendly. (Greater Chicago)

POPS FOR CHAMPAGNE
2934 N. Sheffield Ave.
773/472-1000
Attracting a more chic and monied clientele than many of the city's down-and-dirty jazz clubs, Pops offers high-class jazz entertainment in elegant surroundings. Many of the city's top cabaret singers and jazz musicians perform here. The crowd is largely made up of couples on dates after dinner, enjoying Pops' intimate surroundings and the large selection of champagnes on its menu. Seats are practically on top of the performers, affording the spectator excellent views of great jazz talent. (North Side)

BLUES CLUBS

BLUE CHICAGO
736 N. Clark St.
312/642-6261
and
BLUE CHICAGO
536 N. Clark St.
312/661-0100
These two excellent blues clubs are within two blocks of each other. One cover charge gets you into both, so if the entertainment in one isn't doing it for you, you're bound to be satisfied by the other. Though the atmosphere is a little more immaculate than in some of the city's grittier clubs, and the crowds aren't generally composed of Chicago regulars, the entertainment here is Grade A. Some of the city's best female blues vocalists, often overlooked by some of the other more male-dominated clubs, perform here. (Near North)

Second City, p. 229

B.L.U.E.S.
2519 N. Halsted St.
773/525-6226
Finding a place to sit down in here, especially on weekends, is a tall order. But there's a reason for the overflowing seas of humanity that pack in here every night: the top blues talent in the city. If you come early enough, get a seat near the stage and prepare yourself for some of the best blues entertainment you've ever seen. Keep an eye out for performances here by regulars such as The Kinsey Report (an incredibly talented group that fuses blues, reggae, and funk; led by former Peter Tosh and Bob Marley sideman Donald Kinsey) and Otis Clay (one of the best blues and soul singers around). (North Side)

B.L.U.E.S. Etcetera
1124 W. Belmont Ave.
773/525-6226
Managed by the same people that run B.L.U.E.S., B.L.U.E.S. Etcetera offers the same high-quality entertainment in slightly roomier and

NORTH SIDE

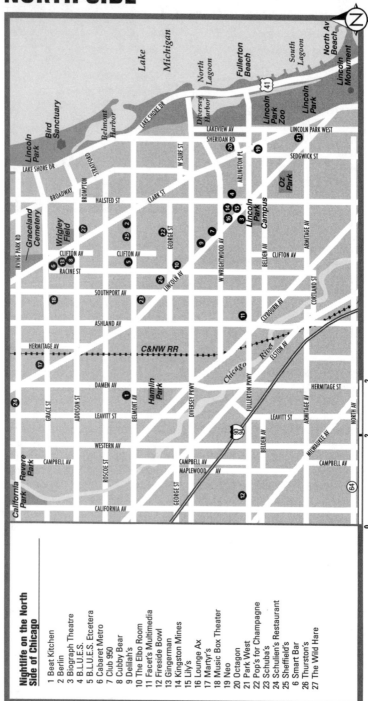

slicker surroundings. Wednesdays are devoted to an open blues jam where local wanna-bes bring their axes and blues harps and try to strut their stuff. Come early in the week if you want to be guaranteed a seat. (North Side)

BUDDY GUY'S LEGENDS
754 S. Wabash Ave.
312/427-0333

Since it's run by Buddy Guy, who may be the best living blues guitarist around, it's not surprising that many of the best Chicago and national blues acts perform here. The surprising thing here is the menu, which features delectable Louisiana items like excellent crabcakes and good barbecue. Even without the comestibles, however, this would still be a great spot. One of the most spacious clubs in the city, Buddy Guy's Legends features many top-name entertainers including Guy himself, whose frequent performances are sold out long in advance. When they are in town, many legendary rock 'n' rollers and bluesmen, including Eric Clapton, come here for impromptu jams with Guy. (Downtown)

CHECKERBOARD LOUNGE
423 E. 43rd St.
773/624-3240

Don't let the neighborhood scare you off. Though 43rd Street is something of an eyesore, and gang activity in the area is high, this is one of the last remaining authentic, gritty South Side blues clubs in the city and, inside, things couldn't be friendlier. This was the prime hangout of Chicago blues legend Junior Wells who, before he died, used to jam here with The Rolling Stones when they came through town. Top-name performers like Otis Clay

still play here. If you are a bit intimidated by the neighborhood, one of the folks working here will notice and offer to escort you to your car. (South Side)

KINGSTON MINES
2548 N. Halsted St.
773/477-4646

A victim, perhaps, of its own success, this is one of the classic Chicago North Side blues clubs and was actually the first in the neighborhood. Unfortunately, on weekends, it's sometimes so crowded with tourists and DePaul students that it's barely worth trying to fight your way in to get a glimpse of the stage. Great acts from Sugar Blue to Billy Branch often perform here, and many national acts have been known to come unannounced to jam (shortly before Kurt Cobain's demise, Nirvana came here to play an impromptu set). Kingston Mines is open way late, though, and if you get here around three o'clock there will still be some entertainment and you're likely to finally find a seat. (North Side)

LILY'S
2513 N. Lincoln Ave.
773/525-2422

The unpretentious and homey Lily's is a classic neighborhood blues spot. The big names don't usually play here, but the music's good, the atmosphere is friendly, the price is right, and the cheap beer flows freely. (North Side)

ROSA'S LOUNGE
3420 W. Armitage Ave.
773/342-0452

The neighborhood is a little dicey, particularly after dark, but the atmosphere inside is so warm and authentic that it's not worth worrying about. The club was founded by Italian immigrant Tony Mangiullo and his mother Rosa, who still tends bar. Mangiullo was so enamored of the Chicago blues scene that he decided to create a blues bar right in the middle of this vibrant Latino neighborhood. He has had great success, attracting all of the city's top blues talent. If you're looking to congratulate Mangiullo on his success in operating a superb blues club, he's the guy with the hat working the door. (West Side)

PUNK CLUBS

FIRESIDE BOWL
2648 W. Fullerton Ave.
773/486-2700
One of the last bastions of punkdom in the city, this bowling alley has turned into a hard-edged club catering to the black-leather jacketed, studded dog collar set. The acoustics are not so hot, but the vibe is authentic. One recent New Year's breakfast celebration featured a performance by legendary

Chicago punk outfit Shellac (led by producer Steve Albini), and free pop-tarts is a tradition that will hopefully continue well into the 21st century. (North Side)

ROCK CLUBS

ARAGON BALLROOM
1106 W. Lawrence Ave.
773/561-9500
In the 1920s this was a beautiful ballroom where all the big bands played. Live broadcasts of Tommy Dorsey and his orchestra were heard on the radio nationwide. The Aragon looks like it hasn't been refurbished or altered ever since, which is part of its appeal. A crumbling relic, the Aragon is now home to many rock 'n' roll and Latin music concerts (David Byrne, Nirvana, Megadeth). A spot favored by up-and-coming bands too big to play clubs but not yet ready for arenas, the Aragon has lousy sound, uncomfortable chairs, a permanent stench of stale beer, and a raucous atmosphere, all of which makes it an absolutely fantastic place to see a

Blue Chicago, p. 219

Blue Chicago

The Ten Best Places in Chicago to See a Rock Concert

by Bill Travis, Chicago rock critic

1. **Cabaret Metro** (3730 N. Clark St., 773/549-0203)—One of the premier rock clubs in the nation, with excellent sound, many vantage points, and a hip crowd. The beer selection is minimal, but then it's not a place to drink. The Smart Bar—spinning the hippest techno grooves—is downstairs.

2. **The Vic** (3145 N. Sheffield Ave., 773/472-0366)—This superb mid-sized theater, catering to national acts and cult faves only, is the best in Chicago. The sound is excellent, and descending levels to the stage make for decent viewing from the back. It doubles as a movie theater.

3. **Empty Bottle** (1035 N. Western Ave., 773/276-3600)—A centrally located stage provides for good sound. A cool place to see a local or independent-label band, this is the hangout spot for the local scenesters.

4. **Riviera** (4746 N. Racine Ave., 773/275-6800)—This is the biggest place one would want to see a band and still be a part of the experience.

5. **Double Door** (1572 N. Milwaukee Ave., 773/489-3160)—This place is primarily for first-album artists, cult faves, and the Rolling Stones. It includes a high stage, an excellent beer selection, and a little balcony with sofas in the back. There's a pool room downstairs.

6. **Beat Kitchen** (2100 W. Belmont, 773/281-4444)—This cool North Side two-room club has a bar in front and a stage in back. While it supports local bands and the sound is fine for the size, the crowd is not too hip.

7. **Buddy Guy's Legends** (754 S. Wabash Ave., 312/427-0333)—Though this is a blues club, it's still a good place to hear some of the best local and national blues artists in the city, and it's dingy enough to be authentic. Tables are placed in front of the stage so patrons can enjoy a bite to eat while listening to the music.

8. **Park West** (322 W. Armitage Ave., 773/929-5959)—This cozy, mid-sized venue offers cool, adult-oriented rock. Sitting in a booth is the key.

9. **Lounge Ax** (2438 N. Lincoln, 773/525-6620)—This small, smoky club caters to local, obscure, and first-album bands, offers a nice beer selection and tends to attract a hip crowd. It's owned by a couple of well-loved and respected scene supporters and is a cool place to hang out if you just want to listen to the music.

10. **Aragon Ballroom** (1106 W. Lawrence Ave., 773/561-9500)—This gymnasium-like theater is the only place where a band who can attract more people than the Riviera will hold can play. It mainly caters to national acts and all-ages shows. There's plenty of beer available on tap and served in Styrofoam cups.

FAR NORTH

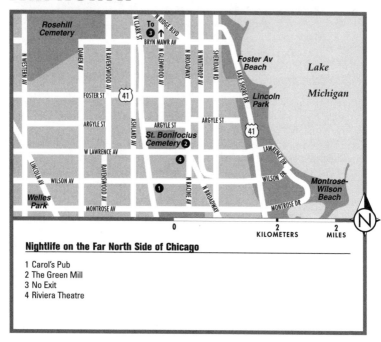

Nightlife on the Far North Side of Chicago

1 Carol's Pub
2 The Green Mill
3 No Exit
4 Riviera Theatre

rock concert. Really. Be wary of neighborhood crime, though, in this uptown area. There was a time when men with fishing lines used to lean out of their apartment windows to try and catch purses. (Far North)

BEAT KITCHEN
2100 W. Belmont Ave.
773/281-4444

The fact that this intimate club is located just a little bit off the beaten path near the Roscoe Village neighborhood keeps away the crowds of cruising singles and fraternity guys. The people generally come to hear the music and, because of that, this is one of the better places to see a rock show in town. With a decent sound system and an eclectic array of acts that usually consist of

local up-and-coming rockers, Beat Kitchen usually has two or three little-known bands a night, which increases your chances of finding a true diamond in the rough. If the music doesn't appeal, there's an upstairs lounge area where you can hang out. (North Side)

CABARET METRO
3730 N. Clark St.
773/549-0203

This is the classic place to see a rock band in Chicago. Though the accent here is on the best local bands, many national acts who could fill much bigger houses than this 1,000-person-capacity bar/concert hall choose Metro for its intimacy. Bob Dylan played here on his last club tour, as have other acts of considerable stature like The Specials, Cheap Trick, Joe Satriani, and Electric Airlines. (North Side)

CUBBY BEAR
1059 W. Addison St.
773/327-1662
The atmosphere here is generally more reminiscent of a sports bar than an honest-to-goodness music club, and the proximity to Wrigley Field brings in as many Cubs fans as music fans. Nevertheless, a number of excellent local and national acts perform here and, if you can keep your eyes on them and not on the big-screen TVs, you'll have a great time. (North Side)

DOUBLE DOOR
1572 N. Milwaukee Ave.
773/489-3160
Owned by the same folks who run the Cabaret Metro on the north side, this is one of the best places in the city to see a rock concert. Loud, crowded, and smoky, Double Door is favored by the best local soon-to-be-signed-to-a-major-label rock performers and by national acts who want to play in a more intimate club setting. On their last "Bridges to Babylon" tour, the Rolling Stones played a surprise gig here. (West Side)

EMPTY BOTTLE
1035 N. Western Ave.
773/276-3600
Once this was just another neighborhood bar in the hip enclave of artists and immigrants known as Ukrainian Village. As Chicago found its way onto the national rock 'n' roll map in the '90s, this quickly became one of the best spots for up-and-coming rock and other avant-garde bands. The talent pool continues to improve, but the neighborhood tavern ambiance

thankfully persists. On weekends, the Empty Bottle frequently plays host to national music industry types looking to find the next Smashing Pumpkins or Veruca Salt. (West Side)

HOUSE OF BLUES
329 N. Dearborn St.
312/527-BLUE
Never mind that this can be a rather oppressive and claustrophobic place to see a concert, and never mind that the rather staid business and celebrity-seeking crowds tend to be somewhat overwhelming here. This Chicago branch of the national chain still provides some of the best national musical talent the city has to offer. House of Blues affords the viewer the opportunity to see many major artists in an unusually intimate setting. Featured performers have included Jerry Lee Lewis, The Ventures, The Fabulous Thunderbirds, Dave Davies, LL Cool J, KC and the Sunshine Band, Eddie Money, and countless others. (Near North)

LOUNGE AX
2438 N. Lincoln Ave.
773/525-6620
There's very little room to sit down here, especially if you want to see the performers. If you step in for two seconds, it'll take a day to get the cigarette smell out of your jeans. However, for seeing on-the-rise local bands and national indie rockers, you can't beat this place. Not every band that plays here is going to make it big, but if a band's gonna make it, this is usually one of the places they start out. Look for performances by The Bells, Steel Blume, Mila Drumke, and other soon-to-be-major acts. (North Side)

MARTYR'S
3855 N. Lincoln Ave.
773/404-9494

Rock 'n' roll purists might scoff at the atmosphere—it's a little more comfortable, clean, and spacious than your average rock club. But if you don't think rock necessarily has to mean cramped and grungy, this is an excellent spot to see some excellent rock, folk, and funk performers. The music here tends to be a little mellower than some of the harder-edged clubs around. Keep an eye out for Chicago pop performers like the Stephanie Rogers Band and Brother Brother. (North Side)

RIVIERA THEATRE
4746 N. Racine Ave.
773/275-6800

Formerly an uptown movie palace and, for a while, a not particularly successful nightclub owned by Chicago Bulls player Cliff Levingston, the Riviera is now an excellent con-

Rosa's Lounge, p. 221

Rosa's Lounge

cert facility featuring national acts in a large but still somewhat intimate surrounding. The mosh pit up front is close to the action, while the upper-level seating area offers great sightlines and excellent sound. Performances here have included a star-studded Ska Against Racism and Collective Soul. (Far North)

SCHUBA'S
3159 N. Southport Ave.
773/525-2508

The accent here is often on more folksy or country-edged rock 'n' roll. However, while the atmosphere may be somewhat mellow, it's still a great place to see a concert. Past the frat-boy bar upfront lies this wood-paneled music hall that recalls as much a Cape Cod seafood restaurant as it does a rock club. But the quality of the performances booked here is uniformly excellent, and great acts like The Bells, Paul Kelly, Kristin Hersh, and Jimmie Dale Gillmore are common. (North Side)

THURSTON'S
1248 W. George St.
773/472-6900

Downstairs there's a neighborhood bar with pool tables and TVs. Upstairs you'll find a loud, somewhat claustrophobic concert facility that plays host to about three bands per night. The quality of the acts varies—usually they're local and not well-known—but sometimes the right band on the rise rocks the house and creates a memorable experience. Look for up-and-coming bands like Henry and Kill Hannah. (North Side)

OTHER CLUBS

THE ABBEY PUB

WEST SIDE

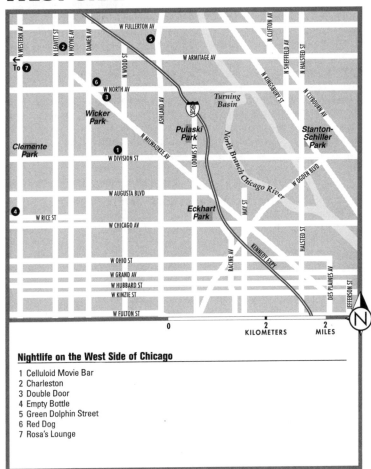

Nightlife on the West Side of Chicago

1 Celluloid Movie Bar
2 Charleston
3 Double Door
4 Empty Bottle
5 Green Dolphin Street
6 Red Dog
7 Rosa's Lounge

3420 W. Grace St.
773/478-4408

Despite the large Irish population in the city, there are few places to go for traditional Irish music. This is one of the best of them. You won't necessarily hear "Danny Boy" here, but you will find plenty of other classic tunes performed by local and national acts and which go quite well with a pint of ale. The

Abbey should definitely be checked out if you're in Chicago for St. Patrick's Day. (Greater Chicago)

BABY DOLL POLKA CLUB
6102 S. Central Ave.
773/525-3091

Just what you might expect from the name. A European party atmosphere pervades this club located on the southwest side of Chicago, a bastion for Polish and Lithuanian families. This is a hot spot on weekend nights. (South Side)

CAROL'S PUB
4659 N. Clark St.
773/334-2402

Chicago is not a country music town boasting only one country music station. But this honky-tonk club located in an unexpected neighborhood on the city's North Side is an exception. Regulars pile into this seedy but friendly bar to pound down beers, shoot pool, and listen to country music either live or on the jukebox. You might even hear a southern act from time to time. (Far North)

CHARLESTON
2076 N. Hoyne Ave.
773/489-4757

Once a neighborhood dive, with the sprucing up of the area around here this has become a funky outpost for great acoustic music. Local folk, bluegrass, and jazz performers play in this cramped but popular little bar, which is overflowing with good spirits and friendly atmosphere. (West Side)

ELBO ROOM
2871 N. Lincoln Ave.
773/549-5549

Everything from rock to jazz to funk to acid jazz shows up here. Located across the street from Thurston's, Elbo Room has a quiet, pristine bar upstairs and a roomy, low-ceilinged music club downstairs. The club features regular jazz and pop performers in a relaxed setting populated by music aficionados and young conservatives. (North Side)

NO EXIT
6970 N. Glenwood Ave.
773/743-3355

A long-time neighborhood favorite in this enclave of aging hippies and '60s refugees, No Exit offers a mellow, Haight-Asbury atmosphere and entertainment that ranges from stand-up comedy to poetry readings to improv to acoustic music. Regulars come here to sip coffee, enjoy the entertainment, read, or play chess. This is one of the only places in Chicago that could accurately be called a beatnik hangout. (Far North)

PARK WEST
322 W. Armitage Ave.
773/929-5959

A nightclub in the old-fashioned sense of the world, this is the sort of place where Sinatra might have played had the club been around in his early days. The place is slick, the drinks are pricey, and the customers come in expensive suits and pay top dollar to see great national performers in an intimate club setting. Entertainment here ranges from progressive rock 'n' roll (Joe Jackson, Elvis Costello) to comedy (Jackie Mason) to the more eclectic (Ziggy Marley and the Melody Makers, Brian Eno, Victoria Williams). (North Side)

THE WILD HARE
3530 N. Clark St.
773/327-0800

This is the best reggae club in the city. Always packed to the walls on weekends, this club sometimes provides an uneasy blend of reggae purists and slumming Cubs fans, but the music is always hot. Drug dealers frequently pass through here and outside on the street corner offering cheap ganja, not an especially good idea given the strong police presence in the neighborhood. (North Side)

PUBS AND BARS

GINGERMAN
3740 N. Clark St.
773/549-2050
Located near the Annoyance Theatre, Cabaret Metro, and the Live Bait Theater, this is one of the friendliest bars in the city and is populated by both theater types and rock 'n' rollers. There's beer available on tap and in bottles, an amusing crew of bartenders, and a lot of room to talk and play pool. (North Side)

RED LINE TAP
7000 N. Glenwood Ave.
773/465-8005
Adjacent to the Heartland Studio Theatre and the Heartland Café, this is a relatively new bar that has quickly become the hangout for the hippie-ish Rogers Park arts and theater crowd. The Red Line Tap includes cheap beer, a pool table, a great jukebox, and occasional live entertainment from local bands. (Greater Chicago)

SCHALLER'S PUMP
3714 S. Halsted St.
773/376-6332
This is the quintessential Bridgeport pub and the oldest bar in the city. Great atmosphere and cheap pitchers of beer are served up in this ultra-friendly bastion of Mayor Daley supporters and White Sox fans. (South Side)

SCHULIEN'S RESTAURANT
2100 W. Irving Park Rd.
773/478-2100
Some people say they come here for the authentic German cuisine that has been served here since 1955. But the people really come here for the bartenders who are almost all professional magicians. Stop by for a beer and a card trick or two. (North Side)

SHEFFIELD'S
3258 N. Sheffield Ave.
773/281-4989
Chicago has so many bars per square inch that bar lovers have to be choosy. This is one of the best and the most eclectic. There's a theater space at the back, a great bar at the front, and a wonderful patio that is one of the best places to enjoy a cold beer in the summer. (North Side)

COMEDY CLUBS

SECOND CITY
1616 N. Wells St.
312/337-3992
The ultimate spot for scripted comedy revues and improv. See the Performing Arts chapter. (Near North)

ZANIES
1548 N. Wells St.
312/337-4027
Despite the overflow of comedy clubs that flooded Chicago in the 1980s, it seems that there are hardly any left. Even eclectic clubs that used to have comedy one or two nights a week have fallen by the wayside. This is essentially the only traditional comedy club that remains within the Chicago city limits. Founded in 1978, this club sticks to the basics: no improv, no lame open-mike nights, no gimmicks; just some of the country's top national acts performing in an

intimate Old Town bar setting. (Near North)

DINNER THEATER

TONY AND TINA'S WEDDING
Pipers Alley
230 W. North Ave.
312/664-8844
Chicago has never been much of a home for dinner theater, but this long-running show is an exception. An interactive comedy, Tony and Tina's affords the spectator the opportunity to actually take part in an Italian wedding ceremony complete with an all-you-can-eat Italian buffet, wedding cake, live music, and dancing. As the folks at Tony and Tina's say, "You're more than a member of the audience; you're part of the family." (Near North)

MOVIE HOUSES OF NOTE

600 N. MICHIGAN
600 N. Michigan Ave.
312/255-9340
This is the best-located multiplex on the Mag Mile, and includes spacious theaters, comfortable seats, great sound, and good popcorn. Most of the major Hollywood and mainstream art house films are shown here. This is also the home of the Chicago International Film Festival, a showcase of some of the best American and world cinema that takes place for two weeks every October. (Near North)

BIOGRAPH THEATRE
2433 N. Lincoln Ave.
773/348-4123
Buffs of gangster lore and curiosity seekers don't always come here for the movies; they come here to check out the alley behind the Biograph. That's where famed gangster John Dillinger, accompanied by the mysterious "Lady in Red," was gunned down by the FBI in 1934 after seeing the movie *Manhattan Melodrama*. The theater looks much the same as it did back in the gangster days and the marquee is worth a look in itself. Inside, several screens in roomy theaters show the latest Hollywood and mainstream indie features. (North Side)

CELLULOID MOVIE BAR
1805 W. Division
312/707-8888
Located adjacent to the hipster groove bar Liquid Kitty, this place combines the best in a bar and a movie theater. There are comfy theater seats in the front and a bar in the back. Until the wee hours of dawn, regulars suck back beers and watch classic, contemporary, and underground films projected on video with a fairly good sound system. Screening choices here range from the expected *(Reservoir Dogs)* to the unusual (local indie filmmaker Jim Sikora's *Rock 'n' Roll Punk*) to cult classics *(Cool Hand Luke)*. (West Side)

ESQUIRE
58 E. OAK ST.
312/280-0101
Carving the interior of this art deco classic theater took away a little bit of its ambiance. The 1930s elegance remains, however, in the Esquire's impressive facade. Inside the theater, four state-of-the-art cinemas screen the latest Hollywood flicks. Lines are long on weekends and, on opening weekends, many movies tend to sell out. (Near North)

NEAR SOUTH/SOUTH SIDE

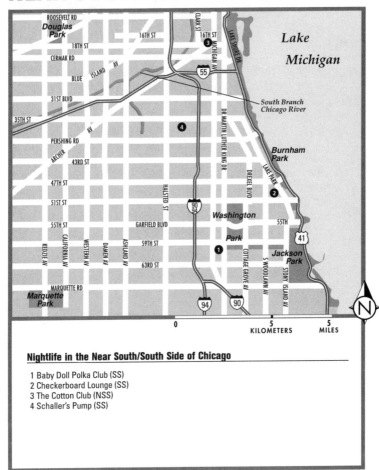

Lake Michigan

Nightlife in the Near South/South Side of Chicago

1 Baby Doll Polka Club (SS)
2 Checkerboard Lounge (SS)
3 The Cotton Club (NSS)
4 Schaller's Pump (SS)

FACETS MULTIMEDIA
1517 W. Fullerton Ave.
773/281-4114
One of the best programmed cinemas in the country, Facets features everything from the most obscure to the greatest overlooked classics. Housed in a small auditorium with a relatively small screen and an unimpressive sound system, Facets

packs in the crowds of art film fanatics with its retrospectives of the careers of major directors (Robert Bresson, Francesco Rosi), premieres of great films without major distributors (Wim Wenders' *Lisbon Story,* Adrienne Shelley's *Sudden Manhattan*), and new prints of classic films (Howard Hawks' *The Big Sleep,* Terence Malick's *Badlands*). The well-respected Chicago

The Best Ten Bars to Be Left Alone to Drink In

by John Covert, Chicago filmmaker and producer
(Films Covert has produced include *The Blind Lead*, *Waiting for the Man*, *Fatty Drives the Bus*, and *The Blank Page*)

Chicago Tribune theater critic Richard Christansen once said that "You can do what you want in Chicago and people will probably ignore you." He was referring to the theater and art worlds. I'm talking about drinking. Unfortunately, I have noticed over the years that more and more bartenders feel it necessary to chat with their customers, and more and more of my fellow patrons feel the same oddly stilted unsocial social pressure. Leave me alone and let me drink! When I'm drinking I'm thinking. And thinking for me is work. I don't bother you when you're working, do I? So, leave me alone, won't you, please?

What follows is a list of locations in Chicago where the bartenders understand the real etiquette of pouring a glass of whiskey and where there is usually no loud TV. Nobody gives a damn if you smoke a cigar and, even better, no one feels obligated to ask you, "Is that a Cuban?"

1. **Hop Leaf** (5148 N. Clark St., 773/334-9851)
   The best beer selection I've ever seen, seriously. But go only on weeknights. Avoid the poseur theater crowds on Friday and Saturday unless you enjoy hearing a Dork on a Date ask for a Miller Genuine Draft after reading a beer list about a mile long. The bartenders are just right with the drinks and their very limited conversation, and they play great music.

2. **Map Room** (1949 N. Hoyne Ave., 773/252-7636)
   Best Sunday mornings in town: pastries, transcendent Bloody Marys, and a free pool. It seems to have the deepest roster of excellent bartenders in town—there's a new face behind the bar every time I go.

3. **Baba Luci** (2152 N. Damen Ave., 773/486-5300)
   A great cozy and dark upstairs. Lounge band and excellent CDs during breaks. The best owner/host in the city—Frank Amanti. Amazing, medium-priced Italian food served at the bar. This place is a must.

4. **Pinkies** (1928 N. Leavitt St., 773/384-8388)
   Authentic neighborhood bar taken over by young owners. Excellent CDs, a pool table, and a cat that feels free to jump onto your lap.

5. **Ginger Man** (3740 N. Clark St., 773/549-2050)
Next to Cabaret Metro and across from the Annoyance Theater. A real-deal, late-night hangout for artists in a sports-saturated neighborhood. Includes a second room with multiple world-class pool tables. Bartenders tend to be a little terse, but who wouldn't be if they had to deal with drunk 22-year-olds wearing backwards baseball caps?

6. **Marie's Riptide** (1948 N. Hermitage)
A Chicago classic. A real-deal local bar that's been around forever and is currently in vogue. Marie is always there with a story and a shot. After-hours it's absolutely packed, but the mood is always friendly and the music is good.

7. **Thurstons** (1248 W. George St., 773/472-6900)
A bit nuts. A big, dark two-level place filled with a younger crowd, tremendous energy, great bands, a couple of pool tables, and good drinks at good prices.

8. **Rose's** (2656 N. Lincoln Ave., 773/327-4000)
Small, intimate, and filled with Rose's knickknacks and memories, a pool table, and a good jukebox. There is a certain sadness that hangs over the place, especially when you find out that Rose's husband died just before it opened and she stepped in never having run a bar before. But often a little sadness makes for just the right mix.

9. **Leopard Lounge** (1645 W. Cortland St., 773/862-7877
A more upscale cigars, martinis, and swingers sort of place. The bartenders are extremely friendly, the jukebox is filled with great music, the pool table is usually open for a game, and it's only two doors down from Jane's, a great restaurant. Julie, Jane's stellar hostess, will actually walk over and let you know when your table is ready. First class all the way around and always quiet enough for talking.

10. **Four Seasons** (120 E. Delaware Pl., 312/280-8800)
The best high-class bar in the city. A wonderful lounge area and a great bar filled with the best liquor money can buy. Cigars are encouraged and you never know who you'll run into. The bartenders are just terse enough to never let you forget that you are at the Four Seasons, and the prices are, well, just what they should be.

CHICAGO FILM FESTIVALS

Chicago, aside from having many fine movie theaters, is also notable for having a good number of excellent film festivals. These include the **Chicago International Film Festival** *(held for two weeks in mid-October), the* **Silver Images Film Festival** *(dealing with films about the elderly, held for two weeks in mid-May), the* **Chicago Underground Film Festival** *(featuring offbeat and underground films, held for a week in mid-August), the Black* **Harvest Film Festival** *(a round-up of African cinema held at the Film Center at the School of the Art Institute for 10 days in early August), the* **Gay and Lesbian International Film Festival** *(held for a week in mid-November),* **Women in the Director's Chair** *(focusing on women directors and held in March), the* **Latino Film Festival** *(held in May), and the* **Chicago International Children's Film Festival** *(see Kids' Stuff). Check the papers for times and actual dates when you're in town.*

International Children's Film Festival and Latino Chicago Film Festival also screen here. Facets also houses the city's best video store (see Shopping). (North Side)

FILM CENTER OF THE ART INSTITUTE
280 S. Columbus Dr.
312/443-3735

There's only one major problem with this theater—a decided absence of popcorn. Other than that, this is an exceedingly well-programmed movie house featuring classics as well as foreign films that don't play the major arthouses. Overlooked masterworks (Michelangelo Antonioni's *Identification of a Woman*), Chicago premieres of new films *(Waiting for the Man, The Blank Page)*, and great old films

(High Noon, Touch of Evil) all play in this comfortable auditorium as part of a number of screening series for the School of the Art Institute students. (Downtown)

FINE ARTS THEATER
418 S. Michigan Ave.
312/939-3700

Located in the fine arts building in what was once a showroom for Studebaker automobiles and later a home to two of the city's major legitimate theaters (The Studebaker and the World Playhouse), the Fine Arts plays a great number of mainstream art house and foreign films. Though the surroundings can get a little lonely—bordering on creepy—at night, the selection of films is generally excellent. (Downtown)

MUSIC BOX THEATER
3733 N. Southport Ave.
773/871-6604

Without a doubt this is the best place in Chicago to see a movie. The Music Box is the sort of theater where you come first for the atmosphere and second for the movie. With a great program of foreign films and independent American cinema, the Music Box dates back to the 1920s. It has maintained its old-fashioned movie-palace splendor with its columns, blinking stars, and moving clouds overhead, as well as with its pipe organ that plays during intermission. Aside from the beautiful main auditorium, the Music Box has recently opened a smaller, less impressive second cinema. Either way, though, this is a classic moviegoing experience. Special events throughout the year include annual Christmas screenings of *It's a Wonderful Life* and *White Christmas* with Christmas carol sing-alongs; midnight screenings of cult classics; the Gay and Lesbian International Film Festival; and a great weekend series of classic cinema, Saturday and Sunday mornings at 11:30. (North Side)

PATIO THEATER
6008 W. Irving Park Rd.
773/545-0206

In the same tradition as the Music Box, this is another beautiful, restored 1920s movie palace. The sound system, though, isn't particularly good; the location is somewhat inconvenient (way west of the city); and the selection of films (basically second-run Hollywood blockbusters) is not imaginative. Still, the surroundings are very picturesque and you can't beat the price ($2 per show). (Greater Chicago)

PIPERS ALLEY
North Ave. and Wells St.
312/642-7500

Located in the Pipers Alley mall next to Second City, this is one of the best first-run movie houses in Chicago. Catering to the yuppie and artsy crowds, Pipers Alley usually sticks to more offbeat Hollywood and indie fare and includes great auditoriums, great seats, and great popcorn.

National Park Service–Indiana Dunes National Lakeshore

12

DAY TRIPS FROM CHICAGO

DAY TRIP: Evanston, Illinois

Distance from Chicago: 10 miles from the Loop (a 20-minute drive)
Though most people think of Evanston as a Chicago suburb (the first suburb to the north of the city), Evanston residents like to think of Chicago as a suburb of Evanston. That's because Evanston has been around a good while longer. Settled in 1826 and incorporated as a town, this picturesque small burg (population: 73,000) is famous all over the world as the national headquarters of the **Women's Christian Temperance Union** (1730 Chicago Ave., 847/864-1396), whose influence is still felt here. Even up until the 1980s you couldn't find a liquor store here. Today there is one. The abundance of bars on Howard Street at the border between Chicago and Evanston is a holdover from the times when beer-thirsty Evanstonians would have to cross over the border into Chicago in order to whet their whistles.

Today, Evanston is better known as the home of **Northwestern University**, a Big Ten school which boasts the most aesthetically pleasing college campus in the Midwest with its serene tree-shaded grounds, its bike trail, its beautiful **Shakespeare Garden** (Sheridan Rd. and Garrett Pl.), and its proximity to Lake Michigan. The university has its own private beach and the athletic facilities look directly out onto Lake Michigan. The campus also houses the **Mary and Leigh Block Gallery** (1967 S. Campus Dr., 847/491-4000), a small but decent art museum with special exhibitions and a sculpture garden, along with a concert facility, **Pick-Staiger Concert Hall** (see Performing Arts).

CHICAGO REGION

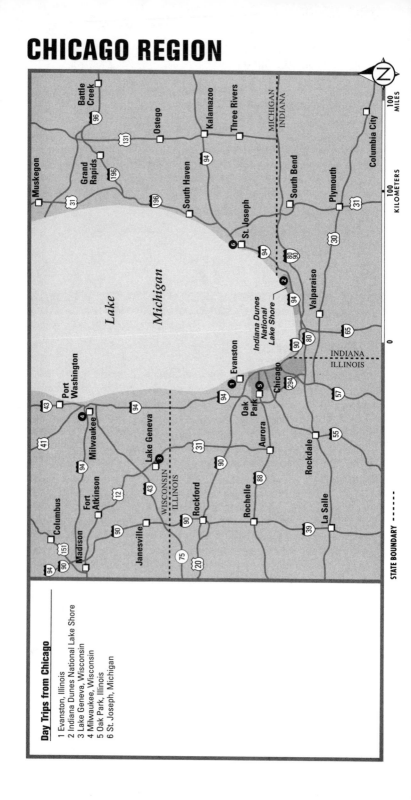

Day Trips from Chicago

1 Evanston, Illinois
2 Indiana Dunes National Lake Shore
3 Lake Geneva, Wisconsin
4 Milwaukee, Wisconsin
5 Oak Park, Illinois
6 St. Joseph, Michigan

STATE BOUNDARY - - - - - -

Downtown Evanston has a bustling college-town atmosphere with its shops, restaurants, bookstores, and cafés. **Sherman Avenue** is home to **The Unicorn Café** (1723 Sherman Ave., 847/332-2312), a pleasant place to enjoy a cappuccino and a scone on a warm summer day; places to buy blue jeans, CDs, and flowers; as well as good spots for rare and used books (**Bookman's Alley**, 1712 Sherman Ave., 847/869-6999), and new books (**Barnes & Noble Booksellers**, 1701 Sherman Ave., 847/328-0883). Around the corner, **JK Sweets** (720½ Clark Street) has delicious baked goods and ice cream. Buy a cone here and either walk north to see the lavish homes of North Evanston or east to check out Northwestern's campus and the lake. A smaller downtown location is to be found on Main Street, home to a number of quaint, old-fashioned general stores and toy shops.

Evanston is also home to some excellent restaurants. For Greek cuisine, check out **Cross-Rhodes** (913½ Chicago Ave., 847/475-4475). For Japanese, **Kuni's** (511 Main St., 847/328-2004) is probably your best bet. For upscale dining, **Trio** (1625 Hinman Ave., 847/733-8746) is an Evanston favorite. **Blind Faith Café** (525 Dempster St., 847/328-6875) has some of the best vegetarian cuisine in the Chicago area. For a perfect college-town dining experience, head straight to **Yesterday's** (1850 Sherman Ave., 847/864-8464) for a foot-long hot dog. For the best Chicago-style hot dog in town, however, try **Mustard's Last Stand** (1613 Central Ave., 847/864-2700).

Serving as a bridge into the highly cultured communities on Chicago's North Shore, Evanston is home to fine theaters and museums. The best professional theater in Evanston may be found at the **Noyes Cultural Arts Center** (926 Noyes St., 847/491-0266), a complex of studios, classrooms, and performance spaces, and home to **The Next Theater** and the **Piven Theater Workshop** (a training facility and performing group where the Cusack family, Lili Taylor, and Jeremy Piven of *Ellen* fame got their starts). Museum lovers should check out the **Mitchell American Indian Museum** (2600 Central Park, 847/866/1395) (see Museums and Galleries).

On a nice day you might want to consider driving further north from Evanston and touring some of the other suburbs along the North Shore including Wilmette, Winnetka, Glencoe, Highland Park, and Kenilworth (which is known as one of the most affluent towns in the country). If you happen to be in Evanston during the summer, be sure to check out its **Custer Street Art Fair**, which has excellent displays from local artists and craftspeople; as well as its old-fashioned **Fourth of July Parade**, which heads down Central Street from the east end of town.

Getting There From Chicago:
Head north on Lake Shore Drive and follow Sheridan Road around the lakefront until you reach the southern tip of Evanston; or follow one of several major streets (i.e., Western Ave., California Ave., Ridge Ave.) north directly into town.

DAY TRIP: Milwaukee, Wisconsin

Distance From Chicago: 81 miles (a 90-minute drive)

Visiting Milwaukee is sort of like vacationing in a miniaturized Epcot version of Chicago. The recipe is simple: Shrink the Windy City down three times, then add frozen custard, beer, and the Violent Femmes. A city of approximately one million, settled in 1835, the bratwurst capital of the Great Lakes region has a decidedly unpretentious shot-and-a-Pabst feel to it along with a fair amount of cultural and culinary diversity.

Lodging in Milwaukee is no trouble whatsoever—it's available in a variety of types and price ranges—and finding a vacancy is usually easy. The city's most prestigious hotel is the **Pfister** (424 E. Wisconsin, 414/273-8222). Erected in 1893, the hotel has the polished marble and brass feel of old-style opulence. Lodging may also be had at the **Hyatt Regency** (333 W. Kilbourn, 414/276-1234), where a revolving rooftop restaurant boasts a large selection of wacky, colorful, and overpriced drinks.

Milwaukee's German heritage still is responsible for its most storied restaurants. The best known of these is **Karl Ratzch's** (320 E. Mason, 414/276-2720), just a hop, skip, and a belch away from the Pfister. Here dirndl-sporting waitresses deliver tasty, if somewhat dense portions of wursts, spaetzle, and schnitzels, and, natch, an excellent selection of beers at about $25 a head. Similar fare at comparable prices may be had at **Mader's** (1037 Old World 3rd St., 414-271-3377), which also affords the diner the opportunity to look at their extensive collection of figurines and other tchotchkes.

During the day there are a fair amount of artsy and other sundry cultural events to choose from in Milwaukee. There are reportedly about 3,000 animals at the famed **Milwaukee County Zoo** (10001 W. Bluemound Rd., 414/771-3040). Another cool spot is the **Mitchell Park Horticulture Conservatory** (524 S. Layton Blvd., 414/649-7800). Also known as "The Domes," the conservatory houses desert, tropical, and other types of plants under geodesic domes that resemble exhibition halls from 1960s world's fairs. The conservatory claims to have 1,200 plant species. The deceptively large **Milwaukee Art Museum** (750 N. Lincoln Memorial Drive, 414/224-3200), located in the War Memorial Building with a cool view of the nearby lake, has what

Milwaukee County Zoo

M. A. Nepper/Greater Milwaukee CVB

might best be termed "a little bit of everything" from a surprisingly number of modern artists.

Nightlife options in Milwaukee generally consist of theater, music, and beer; and, when you mix the three, you're even better off. **Milwaukee Repertory Theater** (108 E. Wells St., 414/224-9490), generally recognized as the city's most respected theater company, features a good roundup of contemporary and classic works.

Located in an up-and-coming, groovy Soho-ish area and led by the nationally renowned artistic director John Schneider, **Theatre X** (158 N. Broadway, 414/291-7800) is thought to be a more cutting edge and adventurous theater. The **Times Cinema** (5906 W. Vliet St., 414/453-2436) shows a different classic film each week. Recent showings have included Kurosawa's *Kagemusha*, Tod Browning's *Freaks*, and Kazan's *A Streetcar Named Desire*.

On the more stodgy and respectable side of things, the **MSO**, the **Florentine Opera**, and the **Milwaukee Ballet** perform in somewhat irregular fashion at Uihlein Hall in the city's **Marcus Center for the Performing Arts** (corner of State and Water Streets, 414/273-7296). The 1895 landmark Victorian-style **Pabst Theatre** (144 E. Wells, 414/286-3663) is a picturesque setting for touring theater productions, jazz concerts, and recitals.

When the major rock acts come to town, you can frequently find them at The Rave, also known as **The Eagles Auditorium** (2401 W. Wisconsin Ave., 414/342-RAVE), a strange but atmospheric place to see (if not hear particularly well) a concert. Rimmed by pink neon, The Rave—the place where Buddy Holly once played—resembles a roller rink or high school gymnasium with bleachers torn out to make room for folding chairs. The washroom is a good place to get into tiffs with bearded guys in Harley jackets.

In the summer Milwaukee belongs to the Brewers and **Milwaukee County Stadium** (2011 S. 46th St., 414/933-9000). While County Stadium may not be the most hospitable baseball stadium in the country, it has loads of atmosphere along with its bratwurst and legendary tailgating barbecues. The Bucks play in the 20,000-seat **Bradley Center** (1001 N. Fourth Street, 414/271-4000); as does the minor league hockey club, the Milwaukee Admirals.

Getting There From Chicago:

Follow I-94 west out of Chicago. The highway leads straight into downtown Milwaukee. Amtrak at Chicago's Union Station offers direct service into Milwaukee (800/USA-RAIL).

DAY TRIP: Lake Geneva, Wisconsin

Distance From Chicago: About 80 miles northwest of Chicago (driving time: less than two hours)

One hundred years ago Lake Geneva was the resort town for the rich and influential of Chicago. The Wrigley family had a summer home here, as did Montgomery Ward. These days some of Chicago's wealthy and famous continue to vacation here, and some have even moved to the quaint lakeside town.

Summers in Lake Geneva are a time for paddleboating, swimming, and sailing. Lake Geneva borders 25 miles of the smooth and serene body of water that bears its name, and the **Lake Geneva Municipal Beach** is one of many beaches in the area suitable for sunbathing, Frisbee playing, or people-watching. **The Geneva Lake Cruise Line** (800/558-5911) offers paddleboat tours of the area. Horseback riding and nature walks are also available here. For riding try the **Geneva Lakes Riding Stable** (414/728-6500); for walks contact the **Geneva Lake Conservancy** (414/248-3358). Strawberry picking is another favorite activity. Just follow the strawberry signs on Highway 94 and Highway 50. Winters are excellent for snowmobiling and ice-skating, and Lake Geneva's Main Street is a good place to shop for fudge, ice cream, and antiques year-round.

Lake Geneva is also famous for its resorts, which offer everything from indoor and outdoor pools to miniature golf. The most venerable of these are **Lake Lawn Lodge** (414/728-5511) and **The Abbey** (414/275-6811). For good, picturesque dining, check out the **Grandview Restaurant** (N2009 State Rd. 120, 414/248-5680.) The Grandview features seafood and great views of the lake.

Riviera on Lake Geneva

Geneva Lake Area Chamber of Commerce

In nearby Williams Bay, the famed **Yerkes Observatory** (414/245-5555) is run by the University of Chicago's astrophysics Department. The facility offers free tours on Saturday mornings. Here you can look at the famed 40-inch refractor, the world's largest lens-type telescope, and take special night tours that offer glimpses of the starlit sky.

Getting There From Chicago:
Take I-94 north from Chicago over the Wisconsin border. Continue for just over five miles, then exit at Highway 50 and follow it west into Lake Geneva.

DAY TRIP: St. Joseph, Michigan, and Environs

Distance From Chicago: 100 miles (a two-hour drive)

When it's cherry blossom time, it's cherry-spitting time, too. Nowhere does that fact take on more significance than in southern Michigan. Taking I-94 north from Chicago into Michigan, one arrives in the middle of St. Joseph, a quaint little town that, along with a number of neighboring resort towns, is a favorite of summer vacationing Chicagoans, including (rumor has it) Oprah Winfrey and Roger Ebert. Here, in May, you'll find the annual late spring Blossomtime Festival, where each city around St. Joe crowns a Miss Blossom, all of whom ride floats in the Great Floral Parade. In early July, as if to signal the coming end of the cherry season, the town holds the International Cherry Spitting Championship, in which spitters try to best the 1988 distance record of 72 feet.

But this area is clearly about more than cherries. And it's about more than delicious cider (although you should try it at **Miller Orchards**, 3265 Friday Rd., 800/457-7892), or comfy lodging in excellent bed-and-breakfasts (though if you have an evening to spare you might want to check out the lovely **South Cliff Inn**, 1900 Lakeshore Dr., 616/983-4881), or the best diner food you've ever tasted (**Ma and Pa's Country Kettle**, I-94 and M140 in Watervliet, has amazing cheese fries, great turkey platters, and delicious fried okra). No, it's about much more than all that. And that's why travelers keep flocking here to the Michigan side of Lake Michigan.

There are more than a handful of towns around here, each with their own sites, many of which are worth day trips in and of themselves. St. Joseph's downtown features the **Curious Kids Museum**, which includes a

Downtown St. Joseph

soap-bubble exhibit in which children may attempt to encase themselves in a giant bubble. There is also a well-designed playground and beach (**Silver Beach County Park**), and the **Krasl Art Center** (707 Lake) has a good selection of changing exhibits by modern artists. In neighboring Benton Harbor, there stands the **House of David**, the remnants of a once-popular cult whose followers preached abstinence and had a famous baseball team in the '30s and '40s. Only a few survivors of the religion remain here; they're awaiting their deliverance in the 21st century.

Though perhaps uncomfortably close to a nuclear power plant, the **Warren Dunes** is a picturesque state park along Lake Michigan. One of the most scenic national parks in the area is **Grand Mere State Park** (616/426-4013) with its lakes, wetlands, dunes, and exotic birds. Not far away, **New Buffalo**, Michigan, is a great spot for antique shopping and winery visits, as is neighboring **Union Pier**. So, position yourself in St. Joseph and make your way through all of the nearby lakeside towns.

Getting There From Chicago:
Follow I-94 east out of Chicago and into Michigan until you see the St. Joseph exits.

DAY TRIP: Indiana Dunes National Lakeshore

Distance From Chicago: 50 miles southeast of Chicago (about a 90 minute drive)

After a few days in the flatlands of Chicago, one may well hunger for hills. There aren't many nearby. But there are dunes. And a great many of them can be found in this national park, where one can spend hours or days roaming through nature, hang-gliding off of **Mount Baldy**, swimming in **Lake Michigan**, or lazing atop the dunes. The **Indiana Dunes National Lakeshore** (1100 N. Mineral Springs Rd., 219/926-7561) is a spectacular natural wonder. Spanning 25 miles along southern Lake Michigan, it is bordered by the former steel capital Gary, to the east, and Michigan City, to the west.

With more than 1,500 plant species (Dunes ranks seventh in plant diversity among all U.S. national parks) including two hundred varieties of wildflowers, the Dunes' 45 miles of nature trails are wonderful for hiking, especially in autumn. Wildlife here include deer, hognose snakes, and more than 300 species of birds. In the park there is the **Bailly Homestead,** the 1830s home site of Joseph-Bailly, a French-Canadian fur trader; and **Chellberg Farm**, an 1874 farm that is still operational today. One of the more peculiar sights near the Indiana Dunes may be found in **Beverly Shores** where five houses stand that were transported and re-located here from Chicago after the 1933 Century of Progress Exposition and World's Fair. These include the **Armco-Ferro-Mayflower House**, the **Rostone House**, the **Florida Tropical House**, the **Cypress Log House**, and the **House of Tomorrow.** The houses are not open to the public, but they are worth a long look from the road.

In addition to these spots, there are bogs (some of which are designated national natural landmarks), prairies, wetlands, and woodland forests. In March there is the **Maple Sugar Time Festival**, while in September there is the **Harvest Festival**. Both festivals involve music, arts and crafts, and storytelling. The main reason that people come to the area, however, are the Indiana Dunes' three magnificent beaches open for swimming May 1 through September 1. If you choose to stay here overnight, there are excellent camping opportunities available. For more information, contact the **National Lakeshote** at (219/926-7561, ext. 225).

Outside the Dunes area, attractions are slim. But if you choose to dine around here, your best bet is probably the venerable **Phil Smidt's** (1205 N. Indianapolis Blvd., 219/659-0025), a classic seafood joint that is such a familiar part of the Midwestern landscape that it probably should be designated a national historic landmark. Other options include a couple of good burger joints—**Pump's on 12** (3085 W. Dunes Hwy., 219/874-6201) and **Wagner's** (361 Wagner Rd., Porter, Indiana, 219/926-7614).

Getting There From Chicago:
By car, take I-80/94 to Indiana and follow the road signs to the dunes. By train, take the South Shore Line from Michigan Avenue and Randolph Street south to the Dunes Park station.

DAY TRIP: Oak Park, Illinois

Distance From Chicago: 9 miles west of downtown Chicago

Oak Park owes much of its historic appeal to two people who lived there almost a hundred years ago. The birthplace of Nobel Prize–winning author Ernest Hemingway and the workplace of architectural pioneer Frank Lloyd Wright (Wright lived here for 20 years around the turn of the last century), this town of approximately 60,000 is loaded with architectural landmarks and historical curiosities. But luckily, it is not just a town living in the past, for Oak Park maintains a contemporary, urban atmosphere with its strong links to its history.

Frank Lloyd Wright Home and Studio

Jon Miller/Hedrich-Blessing

Buildings designed by Frank Lloyd Wright (1869–1959)—one of the founders of the "Prairie School" of architecture—are plentiful here. While most of them are private homes, you can either walk past them on your own or take a tour which begins at the **Frank Lloyd Wright Home and Studio** (951 Chicago Ave., 708/848-1976). The tour will take you past the Tudor-influenced **Nathan Moore House** (333 Forest Ave.); the sleek, low-to-the-ground 1902 **Arthur B. Heurtley House**; and the **Frank W. Thomas House** (210 Forest Ave.); as well as numerous others. More than twenty buildings designed by Wright currently stand in Oak Park. **The Unity Temple** (875 Lake St.), which Wright built in the first decade of the 20th century, can also be toured (see Sights and Attractions). To get a feel for where the author of *The Old Man and the Sea* and *A Farewell to Arms* got his start, tour the **Ernest Hemingway Museum** (200 N. Oak Park Ave.) and the **Ernest Hemingway Birthplace** (339 N. Oak Park Ave., 708/848-2222). See Museums and Galleries for more information.

Oak Park has a vibrant arts and culture scene in addition to its historical landmarks. The **Oak Park Festival Theatre** (1010 Lake St., 708/524-2050) is one of the better summer theater festivals. Works by William Shakespeare and others are performed here by some of Chicago's best up-and-coming actors, including Gillian Geraghty. **The Circle Theater** (7300 W. Madison St., 708/771-0700) in neighboring Forest Park is a very strong professional theater performing classics and new works in low-budget productions directed by well-respected Chicagoans like Kay Martinovich. Oak Park also features one of the best Chicago ice-cream parlors, **Peterson's Ice Cream Parlor** (1104 W. Chicago Ave., 708/386-6130). Dining choices in the area include the Cajun-influenced seafood restaurant **Philander's,** located in the historic Carleton Hotel (1120 Pleasant St., 708/848-4250). The hotel also offers **Poor Phil's Shell Bar** (708/848-0871) with sidewalk dining in the summer.

For more information on places to visit in Oak Park, visit the **Oak Park Visitors Center** (1010 Lake St., 708/848-1500).

Getting There From Chicago:
By car, get on the Eisenhower Expressway (I-290) and follow it west for about nine miles until you reach Harlem Avenue. Turn right off the exit and you'll find yourself in downtown Oak Park. By train, Oak Park is easily accessible via the CTA Green Line.

EMERGENCY PHONE NUMBERS

Police, 911
Fire, 911
Ambulance, 911
Police (Non-emergency)
    708/867-4353
Fire (Non-emergency) 708/867-5428

Major Hospitals and Emergency Medical Centers

Northwestern Memorial Hospital
250 E. Superior
312/908-2000

Rush-Presbyterian-St. Luke's Medical Center
1653 W. Congress Pkwy.
312/942-5000

Michael Reese Hospital
2929 S. Ellis Ave.
312/791-2000

University of Chicago Hospitals
5841 S. Maryland Ave.
773/702-1000

VISTOR INFORMATION

Chicago Office of Tourism,
312/744-2400 or 800/226-6632

WEATHER INFORMATION

312/976-1212

CAR RENTAL

Alamo, 800/327-9633
Avis, 800/879-2847
Budget, 800/527-0700

Dollar, 800/699-4000
Hertz, 800/654-3131

INFORMATION FOR THE DISABLED

Mayor's Office for People with Disabilities
312/744-6673

MULTICULTURAL RESOURCES

Afro-American Cultural Center
773/878-7101

Chicago Area Gay and Lesbian Chamber of Commerce
312/567-8500

Chicago Black Lesbian and Gays
312/409-4917

Chicago Commission on Human Relations
312/744-7911

Queer Nation
773/202-5482

OTHER COMMUNITY ORGANIZATIONS

Chicago Women's Health Center
3435 N. Sheffield Ave.
773/935-6126

Women's Action Coalition
773/918-9161

CITY MEDIA

Daily Newspapers

Chicago Defender
Chicago Sun-Times
Chicago Tribune
Daily Herald
Daily Southtown

Alternative Newspapers

Chicago Reader, weekly
New City, weekly
Windy City Times

Magazines

Chicago Magazine, monthly
Crain's Chicago Business, weekly

Commercial Television Stations

WBBM	Channel 2 (CBS)
WMAQ	Channel 5 (NBC)
WLS	Channel 7 (ABC)
WGN	Channel 9 (Syndicated)
WTTW	Channel 11 (PBS)
WCIU	Channel 26 (Ind.)
WFLD	Channel 32 (Fox)
WCFC	Channel 38 (Christian programming)
WSNS	Channel 44 (Spanish programming)
WPWR	Channel 50 (Ind.)

Radio Stations

WNUR 89.3 FM	Eclectic/North western University
WBEZ 91.5 FM	National Public Radio/talk/jazz/news
WXRT 93.1 FM	progressive rock
WXCD 94.7 FM	classic rock

WNUA 95.5 FM	new age
WBBM 96.3 FM	top 40
WNIB 97.1 FM	classical
WLUP 97.9 FM	classic rock
WFMT 98.7 FM	classical
WUSN 99.5 FM	country
WKQX 101.1 FM	alternative
	top 40
WRCX 103.5 FM	heavy metal
WJMK 104.3 FM	oldies
WCKG 105.9 FM	classic rock/talk
107.5 FM	R&B
WMAQ 670 AM	news/sports talk
WGN 720 AM	news/talk
WBBM 780 AM	CBS news
WLS 890 AM	news/talk
WMVP 1000 AM	news/talk
WSCR 1160 AM	sports talk

BOOKSTORES

Chicago has hundreds of great bookstores—national chains, unique regional independents, special-topic shops, and cozy, hole-in-the-wall used-book sellers that are great for browsing on a rainy (or snowy) Saturday afternoon.

Here is a list of the city's largest general-interest retailers that sell new books.

Barbara's Bookstore
1350 N. Wells St.
Chicago, IL 60610
312/258-8007

2 N. Riverside Plaza
Chicago, IL 60606
312/258-8013

Navy Pier Family Pavilion
700 E. Grand Ave.
Chicago, IL 60611
312-222-0607

Sears Tower
233 Wacker Drive

Chicago. IL 60606
312/466-0223

B. Dalton Bookseller
Downtown Chicago
129 N. Wabash Ave.
Chicago, IL 60602
312/922-5219

222 Merchandise Mart Plaza
Suite 204
Chicago, Il 60654
312/329-1881

175 W. Jackson
Chicago, IL 60604
312/922-5219

Barnes & Noble
659 Diversey Pkwy
Chicago, IL 60614
773/871-9004

1441 Webster Ave.
Chicago, IL 60614
773-871-3610

Book-Line
1958 Damen
Chicago, IL 60647

Booksellers Row
408 S. Michigan Ave.
Chicago, IL 60605
773/427-4242

Borders Books & Music
830 N. Michigan
Chicago, IL 60611
312/573-0564

2817 N. Clark St.
Chicago, IL 60657
312935-3909

Brent Books & Card Ltd.
309 W. Washington
Chicago, IL 60606

312/364-0205

Coopersmith's
900 N. Michigan Ave.
Chicago, IL 60611
312/337-0330

Crown Books
26 N.Wabash Ave.
Chicago, IL 60602
312/351-1150

144 S. Clark St.
Chicago, IL 60603
312/857-0613

1714 Sheffield Ave.
Chicago, IL 60614
312/787-4370

3322 Western Ave.
Chicago, IL 60618
773/529-2753

Earful of Books
565 W. Diversey Pkwy.
Chicago, IL 60614
773/388-9843

Epicenter Bookshop
7540 S. Halstead
Chicago, IL 60607
312/413-5526

57th Street Books
1301 57th St.
Chicago, IL 60637
773/-684-1300

Lincoln Park Bookshop
2423 N. Clark St.
Chicago, IL 60614
773/477-7088

Modern Bookstore
3118 Halstead
Chicago, IL 60608
312/225-7911

Reading on Walden
9913 S. Walden Pkwy
Chicago, IL 60643
773-233--7633

Rizzoli Bookstore
Water Tower Place
835 N. Michigan Ave.
Chicago,. IL 60611
312/642-3500

Sandermeyer's Bookstore in Printer's Row
714 S. Dearborn
Chicago, IL 60605
312/922-2104

Seminary Cooperative Bookstore
5757 S. University Ave.
Chicago, IL 60637
773/752-4381

Super Crown Books
105 S. Wabash Ave.
Chicago, IL 60603
312/782-7667

801 W. Diversey Pkwy.
Chicago, IL 60614
773/-327-1551

Waldenbooks
127 Madison St. & LaSalle
Chicago, IL 60602
312-236-8446

Ford City S./ City Center
7601 S. Cicero
Chicago, IL 60652
978-236-4833

INDEX

You'll Feel like a Local When You Travel with Guides from John Muir Publications

CiTY·SMaRT™ GUIDEBOOKS

Pick one for your favorite city: *Albuquerque, Anchorage, Austin, Calgary, Charlotte, Chicago, Cincinnati, Cleveland, Denver, Indianapolis, Kansas City, Memphis, Milwaukee, Minneapolis/St. Paul, Nashville, Pittsburgh, Portland, Richmond, Salt Lake City, San Antonio, St. Louis, Tampa/St. Petersburg, Tucson*

Guides for kids 6 to 10 years old about what to do, where to go, and how to have fun in: *Atlanta, Austin, Boston, Chicago, Cleveland, Denver, Indianapolis, Kansas City, Miami, Milwaukee, Minneapolis/St. Paul, Nashville, Portland, San Francisco, Seattle, Washington D.C.*

TRAVEL✦SMART®

Trip planners with select recommendations to: *Alaska, American Southwest, Carolinas, Colorado, Deep South, Eastern Canada, Florida Gulf Coast, Hawaii, Illinois/Indiana, Kentucky/Tennessee, Maryland/Delaware, Michigan, Minnesota/Wisconsin, Montana/Wyoming/Idaho, New England, New Mexico, New York State, Northern California, Ohio, Pacific Northwest, Pennsylvania/New Jersey, South Florida and the Keys, Southern California, Texas, Utah, Virginias, Western Canada*

Rick Steves' GUIDES

See *Europe Through the Back Door* and take along guides to: *France, Belgium & the Netherlands; Germany, Austria & Switzerland; Great Britain & Ireland; Italy; Russia & the Baltics; Scandinavia; Spain & Portugal; London; Paris;* or the *Best of Europe*

ADVENTURES IN NATURE

Plan your next adventure in: *Alaska, Belize, Caribbean, Costa Rica, Guatemala, Honduras, Mexico*

JMP travel guides are available at your favorite bookstores. For a FREE catalog or to place a mail order, call: 800-888-7504.

John Muir Publications • P.O. Box 613 • Santa Fe, NM 87504

ABOUT THE AUTHOR

Adam Langer is a third generation Chicagoan. His grandparents came to Chicago from Russia and Austria in the early 20th century and set up businesses here—a soda pop factory on the South Side, a deli on the West Side. Born and raised in the city, Langer left to study political science at Vassar College but returned to pursue a career in journalism. He later received his graduate educa-

Beate Sissenich

tion in English literature from the University of Illinois at Chicago.

Currently a resident of Chicago's North Side, Langer is an accomplished journalist and playwright. He is a features writer and theater critic for the *Chicago Reader*, an editor at *Book* magazine, and a contributor to numerous local and national publications, including *Chicago Magazine*, *Inside Chicago*, *Mother Jones*, *Chicago History*, *Chicago Tribune*, *Rolling Stone*, *Request*, *Visions*, *New City*, and *Merian*. He's also the author of numerous plays, including *The Blank Page*, *Crime in the City*, *Film Flam*, *The Critics*, and *Three Glasses of Sherry*, which have been performed in New York, Los Angeles, San Francisco, Connecticut, Massachusetts and Chicago. Other books by Langer include *The Madness of Art* (Chicago Review Press), *The Film Festival Guide* (Chicago Review Press) and *Indie Jones* (to be published soon).

JOHN MUIR PUBLICATIONS
and its City•Smart Guidebook author
are dedicated to building community
awareness within City•Smart cities.
We are proud to work with
Literacy Chicago as we publish
this guide to Chicago.

Literacy Chicago is dedicated to improving the
literacy skills of adults and their families in the
Chicago area. The agency's free programs are
geared to both English-speaking adults with limited literacy skills and those whose first language is
something other than English. Program services
include one-on-one and small group tutoring, pre-GED
and GED classes, family literacy services in schools and
domestic violence shelters, and on-site workplace literacy services. Literacy Chicago is also the local coordinator for Reach Out
and Read, a national parent–child early reading program.

Each year, with the help of over 500 trained volunteer tutors, about
1,300 adult learners gain new skills and develop greater self-
reliance by improving their literacy skills.

LITERACY Chicago

For more information, please contact:
Literacy Chicago
70 East Lake Street, Suite 1500
Chicago, IL 60601
(312) 236-0341